Praise for *The Integrity Dividend*

"Living and leading by your words is so very difficult, but is critical for great leadership. This book has excellent real-life examples that will reinforce the value of the integrity dividend."

—**Doug Brooks,** chairman, CEO, and president,
  Brinker International

"A culture of promise-keeping is a competitive advantage for any great company. If you want to lead such a company, read this book and take its message to heart."

—**Carl Camden,** president and CEO, Kelly Services

"Living by your word makes good sense. Doing it in today's business climate is another thing. Are you ready to take this journey? *The Integrity Dividend* is the only guide you will need."

—**Dick Axelrod,** author, *Terms of Engagement*

"*The Integrity Dividend* is a delight, packed with practical advice and crystal-clear, proven insight. It should be read by all leaders and future leaders. You will be surprised to learn how powerful it is 'to be *seen* as living by your word,' and how much the integrity dividend means to you and your bottom line."

—**Allen S. Ibara,** CEO, Phiam Corporation

"Dr. Simons's groundbreaking work demonstrates the cost of not keeping our word to staff and, better yet, proves the economic benefits of integrity. Every executive I have introduced to his work has been impressed. You will be too."

—**Robert J. Wright,** CEO, the Wright Business Institute

"*The Integrity Dividend* is a great book with an incredibly important message and helpful guidelines. I can see myself referring to it again and again in helping leaders bring more integrity to their role. This is an outstanding work!"

—**Jeff Balin,** leadership coach and facilitator

"*The Integrity Dividend* should be read by all leaders, and those whose goal is to become a leader. The examples were so clear and powerful, I felt I was having a personal discussion with top industry leaders."

—**Jack Gillis,** president, Insurance Negotiating Service

"Tony hits the nail on the head with this book. If our sales managers all read his book and then followed the practices he lays out, I know we would see an immediate reduction in turnover and an improvement in productivity. A must-read for anyone responsible for developing leaders in their organization!"

—**Tom Chelew,** vice president, Fleet Management,
    Enterprise Rent-a-Car

"Integrity is in short supply in today's professional world. Tony Simons offers a practical and insightful work for leaders in all walks of life!"

—**Roy J. Lewicki,** coauthor, *Mastering Business Negotiation*

"Finally! A book that connects behavioral integrity and results. Tony Simons's book should be mandatory reading for anyone who seeks to lead others!"

—**Lloyd Hill,** former chairman and CEO, Applebee's
    International, Inc.

"It's about time that integrity in business has moved into the category of critical success factors. This book is an important contribution to this expanding conversation."

—**Steve Zaffron,** CEO, the Vanto Group

"Tony Simons richly illustrates a powerful benchmark of leadership credibility. *The Integrity Dividend* vividly shows how an impeccable commitment to your word can affect business relationships, cultures, and performance. Then it shows how to get there."

—**Stanley T. Myers,** president and CEO of SEMI
    (Semiconductor Equipment and Materials
    International)

"Tony Simons has taken enormously valuable academic research on trust and translated it into language accessible to all of us. I particularly commend this book to executives, managers, and others who seek to lead with integrity in corporate and public life. I will certainly be recommending it to clients of mine."

—**Charles Feltman,** executive coach, Insight Coaching

"In *The Integrity Dividend* Simons captures the inherent value of a much-needed leadership practice: ensuring that your actions match your words."

—**Amy Lyman,** chair, board of directors, Great Place to Work Institute, Inc.

"Given the volatile environment of business ethics today, and the daily reminders in the headlines, this invaluable resource should be in the back pocket of every executive who dreams of long-term business results."

—**Kerry Miller,** Kerry Miller Executive Search

"Leadership integrity—often talked about, never objectively valued. Now Tony Simons is demonstrating its bottom-line impact. Every aspiring leader should own a copy, and some existing ones too."

—**Michael Z. Kay,** retired president and CEO, LSG/Sky Chefs

"As leaders of people, 98 percent of how we produce results is by managing our conversations with others as well as with ourselves. Tony powerfully demonstrates the huge payoff when we align our actions with our words, and also the significant cost when we don't."

—**Ted Teng,** former president and CEO, Wyndham International, Inc.

"In light of the Enron horror, Simons's powerful research in *The Integrity Dividend* is a must-read for any executive who wants to enhance her or his success in dealing with people."

—**Gary Patton,** executive coach and adjunct professor of human resource management, York University, Toronto

"Tony Simons has revealed a fundamental but often ignored truth—that word-action consistency is at the heart of trustworthy relationships. Integrity drives engagement, commitment, satisfaction, productivity, and profitability."

—**John Lazar,** executive coach and coexecutive editor,
  the *International Journal of Coaching in Organizations*

"This book is full of valuable wisdom and practical insight."

—**Philip Truelove,** owner, Island Inn, Monhegan Island

THE INTEGRITY DIVIDEND

Leading by the Power of Your Word

Tony Simons

Foreword by Jim Kouzes

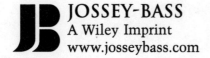

JOSSEY-BASS
A Wiley Imprint
www.josseybass.com

Published by Jossey-Bass
A Wiley Imprint
989 Market Street, San Francisco, CA 94103-1741—www.josseybass.com

Jossey-Bass books and products are available through most bookstores. To contact Jossey-Bass directly
call our Customer Care Department within the U.S. at 800-956-7739, outside the U.S. at 317-572-3986,
or fax 317-572-4002.

Jossey-Bass also publishes its books in a variety of electronic formats. Some content that appears in
print may not be available in electronic books.

Library of Congress Cataloging-in-Publication Data

Simons, Tony.
  The integrity dividend : leading by the power of your word / Tony Simons ; foreword by Jim Kouzes.
     p. cm.
  Includes bibliographical references (p.   ) and index.
  ISBN 978-0-470-18566-7 (cloth)
 1. Business ethics—Economic aspects. 2. Leadership. 3. Integrity. I. Title.
  HF5387.S568 2008
  174'.4—dc22   2008023798

Printed in the United States of America

FIRST EDITION
HB Printing 10 9 8 7 6 5 4 3 2 1

CONTENTS

FOREWORD

"Credibility is the foundation of leadership."

I must have delivered this line five thousand times over the twenty-five years Barry Posner and I have been researching and writing about leadership. Maybe more. This is no idle claim. It's exactly what we've found after asking hundreds of thousands of people what they look for and admire in a leader, someone whose direction they would willingly follow. People tell us that, above all else, they want leaders who are credible. They want leaders in whom they can believe. And just what is credibility behaviorally? When we've asked people to define it, they consistently use one simple phrase to sum it up: when you are credible you *do what you say you will do*. DWYSYWD. Remember that phrase. It's the most important leadership lesson you'll ever learn.

Now Tony Simons has come along and nailed the manifesto to the door. He's taken this commonsense notion of doing what you say you will do, tested it in the real world, crunched the numbers, and discovered something profoundly meaningful to businesspeople. Without giving away the richness of this book, here's the punch line: if you walk the talk, practice what you preach, stand up for your beliefs, put your money where your mouth is, follow through on your promises—do what you say you will do—your business will make more money. You will also be more trusted, more powerful, more personally successful; have more loyal and committed people; and be more at peace with yourself. Tony calls this the *integrity dividend*. It's what you get in return for behaving in ways that are consistent with your, and the organization's, stated values.

In this book, you'll meet influential leader after influential leader who testify to the power of behavioral integrity. You will read story after story about the payoff of living by your word.

You'll see why promising less but doing it more often is a far better way to maintain your integrity than promising more but doing less. You'll understand why those who take strong stands and really mean what they say are far more credible than those who have trouble clearly stating their beliefs. You'll discover that none of this is easy and that you can't have personal integrity without personal discipline. It means that once you make a promise, you have to organize your life around ways to keep that promise. Simple things like a meeting agenda, the people you see, the stories you tell, the rewards you give, the language you use all send signals about what matters to you.

Tony also addresses the realities we all face in our organizational life. He knows that middle managers often feel tension around the personal values that guide them, or a corporate mission that inspires them, and certain organizational policies they must champion. He knows that this conflict can sap personal energy and weaken resolve. He dispenses no cheap drugs to ease the pain. Speaking the truth to power requires personal courage, and you have to make your own decisions about the "bright line" that defines the boundary you won't cross. Just knowing that can help you retain control of your own life. But Tony also asks us to consider the possibility that we may not always have all the data and that if we've chosen our organizations well, then there are times we just have to trust our leaders.

In the end, to have an organization full of people who behave with integrity, we have to be able to create a culture of accountability. That means, dare we say it, appraising people's performance against the values that are espoused. None of us needs a lot of research to understand how behavior changes when you measure performance. If we truly believe in what we say, then we're willing to be measured against it. There have to be clear, visible, and understandable metrics for our behavior. After all, if you're going to count on me for something, then I want to know what counts.

There is one final observation, though, that I'd like to add to Tony's treatise on the importance of doing what we say. Leadership is a humbling experience. Anyone who's ever been in a leadership role quickly learns that you're squeezed between others' lofty expectations and your own personal limitations. You realize that while others want you to be of impeccable character, you're not always without fault. You find that you sometimes get angry and short, and that you don't always listen carefully to what others have to say. You're reminded that you don't always treat everyone with dignity and respect. You recognize that others deserve more credit than they get and that you've failed to say "thank you." You know that sometimes you get, and take, more credit than you deserve.

In other words, you realize that you're human.

The people we work with and count on are also human, and despite their best intentions, they don't always do what they say they will do. We need to give them the same opportunities we afford ourselves to try and fail and try again. We need to give them the chance to be the best they can be, even to be better than they thought they could be. We need to support them in their growth and help them to recognize that the journey is not about perfection but about becoming fully human.

Reading Tony Simons's book, *The Integrity Dividend,* is a wonderful place to begin the exploration of what it means to live by our word. The rest is up to us.

Orinda, California   JIM KOUZES
July 2008   Coauthor of *The Leadership Challenge*

PART ONE

WHAT IS THE INTEGRITY DIVIDEND?

CHAPTER ONE

THE DOLLAR VALUE OF YOUR IMPECCABLE WORD

Stan Myers, president and CEO of SEMI, a global semiconductor industry association, tells the following story about the impact of keeping his word. When he was CEO of Mitsubishi Silicon America, he had to move his R&D department from the San Francisco Bay area to Salem, Oregon. Many employees were not interested in moving, so he offered an incentive: a retention bonus to people who would stay the full eight months until the move and help to recruit their replacements. If they took another job before the eight months, they would still get a severance package but not the retention bonus. One young engineer, Alan, got another job, did not get his retention bonus, and finance did not pay him his legitimate severance of several thousand dollars. He never asked for it. About a year later, Stan, the CEO, learned about the mistake. He had his people cut the check, found and visited Alan's new workplace, and asked the president of the company to bring Alan up to the conference room for a conversation.

Alan came in, and he said, "What are you doing here? I haven't seen you for a while."

Stan said, "Yes, Alan, but I wanted to tell you that we forgot to pay you your severance."

Alan was overwhelmed. More than fifteen years later, Stan heard again from Alan, who had started up a successful electronics company. He sought out Stan to present him with an engraved iPod Nano, thanking him for his leadership and friendship.

I draw two points from this story. One is that the simple act of keeping a promise can have a huge impact on a person. The second point gives pause: Alan did not expect his employer to keep his word. The fact that Stan acted as he did struck Alan as extraordinarily unusual. CEOs are very busy, and nobody likes to admit a mistake. There probably would have been no fallout if the check had never been written. There would have been understandable reasons for Stan Myers *not* to have acted as he did. But the fact that he did says something about the man as a leader, and it helps to explain his great success in that role.

It's easy to break a promise, and it's even easier to forget the price of breaking it. After all, who can measure that price? Few would deny that a broken promise lowers the morale of employees, but what's the real dollar cost—the bottom-line impact? Or what is the payoff of keeping a promise? It should be simple to align your words and actions in a way that employees can see. But if it's so simple, why do most employees say their managers do not do it? Maybe it is not so simple.

Consider how two executives described to me the benefit of an impeccable word—and the cost of lacking one:

> Good leadership is, "Whatever I say I'm going to do, I'm going to do." That means I have to know what my limitations are and what I'm capable of delivering. As a leader if you don't fulfill your commitments, I can't think of anything that can hurt you more than that.—Frank Guidara, president and CEO, Uno's Chicago Grill

> If your staff see you cutting corners, then they're not going to take you seriously. And then they're not going to take the values you're trying to instill seriously. Because *you're* not taking the values seriously.—Deirdre Wallace, President, The Ambrose Collection

Like these successful executives, you too most likely want to be an honest and respected leader. But this book is about more than being respected. As its title says, it's about the *integrity dividend*—and why and how keeping your word as a leader pays off on the bottom line. One thing that sets this book apart from others that discuss the importance of integrity is that it tells how I have been able to accurately measure its positive dollar impact. As you will see in later chapters, successful executives I talk to recognize the dividend too, but until now it has not been well measured.

I am not asking you to be motivated by any intrinsic payoff, though I think there are several. Integrity for me is about being more effective, because people see you as consistently following through on your word and demonstrating the values you profess: more effective as a leader, because you more readily capture the hearts of your followers; as a communicator, because people know you mean what you say; as a partner, because you can be counted on; as a customer, because you complete business transactions efficiently; as a supplier, because buyers know what they will get; and as a brand, because you keep your promises—and promises are all that a brand is. Integrity contributes hugely to executive effectiveness.

Behavioral Integrity: A Recognized Fit Between Words and Actions

Most successful executives intuit the importance of a reputation for integrity. It plays a major role in our public discourse, as politicians of all stripes revel in accusing their opponents of lacking it. People sense its importance, perhaps especially in today's climate, as corruption scandals break careers, lives, bank accounts, and the faith of millions. But in 2005, *integrity* was the single most looked-up word on Merriam-Webster's Dictionary Web site, which implies that people are not exactly sure what integrity means. Think about that for a minute: *people know integrity is important, but they are not sure what it means.*

Often people use the word *integrity* to describe a general quality of acting ethically. Ethics are important, but they are not what this book is about. For the purposes of this book, *integrity* means the fit between words and actions, as seen by others. It means promise keeping and showing the values you profess. This book is about keeping your words lined up with your actions—keeping promises and living by the same values you talk about—seamlessly, as in the *integrity* of the hull of a boat. It means being seen as living by your word.[1]

Behavioral integrity is not about the content of a person's values, though I believe that content is very important. It is about how well a person follows through on the values he or she espouses. I can judge people despicable for what they value, but if they walk their talk and keep promises, I will—grudgingly—concede that they have behavioral integrity. A colleague of mine once proclaimed at a department meeting that his decisions would be guided strictly by self-interest and that he had no concern for what the department or the school needed. I did not like working with him, and I did not trust him. But he was living up to his word, and I had to give him credit for behavioral integrity.

It is not enough to keep your word; others have to be aware that you are doing it. And here is where it gets sticky. Like beauty, behavioral integrity is in the eye of the beholder. Consistently keeping promises and living by your stated principles are difficult tasks. Being seen as consistently doing these things is harder still. People we manage spend a lot of time watching us and trying to figure us out. They generally notice and understand more than we realize, but they also carry their own baggage—their own hurts, cynicisms, and biases. Their judgments about our integrity are colored by everything from their own parental issues from childhood to previous bosses to personality to the particular moments they happen to witness. As effective leaders (or business partners, or suppliers, or board members, or whatever else), our challenge is to penetrate the veil of others' subjective perceptual processes and convey integrity regardless of them.

The added step of managing others' perceptions makes the challenge more difficult than it might have seemed. It is not enough to manage your own level of consistency. You have to manage others' perceptions of it without lapsing into cynical manipulation, which probably would not work anyway.

LEADERSHIP, TRUST, AND THE INTEGRITY DIVIDEND

It is difficult for anyone to define, measure, and develop leadership, in part because leadership involves trust, inspiration, challenge, strategic vision, and much more. But leadership is critical to just about any company's performance, and there are numerous books about it, many offering terrific insights. Still, I suggest that the basic insight of this book—a fundamental, challenging one with a demonstrated financial dividend—has not received the kind of attention it warrants.

Consider the issue of trust, which has recently been a popular topic. Most agree that trust is a critical ingredient for leadership, since few people follow someone they do not trust. Most also agree that trust is complicated, encompassing reliance, emotion, respect, and a sense that the trusted person will look out for you. This book argues for looking particularly hard at reliance as a crucial ingredient for building and keeping trust. Reliance is the belief that leaders keep their word, fulfill their promises, and show the same values they profess. That is what "walking the talk" means. If people do not see this consistency, leadership cannot happen at all. You cannot even get out of the starting gate as a leader if others do not believe your words. Behavioral integrity is a simple idea, but it is hard to put into practice. To the extent that you do so, your powerful word pays off in powerful, concrete dividends.

Later chapters of this book say how to capture the integrity dividend. Before moving on to them, however, let's look at some of the growing evidence that the dividend exists.

A Scientific Study: The Dollar Value of an Impeccable Word

A few years ago, a colleague of mine at Cornell University's Hotel School, Cathy Enz, was fascinated by the idea of clear corporate values as a powerful tool for contributing to effectiveness. At the time, I had not yet latched onto behavioral integrity as a key to leader effectiveness. Through many of our conversations, I kept coming back to the notion that talking about values was one thing, acting on them was another, and aligning those words and actions might be the most powerful combination by far. By that time, I had also begun to regard as toxic the common exercise of drafting up a statement of values that sits in a desk drawer. It gives rise, I thought, to cynical employees who see their bosses pretending to adhere to values they do not implement. Cynicism kills spirit, and so undermines the company's bottom-line performance in a thousand small and large ways. But at that point, my thoughts were just theory; I had no clear supporting evidence.

Management scholars have generated significant recent research on several concepts related to the alignment of words and actions. Trust is widely recognized and demonstrated as a key performance factor in teams and leadership in general. A study of National Collegiate Athletic Association college basketball teams found that players' trust in leadership drives the quality and consistency of team performance.[2] Several studies have shown that trust in leadership drives subordinates' positive attitudes and their willingness to expend effort beyond formal job definitions.[3] Fairness perceptions[4] and perceived violations of "psychological contracts"[5] have also been shown over many studies to affect employee attitudes, discretionary effort, and retention. But with a very few exceptions, the previous relevant research had focused on individual outcomes rather than companywide outcomes. No one had zeroed in on the idea of leaders living by their word and linked it to company performance as its final outcome.

I began to look for ways to test the bottom-line impact of word-action alignment. Testing the bottom-line impact of anything in the real world is not easy. To test a single factor like integrity, you need a lot of businesses that you can compare directly to each other. Franchises make a good testing ground, as you can filter out a lot of variation, comparing the performance of independent business units that are very similar in most ways but have different managers who lead with different styles.

I found help in this investigation from Pete Kline, then the CEO of Bristol Hotels and Resorts, which operated over 110 hotels in the United States and Canada. Pete is a brave man who also intuited the truth of the claim I wanted to test. We focused on 76 of his Holiday Inn franchises that were in the United States and not unionized. Bristol agreed to share the financial performance, employee turnover, and guest satisfaction information for each hotel. Pete asked me to design an employee survey to include penetrating questions about how much people trust their bosses and how good they think that boss's word is.

For the project, I collaborated with Judi McLean Parks of Washington University, an expert at measuring employee perceptions of their implicit and explicit employment deals—what she calls the "psychological contract." By applying solid scientific practice (focus groups, careful pretesting, prevalidated questions where feasible, multiple questions triangulating on each underlying idea, and objective operational performance measurement), we created a survey that could measure a chain of impact running from behavioral integrity perceptions to employee attitudes to behaviors to the business unit bottom line.

At a few hotels, we ran focus groups about what behavioral integrity looked like and pilot-tested the survey, which had been translated into five languages. Then we asked employees at all seventy-six hotels to complete the survey. They did so anonymously, on company time, with a raffle for sweatshirts and dinners out as an incentive. Most employees filled out paper surveys, but we set up "read-aloud" tables for the roughly 7 percent of employees with limited literacy.[6] At each hotel, we asked line employees, supervisors, department managers, and the general manager to say how strongly they agreed or disagreed with statements like these:

- My manager practices what he/she preaches.
- When my manager promises something, I can be certain that it will happen.
- I would be willing to let my manager have complete control over my future in this company.

The first two questions measure behavioral integrity and the third measures trust. The questions are phrased as extremes, so that a statement of strong agreement indicates a deep belief in integrity or a deep feeling of trust. I did not want to ask questions with which it would be easy to agree.

Each hotel employed about one hundred and thirty employees spread over six to eight departments. Typically the biggest departments by far were housekeeping and front office. Around two-thirds of all employees (more than sixty-five hundred total) completed our surveys. For every manager with four or more employees, we generated feedback reports that described employees' relationships with that manager. For each hotel, we collected employee turnover information, the results of independently conducted customer satisfaction surveys, and financial performance information for the months following the employee survey.

We averaged employee perceptions at each hotel and applied path analysis to evaluate all the links in the proposed chain of impact at the same time. We expected to find a chain that runs from employee perceptions of their managers' behavioral integrity, to employee trust in their managers, to their commitment to the company, which in turn would drive both employee turnover and discretionary service behavior. We expected, furthermore, that discretionary service behavior would drive customer satisfaction, and profit would be affected by both employee turnover and customer satisfaction.

The results of the study were so clear that they surprised even me. As Figure 1.1 shows, the average employee perception of how much the employee's manager kept promises and lived by stated values drove hotel profitability more strongly than the five other attitudes measured by the survey.

FIGURE 1.1. STRENGTH OF ASSOCIATION BETWEEN BUSINESS
PROFITABILITY AND DIFFERENT EMPLOYEE ATTITUDES.

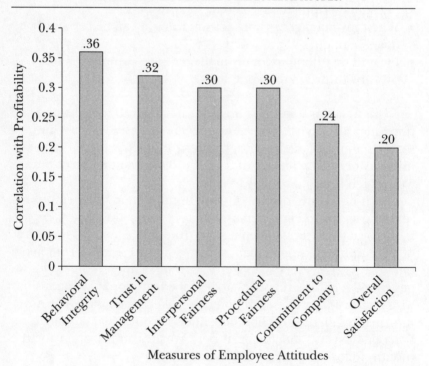

Let's take a minute with that result alone: how strong your employees feel their managers' word is—their assessment of their managers' behavioral integrity—is more important to your company's financial performance than employee trust, sense of fairness, commitment, or satisfaction. These other attitudes also matter, to be sure, but behavioral integrity came out as the single most powerful driver of profit. It might be more important that the workers know you mean what you say than whether they like you or the company or their work. First comes the word. Everything else follows.

The survey had asked employees to respond to statements with a number from 1 (strongly disagree) to 5 (strongly agree). Results showed that one-eighth of a point difference between two hotels in the average employee behavioral integrity ratings pointed to a difference in profits of around 2.5 percent of revenues. The difference raised the portion of each dollar of revenue that the company got to keep as profit by two-and-a-half cents. Typical revenue streams for that size and tier of hotel run around $10 million annually, so that difference in behavioral integrity could be expected to raise profit by an average $250,000 per hotel per year. Many of the hotels with high management integrity converted over ten cents more of each revenue dollar into profits than others. Does behavioral integrity make a difference to the bottom line? The evidence said emphatically—and hugely—yes. We had detected the *integrity dividend*.

Here are the details of the chain of impact that we saw:

- Where employees feel their managers keep promises and live by the values they describe, they trust their managers more.
- Where they trust their managers more, they become more emotionally committed to the company—caring more deeply about its mission and taking pride in working for it.
- Where they feel greater emotional commitment to the company, they are more willing to stay in their jobs and to go beyond their formal job descriptions by providing discretionary service to satisfy guest requests.
- Guests who experience discretionary service from hotel employees like it and feel more satisfied.

- Satisfied guests translate to repeat business, which boosts profits. Employee retention boosts profits as well.

Here is a simpler way to describe the chain: where employees reported high integrity on the part of their managers, we saw:

- Deeper employee commitment, leading to
- Lower employee turnover and
- Superior customer service; all leading to
- Higher profitability.

This study took place in a single industry: the hotel business. Is there evidence of a similar bottom-line integrity dividend in other industries? After all, the hotel business is unique in some ways. It is a service industry that sells positive guest experiences. The pivotal role of customer contact in determining the quality of the final product suggests that employees' emotional response to their work might be more important for hotels than for, say, a manufacturing business. Hotels also employ a less educated labor force than most other white-collar businesses. However, there is no evidence that sensitivity or response to managers' integrity issues depends on education level.

As a framework for systematic studies, the notion of behavioral integrity is new, even if the essential idea has long been discussed as an element of good leadership. Other scholars have already started to build on this initial work and are creating a research community with sessions devoted to the topic at annual Academy of Management conferences. In coming years I expect to see similar research results in other industries as more scholars explore the causes, consequences, and management of the issue. Apart from that future research, there is already strong evidence that the behavioral integrity effect holds true in other industries as well. For one thing, the attitudes and behaviors that are driven by behavioral integrity—trust, perceived fairness, employee commitment, turnover, and discretionary effort—are already well-demonstrated performance drivers in a variety of both service and manufacturing industries.[7] Furthermore, all the executives I spoke with, in a wide variety of industries, agreed that behavioral integrity plays a pivotal role in determining attitudes toward leadership and, ultimately, driving performance. Chapter Two begins to discuss what the integrity dividend looks like in other industries.

THE INTEGRITY DIVIDEND IN PRACTICE: CHECKING WITH EXECUTIVES

Braced by my evidence that managers' promise keeping and living by stated values drives profitability, I interviewed about a hundred successful executives to learn more about how behavioral integrity works. I spoke with leaders in high-tech manufacturing, health care, real estate, restaurants, hotels, food service, and nonprofit, as well as union leaders and a handful of executive coaches and consultants. My primary criterion for selection was that the executives be successful in their chosen fields, as shown by a pattern of promotions and executive positions. I sought to understand the payoffs and the challenges around behavioral integrity through their eyes, figuring that most successful managers have something to teach me and others working on this issue.

I conducted hour-long interviews, usually by telephone. The result was over two thousand pages of transcription, which my research team and I broke down into discussion themes. We looked for patterns, extracted and developed stories that related to those patterns, and massaged the pooled insights of these many executives to yield the book you are now reading.

I asked the executives about how they perceive the challenges and consequences of word-action alignment or its lack. I also asked them for both general and specific advice. Their responses are valuable in two main ways. First, they demonstrate that the integrity dividend is not unique to the hotel industry. Second, they flesh out the whys and hows of behavioral integrity in deeper, more practical detail. The techniques the executives propose are grounded in the sense that they drive the kind of integrity perceptions that create the dividend shown in the Holiday Inn research. However, it is also true that the process of talking to these executives and drawing out and combining their insights may resemble art more than it resembles science. I am learning about integrity along the way. I expect that you will too.

The interviews yielded four main themes, which we explore in coming chapters:

- The payoff of behavioral integrity is greater personal and organizational effectiveness. It builds personal credibility and trust, which contribute to your ability to get things done through people.
- Employees who trust their leaders work harder and with clearer direction. Trust also leads to greater efficiency in customer relationships, supplier relationships, and union relationships.
- Some of the greatest challenges of behavioral integrity management come down to recognizing and reckoning with our own personal habits and the ways we have learned to interact with people. Some of our well-intended actions serve to undermine our integrity and thus our credibility. Elements of self-knowledge and self-control are integral to managing behavioral integrity. You have to be willing to occasionally sacrifice in the service of keeping your word. To create a word as good as gold, you sometimes have to demonstrate the value of your word by paying for it.
- Executives can extend behavioral integrity and its dividends through leaders and practices throughout the organization. It is not just about personal relationships. Through careful modeling, training, coaching, accountability and incentives, impeccable follow-through can become a mutual expectation that forms part of the structure and the culture of the company. Make it a shared priority, and watch your effectiveness build.

CHALLENGES RATHER THAN EASY ANSWERS

You may be thinking that behavioral integrity cannot be easy. It isn't. Accepting one's word as one's absolute bond and making that bond as solid as steel is hard work. The payoff, of course, is that your word of steel is as valuable as gold, because great integrity is rare and people are drawn to it. The challenge is especially great for people who take on the job of managing others in a company hierarchy. Most managers' days are filled with brief tasks, noise, and fires that need putting out. It isn't easy to keep track of commitments. Sometimes your boss countermands your decisions—at the cost of your own credibility. Sometimes the need to keep relationships smooth leads you to sugar-coat the truth, and sometimes that sugar coating causes feelings of betrayal on the part of those who mistook the frosting for the cake.

Managing behavioral integrity demands careful communication, as described in Chapter Five. People misunderstand each other all the time, and they feel no less betrayed when the promise that was broken was wrongly understood. People often ignore the escape clauses we insert into our promises, such as "I'll try" or "I hope" or even "probably." They often hear the message they hope to hear or the message they expect. They bring their own cynicism and other kinds of baggage to interactions and sometimes they assume you are lying before you speak.

Your position within the company sometimes adds other challenges to living by your word. Leaders are sometimes expected to project confidence and certainty even when they lack it. Managers are sometimes asked to produce short-term results at any cost or publicly endorse policies with which they do not agree. As subordinates, leaders and managers sometimes face bosses who prefer deference over honesty. As negotiators, they often fear that truthfulness sacrifices a competitive edge.

When companies face change, the challenges become greater still. Policy shifts are often confusing, and sometimes, as a manager, you have to introduce changes that violate values you yourself promoted. Sometimes in your ambivalence, you send mixed messages. And sometimes the policies themselves seem to contradict each other in the values they imply. Then there are initiatives about which you may not be allowed to speak, like layoffs, acquisitions, and mergers.

These challenges are often attended by other difficulties you must face, including trade-offs, the need to forsake expedient solutions, hard conversations you must have, and personal weaknesses you (like all of us) must acknowledge and confront. The executives and coaches I interviewed for this book have faced them too, and sometimes they made mistakes. But more often they overcame them—and collected the integrity dividend.

I cannot say with certainty that integrity will always yield the practical outcomes you want. But I can say that over time, its lack kills spirit among those who follow and that excellent leadership is fundamentally about building and focusing spirit toward extraordinary achievement.

As a leader, you should finish this book a little wiser, a little more insightful, and a little more effective. It is not about how you can feel better about yourself or how you can better live up to your moral values or those of society. It is about creating more effective relationships and more effective businesses through alignment. Develop a powerful word, because it will serve you well.

SUMMARY

This book is about building an impeccable word in order to increase your effectiveness and that of the people around you. Behavioral integrity is about having that impeccable, powerful word. It is about keeping promises, showing the values you profess, and being seen as doing so. It is not at all easy, especially as the goal is to do so all the time.

Make no mistake: others evaluate your integrity constantly. And the challenge is harder still when you consider the subjective biases they bring to that evaluation.

Behavioral integrity is not the whole challenge of leadership; there are many other skills and abilities involved in leading. It is not even the whole challenge of building and maintaining trust; there is more involved in that too. But neither trust nor leadership happens without behavioral integrity—without certainty that the leader means what she says. Behavioral integrity is, in the language of logic, a necessary but not sufficient condition for trust or leadership. It is a cornerstone on which trust and leadership must be based.

A careful scientific study tracked the consequences of behavioral integrity and measured the dollar impact of it as it operated through hotel worker attitudes and actions, affecting service delivery and the bottom line. The study suggested that employees' sense of their boss's strong behavioral integrity might be a more important performance driver than employee satisfaction, commitment, sense of trust, or feelings of fairness.

Extensive conversations with executives have confirmed both the impact and the challenge of behavioral integrity and have provided ideas about how others have met the challenge. This book is aimed at helping you to master that challenge and so to reap the integrity dividend.

Chapter Two explores the integrity dividend in a variety of industries. Chapter Three deepens our model of behavioral integrity's drivers and payoffs. Chapters Four through Six explore common challenges to managers' behavioral integrity and how to address them. Chapters Seven through Nine focus on developing behavioral integrity at the company level. Chapter Ten briefly applies the same framework to relationships outside the company.

Each chapter ends with brief points designed to help you apply these ideas to your workplace. The first three chapters have a set of questions labeled "consider." Later chapters add a section with specific tools and techniques, labeled "act."

Into Practice

Consider

- Where have you seen high or low behavioral integrity on the part of your current or a previous leader or boss? How did it affect your work attitude? Your level of discretionary effort? Your peers?
- How high a priority is keeping your word? How much would you sacrifice in order to keep your word?
- Where do you find it challenging to keep promises or live up to stated values? How much does the resulting gap cost you?

CHAPTER TWO

EXECUTIVE SIGHTINGS OF THE INTEGRITY DIVIDEND

I interviewed about a hundred successful executives to learn more about how behavioral integrity works. I spoke with leaders in high-tech manufacturing, utilities, real estate, restaurants, hotels, food service, financial management, and nonprofit, as well as union leaders, and a handful of executive coaches and consultants. In essence, I asked them questions about consequences, challenges, and guidance:

- What consequences have you seen for word-action alignment or its lack?
- What situations arise that challenge your own word-action alignment? When are good managers inclined to be less than forthright, to break promises, to fail to live up to their stated ideals?
- What is your advice about how to manage these pitfalls?

In the interviews, managers described the integrity dividend as it shows up in different business contexts: daily operations, change management, service delivery, union relationships, supplier relationships, and brand management. These executives and executive coaches talked about challenges managers face in a host of different business settings. There are unique elements to different industries, but there are also common threads, and the integrity dividend is one of them. Every manager and coach I spoke with reported grappling with integrity issues and seeing their consequence.

Michael Kay, former president and CEO of LSG Sky Chefs, describes the integrity dividend like this:

> It's all about results time. It ain't about feeling good. It ain't about being a nice place to come to work. It's that heightened levels of trust produce heightened levels of results. Because people feel better, work better, *are* better, in a trusting setting and environment than they are in one where distrust saps their energy.

The reason to read this book is not to feel better about yourself or to create a happier workplace, although those outcomes may well follow. The reason to read this book is to get better results—to be more successful.

Lin Coughlin, CEO of Great Circle Associates and former chief administrative officer of Cendant Corporation, speaks about transparency, a close cousin of behavioral integrity:

> The way you enact transparency has an awful lot to do with the frequency, consistency, and clarity of your communications. The more transparent you are as a leader, the more you will engender trust; and so the more productive, effective, efficient, and innovative your organization will be. And the convergence of those factors gets you to the breakthrough results.

Lin and Michael see the integrity dividend every day. Lin says simply that people work better when they understand what their boss is doing—because he is doing exactly what he said he would do. As a result, the company works better than the competition, and the dividend shows up in performance. When I talk with Lin and Michael, I do not get any sense that they are naive in their approach. But some readers, I am sure, will think they are. Let's look behind their claims. Here are some of the mechanisms by which executives in various industries say that behavioral integrity drives performance.

INTEGRITY DRIVES EFFECTIVENESS

Behavioral integrity forms a foundation for trust and interpersonal warmth and loyalty. It builds credibility and leads to a personal reputation. By creating predictability, it enables others to predict your judgments and act on reliable, accurate information. It all but eliminates the need for employees to wonder about and discuss what your true agenda might be and whether you mean what you say.

These immediate consequences of integrity echo far beyond the attitudes and behaviors of employees. Improving their attitudes and behaviors would be enough. But leaders' behavioral integrity also affects the culture of the organization and its managers. It determines the effectiveness of change efforts. It profoundly colors relationships with organized labor. It shapes supplier relationships and their potential value contribution. It determines the efficiency of negotiations and problem solving with all stakeholders. And it goes to the heart of the value of your brand. In short, this issue touches every aspect of your business. Managed properly, behavioral integrity stands to enhance value at each of these connection points. Consider these as the many forms of the integrity dividend.

THE DIVIDEND AND LEADING

This section centers around employees and the ideas of trust, relationships, clear direction, and engagement, as shown in Figure 2.1. Integrity allows a leader to build deep, trusting relationships with followers. It also allows that leader to send clear, unmixed signals to guide people. And the combination of these two consequences promotes workers' engagement—their willingness to work hard and to go the extra mile to get the job done with excellence.

FIGURE 2.1. TRUSTING, WELL-DIRECTED EMPLOYEES ARE MORE ENGAGED.

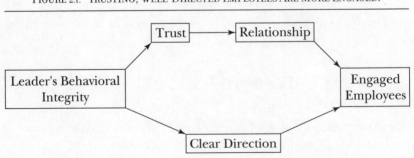

Integrity and Trust

As with everyone else in our work and personal lives, trust is central to our relationship with bosses, and our trust in them depends on our faith that they will keep their word. As a boss yourself, keeping your word is not all it takes to win and maintain trust, but you do not win trust without it. Keeping your word means keeping promises, both the concrete ones about when something will happen and the more abstract ones about what values you say are important. Trust is important in all your relationships, and especially when you are vulnerable to someone— when someone has the power to hurt you badly. That is when trust becomes critical. In fact, scholars have started to define trust specifically as *a willingness to accept vulnerability to another.*

Lloyd Hill recently retired as the chairman of Applebee's International and formerly served as chief operating office (COO) and as CEO. He says:

> Genuine leadership incorporates a number of attributes, but none of them works until there is trust. If as a leader—as a leader of restaurant unit or the leader of a $4.5 billion chain like Applebee's— people can't trust my integrity, I mean in the smallest sense, it creates problems. And I think that goes to an issue so small that if I say, "I'm going to call you at ten o'clock," and I am unprepared to call you at ten o'clock, or if I've had an accident and can't call you, I better have someone call you and say, "Lloyd cannot call you and he wants to reschedule." Or I better call you at ten o'clock and say, "I don't have the information."
>
> Two or three of those missed appointments erode trust in an organization. Then if I'm going to ask the organization to go somewhere that it might be frightened to go, if I'm going to ask an individual to step up and take on a job that he or she doesn't feel qualified to take, or I may be asking you to take a family risk. . . . you may see it as a career risk. And if you do not trust me, you will not do it. You just will not.

A perceived lack of behavioral integrity has a nasty way of contaminating other judgments so as to profoundly undermine trust. Once I question your word, I come to question your goodwill and your ability as well. Mistrust tends to gather momentum and paints future events with sinister colors. A single perceived broken promise can sow the seeds of destruction to goodwill in any relationship. Small events can have big consequences.

INTEGRITY AND RELATIONSHIP

Given how much damage a malevolent or careless boss could do to a typical employee's life and career, it is not hard to see why trust should be so important to a productive leadership relationship. Having a strong word is essential for any respectful relationship, and many managers are coming to the realization that relationships are essential to their business model. As Paul Hortobagyi, general manager at the luxurious Le Marigot Beach Resort in Santa Monica, California, says:

> In my opinion, we are not in the hotel business. We are in the relationship business. A relationship with your front desk agent, a relationship with your bellmen, a relationship with the high roller who comes in and gives hundred-dollar tips to the bellmen, or the person who comes in on the per diem break. It doesn't really matter. It should never, ever change. You have to project the same style and the same relationship-building process that you do with your staff member. I don't know why, but it's going to come back twofold or even threefold to you in various ways.

Paul is offering a business philosophy of striving to build positive, lasting, trusting relationships with everyone with whom you interact. For many of us, that is a daunting prospect. Personally I am a little shy and sometimes stingy with my time. But Paul pulls it off with style and grace. After only a few conversations with me, he has inspired in my heart a deep respect and a fierce loyalty. Paul says he does not know why the dividend comes back to him. I submit it is because he has that effect on most people he encounters, and it makes them want to do business with the man.

Like Paul, Lloyd Hill thinks about leadership as a deeply personal relationship. He even uses the word *love:*

> I think there's got to be a certain love for not only *what* you do but *whom* you do it with. When you find that kind of emotional attachment, it makes a huge difference. I don't think we yet know

the depths of people's capacity. It's pretty much infinite if they're engaged around a vision that causes them to reach down within themselves and tap that infinite power. If they trust and there's clarity around the rewards, I think people are capable of just about anything.

When you think of leadership this way, the importance of keeping your word jumps out. Keeping commitments small and large is fundamental for the trust that is necessary when, as a leader, you ask someone to take a risk. As Lloyd said later in the conversation, he asks people to take risks all the time, and so do we. Even simply asking someone to do his best work is to ask him to take a risk. As Lloyd suggests, the emotional connection that is made possible by trust and promise keeping opens new vistas of possible extraordinary performance.

Integrity and Clear Direction

In addition to building empowering trust, a second consequence of an impeccable word is that you equip people to deliver the results you want, in the ways you want, because there is no mixed message. Michael Kay, whom I quoted at the outset of this chapter, says, "When it's easy for the people who work for you to figure *you* out, when you're clear about who *you* are, it is easier for the people who work for you to decide how most effectively to work with you." You are telling people how to succeed and how best to support you and your company. And since your actions have supported your words, the message is unified—and therefore potent.

One prerequisite for giving clear direction is credibility. Through innumerable daily actions, an effective leader erects signposts for others to follow. What is valued here? What is out of bounds? But the signs work only if the leader is credible. President and CEO of the Uno's Chicago Grill chain of restaurants Frank Guidara describes how this direction-setting aspect of leadership depends on behavioral integrity.

> The laying out of consequences, good and bad, is fundamental to leadership. When, as a leader, you say you're going to do something and you don't do it, it's not going to destroy your leadership status, but each time there will be a little bit more erosion, and a little more, until finally you really can't lead any longer.

When a leader fails to follow through on a stated consequence—a raise, a promotion, a firing—her credibility diminishes. The next time she lays out a consequence, her followers consider it only a possible consequence; it is no longer clear what will happen. Without follow-through, the third time it becomes an empty promise or an empty threat. That trend might seem obvious, but absolute consistency on the part of managers is really rare, for good reason.

Here is a story about credibility and why some leaders' words get followed while others' do not. Consultant Darryl Stickel is a principal for Trust Unlimited, a consulting firm that specializes in its namesake. Early in his career, he worked at a drop-in center for troubled street teens. As you might expect, the center had policies against the kids' bringing in weapons, fighting, intimidating others, drug use, swearing, and so on, and the credibility of those policies mattered. Many of the other staff failed to consistently enforce these policies because they wanted to be liked, but Darryl earned respect precisely because of his consistency. The center was open from noon until eleven o'clock at night, so there were two shifts:

> If I came in for the noon shift, as I came in guys would drop off their weapons with me. If I came in for the late shift, when I came in, there'd be a lineup of guys who would drop off their weapons with me. I'd say, "You guys have been here for hours." They'd say, "Well, yeah. But you weren't here." Folks got so that they knew "if you show up stoned, he's not going to let you in." There was this incredible power to being overwhelmingly consistent, and never making a statement that I didn't intend to follow up on. So if I would see someone doing something, I would say, "You know you're not allowed to do that. Stop it, or you'll have to leave." And they would stop.

The simple power of keeping one's word consistently and predictably is huge. Yet strikingly few people capitalize on it. Managers who compromise their credibility and clarity by failing to follow their word are blunting their most useful tool.

INTEGRITY AND ENGAGEMENT

So far I have argued that integrity fosters emotional connection with followers and that it allows a leader to send signals that are clear and unmixed and so get followed. This combination of strong connection and clear communication also engages followers' hearts. Employees become more willing to go an extra mile to satisfy a customer, solve a problem, or get the job done right. Employees (or others) whose hearts are fully engaged in their task bring everything they have to it. Contrast that approach to one more typically seen when employees are more concerned with following rules, staying out of trouble, and keeping their head low.

I submit that the engagement workers feel when they are in a trust-based relationship with their leader and have a clear sense of direction trumps even the inspiration that charismatic leaders can generate. Celebrity and charisma are not bad things, but they cannot substitute for behavioral integrity and its fruits. Kerry Miller, an executive search consultant and former vice president of people development for Bertucci's Restaurants. explains:

> People have grown accustomed to celebrity. And they aren't as engaged under celebrity leaders: they're more into what goes on inside the four walls of their house. That being said, when you find true leadership—and true integrity in leadership—that, to them, is an aphrodisiac more than celebrity leadership. I think that when you get behind a true leader, you're more jazzed up to get into work every day because you know that person is supportive of what you're doing. It's more about the team than it is about the individual.

The relationship that emerges from strong word-action alignment has the potential to generate deep enthusiasm and stir the soul. Workers who feel that way have the potential to work miracles.

Some leaders witness such miracles on a regular basis. It all comes down to exciting people, getting them to accept ownership of the success or failure of the company's endeavor, getting them very deeply engaged. Frank Heinz is the former president of Baltimore Gas and Electric. He describes engagement in terms of employees' taking initiative in the service of the company:

> I think that employees who trust management are just more likely to take positive initiative. They see an issue, and they know they are part of the team that remedies issues. Or they

see an opportunity—they know they are part of a team that seizes opportunities. And that initiative—cumulatively, among many employees, over time—can make a big difference in the effectiveness of the use of human resources, of capital resources, and the effectiveness, if you will, of the cohesion of the total team. . . . I've seen it occur in ideas about software, I've seen it occur in ideas about how to refurbish or underline gas pipe in a more productive way. And I've seen it occur in areas of customer interface and how to craft messages that are clearer or more understandable for customers, to be used by telephone or in the monthly mailings to customers.

When your people are engaged, they take initiative to solve problems and capitalize on opportunities. You cannot force them to do those things, and you cannot require them. You can only lead in a way that engages their hearts and inspires them to care and go beyond their formal job description in performing the functions of the company.

The initiative of engaged employees does not just drive problem solving; it drives customer service as well. When employees are not deeply engaged, service quality suffers. Deirdre Wallace is the president of the Ambrose Collection, a green hotel operator. She presents the link between behavioral integrity and customer service in a way that closely reflects the chain of impact shown in my study of hotel employees and performance:

> If your actions fall short of your ideals, your employees just
> don't take you seriously. And then they just don't care. Then
> they're just there for the paycheck. I'm in the service industry.
> If my employees don't care, then that affects my guests directly.
> And believe me, guests don't tell you when they're happy.
> They tell you when they're mad. So you want your employees
> to be behind the product and your philosophy, or else your
> guest is going to react to that, because disgruntled employees—
> they don't smile.

Employees who do not feel inspired and trusting of their leadership and are not engaged can still perform their jobs, but they won't excel. Bob Fox is the vice president of human resources for Carlson Hotels Worldwide. He describes how leaders who fail to

maintain trusting relationships drive workers to operate in survival mode—the exact opposite of engagement:

> If the leader doesn't have trust, respect, authenticity, credibility, the
> level of followership is going to be much lower. Workers and man-
> agers will do stuff, but their level of commitment, their willingness
> to appropriately do whatever it takes, is going to be lower. People
> are going to survive. They're not going to go the extra mile on
> behalf of *that* person because that person doesn't deserve it. The
> survival strategy is, "I'm just going to do my job, keep my head
> down, not raise any issues, and just try to help out the team and
> other people in the organization as best I can." Most people in
> most companies operate like that because that's the situation.

How many people in most companies operate in survival
mode? Bob would argue, and I agree, that most employees carry
some element of survival mode through their daily work lives.

What makes these employees cynical and unhappy is typically
not malice or incompetence on the part of managers. Managers who want to make others feel bad, for whatever reason, exist,
but they are in a dramatic minority. The reason the number of
survival-mode employees is high, and the reason so few people
report impeccable integrity on the part of their managers, is that
well-meaning and thoughtful managers make integrity mistakes.
The challenge, then, is one of discipline and skill, not character.
R. J. Dourney is president of Hearthstone Associates, a restaurant
franchisee, and the former head of operations for Au Bon Pain
Restaurants. He points out how difficult it is for managers to get
this right:

> One of the things I think leadership all too often misses is that
> there is no malice aforethought on the part of a manager when he
> doesn't walk the talk. I think very often, he either doesn't know
> how, or is afraid to.
>
> For instance, one of the keys in our industry—possibly in any
> industry—is getting your arms around your people to help them
> grow. When your people are happy and they feel like their careers
> are moving forward, they do amazing things. Very often as leaders,
> we say those things. But when it comes to taking the time to do
> one-on-ones, and helping somebody grow, and getting them into

a development program, we fall down. If the person is a manager, maybe you're just spending quality time with them. If he or she is an executive, you push them into an M.B.A. program.

You start the flywheel when you tell that individual that his development is important to you. So you do their review. But then you fail to follow up. I think, all too often, that lack of follow-up is linked to the fact that either you're afraid to or you don't know how. The net result is where you see that sense of betrayal: "My boss says that he cares about me, but he really doesn't. He just wants me to go in and do a job."

"My boss just wants me to go in and do a job" is not the language of a fiercely engaged spirit. It is what you say as you enter survival mode, preparing to plod through your days with clay feet and lowered head. As managers and as leaders, too often we unwittingly break the spirit of those who might otherwise propel our companies to excellence, and that spirit is perhaps a leader's most important charge and most effective tool.

THE DIVIDEND IN THE ORGANIZATION: BUILDING A CULTURE AND MANAGING CHANGE

As I spoke with executives, I came to realize that their behavioral integrity has impact well beyond the trust, direction, and engagement of their immediate followers. That impact echoes through the company in both formal and informal ways. It affects and is affected by policy decisions and unwritten norms. Behavioral integrity is itself an aspect of the organization's culture that managers learn, for better or worse, by observing their bosses. Furthermore, it allows managers to shape the culture toward professed values by modeling those values. This facilitation likely also extends to all forms of change: workers will respond more nimbly to new directives when they are fully confident that leaders' words lead to action.

Let's consider separately these two areas: integrity as an influence on general company culture and the effect of integrity when change efforts are under way.

INTEGRITY AND COMPANY CULTURE

Executives' integrity affects the culture of their organizations as aspiring managers imitate their bosses' approaches to managing the strains and trade-offs of the job. It trickles down. Furthermore, executives who routinely enact the culture do far more to convey and reinforce that culture than all the exhortations in the world. Integrity also affects culture in that it allows potential employees to better self-select. Where managers are equipped to present actual operating values (as opposed to those to which the company aspires or presents for publicity), employees know what they are going to get. This knowledge allows them to appropriately choose to "play" or not. By noting who chooses to play or not, you can collect the people you want—the ones who buy into the culture.

Executives set the tone for those around them. Ed Evans, executive vice president for human resources and organizational development at Allied Waste Industries, points out how leaders' poor choices about integrity can affect integrity throughout the company:

> You can't pick and choose when behavioral integrity is key. You can't say, "Well, it's a white lie; it didn't hurt anybody, didn't materially change the financial reporting, didn't hurt the customer. . . ." Once you start making excuses, the slip or slide starts. And in most organizations, everybody looks up to see how the next level of executive behaves—not necessarily with regard to them, but on issues that may have no impact directly on them or their customers.

Skip Sack, founding partner of Classic Restaurant Concepts and former executive vice president of Applebee's International, believes integrity "starts at the top. The type and the style of leadership permeate an organization. If I'm the number one guy and I am truthful to my subordinates, honest, and tactful, then they will be truthful, honest, and tactful to the people they have reporting to them." The fact is that executives serve as role models for those who report to them. As a result, small actions have big consequences as they trickle down through the company and shape the style of leadership that managers and supervisors adopt.

When managers act consistently to keep promises and enact stated values, employees develop a climate of trust. Then the values that management models come to permeate the company. Jay Witzel, president and CEO of Carlson Hotels Worldwide, expands on this idea:

> It doesn't matter what you write down on a piece of paper for your vision statement or your mission statement. It doesn't matter what you list for your values. It matters what you do. This gets down to execution, and that's why it gets so complicated. It's not just execution in the sense of "I walked over and cleaned the carpet," or "I walked over and picked up the piece of paper." It gets down to whether you embody the values of the organization. Do you embody the mission and vision of the organization? Do you do what you say you're going to do? Actions that are trustworthy in nature build trust.

Integrated Project Management Company is a consulting firm that serves multiple industries. Its CEO, Rich Panico, agrees with Jay that leaders' actions convey values better than words and that employees will act on the company's professed values only if they see their leaders doing the same. If you want to see your company's values put into practice, leadership means showing the way by doing it yourself so others can see it.

> Many organizations have value statements and missions. However, how many make these the focal point of operations and interactions? Leadership is responsible for making these principles real and effective. Certainly value and mission statements are important, but leadership behavior telegraphs more. Leaders who do not act in accordance with prescribed values in personal and professional lives cannot expect their organizations to be compliant.

Culture is more surely shaped by managers' actions than by their words. Where the two are aligned, the culture of the company becomes what you say you want it to be, and bonds of trust are strengthened with employees at all levels. Where actions and words are not aligned, you engender cynicism.

INTEGRITY AND CHANGE EFFORTS

The idea that followers respond to leaders' actions more than their exhortations applies not just to culture but to company change efforts as a whole. Pete Kline, a former CEO of Bristol

Hotels and Resorts and current managing partner of Seneca Advisors, offers this perspective on change:

> One of the biggest mistakes that happens over and over again, particularly in big companies, is that senior management expects behavioral patterns or attitudes to originate in the middle of the company, as opposed to from the top of the company. They try to operate with two different sets of rules. But the behavior of the entire company is going to reflect the behavioral pattern of the people at the very top. At Enron those problems didn't start in the middle of the company. There is a tendency, when people reach the executive suite, to say they have already paid their dues and they can live a different existence from the people who are doing the real work. Leading by example is probably the cornerstone of any behavioral pattern that you are trying to put into place within a company.

Pete speaks with pride about how Bristol Hotels implemented an important change (an open-office policy) starting with the senior executives. The cultural message was transmitted, and the change effort was successful in large part because the company took care to start it at the top.

Anyone who has been around organizations for a few years and participated in a few change efforts will say that conceiving an organizational change is one thing and seeing it through to reality is quite another. In fact, most change efforts fail. Companies seldom succeed in recreating themselves and almost certainly never succeed when the team at the top is unwilling to change the way it does business and lacks an emotional connection with the rest of the employees. Trust Unlimited principal Darryl Stickel provides a good metaphor related to connection:

> The analogy I heard in one of the mutual fund companies that I was working with was that upper management felt that they were in a Porsche. They had these great ideas and were ready to drive! But everyone else was in a trailer behind them, and they had a faulty hitch. So they couldn't drive too fast or take too many sharp curves because they would lose everyone.

How to tighten or repair the hitch? Here is another aspect of the integrity dividend: integrity tightens the linkage between your Porsche and your trailer. You show the way, as a leader should, and your people are more willing to follow you into the great unknown. You become better able to create change in your company.

THE DIVIDEND WITH OUTSIDE STAKEHOLDERS

Outside your own organization, behavioral integrity also builds your relationship efficiency, quality, and loyalty with customers, suppliers, and unions. Here is a general preview of the topic, which is explored much more in Chapter Ten.

INTEGRITY AND CUSTOMERS

The executives I interviewed pointed out two primary ways that consistently keeping one's word pays a dividend with customers. First, a reputation and history of consistently following through on promises helps dramatically when you need to address an unanticipated challenge or conflict. Second, staying true to values that drive your brand, even under adverse circumstances, helps to cement the brand in the minds of consumers—and of employees.

Good, collaborative, mutually satisfying problem solving requires open and honest communication. Such communication requires a basis of trust, and trust requires integrity. Rich Panico recalls telling a client that there would need to be a shift from the initial project manager to another:

> Of course, the client was very concerned that the transition would cause inefficiencies and that the new project manager wouldn't be as good as the first. I said to him that even though I'm sure he'd heard this from other consultants, "There's just no way in hell that we would ever let you down. Please trust me, because we have never ever let any of our clients down in managing a transition."

> Reflecting on his prior experiences with other consulting firms he said, "Yes, everybody says that, but in the end, I've always been caught short."

The other individual at the meeting, a guy with whom we've had a relationship for fourteen years and for whom we've managed several projects, turned to the client and said: "Let me tell you something about Rich. Rich and I have butted heads. We've had disagreements. But he will never ever lie to you. And his organization has never failed to live up to their commitments. As much as this may sound too good to be true," he said, "it is absolutely fact."

In this situation, the trust I had developed over the years was all I had to convince the client, because the client, whom I'd just met for the first time, could only compare us to others.

Rich's history of impeccable integrity made the difference in managing a potential client crisis. The reassurance created by such consistency allows the relationship to work on it with faith and goodwill. Such a reputation is hard earned, to be sure, but it does reap a dividend in the relationships that are preserved and protected and in the efficiency of doing business.

Behavioral integrity also creates customer relationships through branding. Duane Knapp is chairman and president of BrandStrategy, a strategic marketing consulting firm and is the author of several books, including *The BrandMindset* and *The Brand Promise.*[1] He argues that a true brand is fundamentally based on a promise about the consumer experience. He says that consumers will consistently choose a product or service with a credible promise attached over competition that lacks it. As a result, companies that make credible promises to their customers tend to be far more profitable than companies that do not.

Omni Hotels faced a challenge to its fundamental brand promise of excellent service in the wake of 9/11 as travel demand dropped and cost pressures mounted. Joy Rothschild is senior vice president of human resources for Omni Hotels. She describes the problem and how it was handled:

> After 9/11 a lot of companies were cutting services and cutting amenities and cutting everything. We had all these contingency plans because business was horrible. And we went to ownership, and said, "You know, if we really want to squeeze some more money out of the company we can eliminate doormen. We can take some of the amenities out of the room. We don't have to have a concierge." And to me, that was a watershed moment in

the company's history, because ownership decided not to touch service. Because this thing is going to end. And how are you going to explain to everybody, "Oh, now we're about service again. We're about service. And we weren't when times were bad. But now we are when times are good. You have to be *for* whatever you're going to be for, no matter what happens." And so we didn't cut back service.

As a result, we preserved the brand. We won J. D. Powers twice since then. And we really think we did that by not touching things for 2001 and 2002 and 2003, like a lot of other people did. It served us well for our long-term strategies.

If, as Duane Knapp powerfully suggests, a company's brand is its promise, then staying true to that promise, even when short-term circumstances make it costly or inconvenient, is another profit-driving form of behavioral integrity.

INTEGRITY AND SUPPLIERS

Supplier relationships are also strongly affected by perceived promise keeping, and in a way that directly feeds the bottom line. Here is another one of those ideas that seems obvious until you realize how seldom it is put into practice: suppliers really love it when you pay your bills on time. And if you play it smart, you can get them to reward you for it. Here is Pete Kline talking about his time as CEO of Bristol Hotels and Resorts:

> We had a great relationship with our vendors. Even as a small company with ten hotels, we were buying most product at Marriott pricing. The reason we were able to do that was our vendors knew we always paid our bills on time. And in an industry where that is not the norm, that really set us apart with our vendors. The way we built trust with our vendors was they knew we were going to be tough; we were going to demand the best pricing we could possibly get. But they also knew that if they gave it to us, we were going to pay on time.

The same dynamic with suppliers was described by Marty Belz, the president and CEO of the Peabody Hotel Group, which successfully differentiates itself from other buyers in the same way. He says he gets better service and better prices because of it. Chapter Ten describes other ways that behavioral integrity can make supplier relationships more productive.

INTEGRITY AND LABOR RELATIONS

If you have ever suffered through labor negotiations characterized by mistrust, the following stories may seem truly magical.

The first concerns a negotiation several years ago between labor and management at a mining company in the Peruvian Andes. The company had formerly been run by the government, and an American company had acquired it. The past relationship between the unions and the government had been so poor that in the late 1980s, union members had kidnapped the mine manager for ransom money they felt they were owed and the government responded by sending in troops. Steve Zaffron, CEO of Vanto Group (formerly Landmark Education Business Development), describes how he and his consulting team worked with the top union leaders and the new company executives to build a relationship that minimized the impact of a difficult history.

The union leaders' initial attitude toward the new management was understandably cynical and often adversarial. Steve says, "Before we started working there, this company's standard union contract was a one-year contract that took six months to negotiate." His team conducted workshops to establish a common language and framework for discussing issues. It then orchestrated a series of conversations about the ground rules that the target deal had to be long term and had to have what amounted to behavioral integrity: all parties staked their reputations on fully honoring the deal and getting their people to do so. The union-management group developed a five-year contract within one month, which Steve calls "unheard of in the mining industry in South America."

Integrity can be a source of competitive advantage. Says Steve, "Companies would send representatives to study the agreement but they never got what was the source of the agreement. They looked at the document and tried to copy it, and it didn't work very well." He says the underpinnings that made this deal possible were the open process and the agreed-on level of integrity that he had demanded as ground rules for both sides. When competitors tried to import the contract without those bases, it did not work.

Here is a story from an international hotel chain about the day-to-day impact of integrity in labor relations, told to me by the senior human resource (HR) executive, whom I will call Nancy Kimber. It too suggests that integrity can create competitive advantage:

> We had a labor strike in a major city several years ago. We were offering the same money as everybody else in the city for the renegotiation. I'm like, "What is wrong here? There's something *wrong* here." The employees were demanding, in the union contract, that I would personally come meet with them four times a year. My first reaction was, "Why do I have to do that? I don't have that in any other contract. I've never heard of that."

> I went up and met with them and said, "Why is this so important?" And they said, "Because we don't trust that your local management team is going to treat us with integrity in between the contracts. So we want to make sure that you come up and meet with us four times a year, because at least we think we'll have a better chance of getting a fair shake." So I said, "You know what? Put it in. I'll do it."

> Now shortly after the contract negotiations concluded, we made a change in leadership. I went up there a few months later. We had a new general manager. I met with the union for one of my mandatory meetings. They said, "Ms. Kimber, we can't tell you what a change there is in this hotel and in the way we're being treated." And I said, "What is different?" They said, "Ms. Bunson, the general manager, is sincere. She talks to us. She listens to us. And she doesn't give us everything we want, but she tells us why she can't do something if she can't do it. And she answers us. And if the answer is no, she tells us immediately. We know we're not going to win every battle, but we're getting the truth."

> It was such an eye-opener because even within a company that's so well intentioned, if the local leader does not treat the people with integrity, it doesn't matter what your company stands for.

In Chapter Ten I describe the labor-management relationship at Boeing before, during, and after the first (and thus far only) full-scale engineers' strike in 2000. That discussion will show how the engineers' perceptions of their managers' integrity—their promise keeping, their transparency, and the extent to which they demonstrated their espoused values—played a vital role in causing those relationships to sour and, later, to improve.

Those I have spoken with, on both the management side and labor side, have argued that behavioral integrity represents a golden key in labor relations. It will not resolve all challenges, but it makes resolution possible.

SUMMARY

As I spoke with executives about the benefits and challenges of behavioral integrity, they reported an astonishing variety of settings and ways in which the integrity dividend emerges. Leaders' consistency between word and action supports employee trust and gives them clear direction. It promotes the engagement of employees' hearts in their work, which leads to a host of discretionary contributions, from enhanced initiative and problem solving to customer service. It trickles down through the organization to create a leadership culture of integrity. It may be the only way to implement espoused values throughout an organization, and many change efforts seem to fail from its lack; the exhortation to "do as I say, not as I do" never works. Behavioral integrity increases the strength and efficiency of relationships with customers, suppliers, and unions. And all of these improvements can be expected to show up on the bottom line as the integrity dividend.

The next chapter offers a few more basic insights from a general model of behavioral integrity in business. Then we return to more that executives can tell us about the challenges of achieving behavioral integrity and how to overcome them.

Into Practice

Consider

- Is your word impeccable? Do you know anyone whose word is impeccable? How do others respond to him or her?
- What level of behavioral integrity have you learned from your leaders? How does your leadership style reflect theirs?
- To what extent does excellent performance in your business depend on the discretionary efforts of workers?
- To what extent are people in your company putting their best efforts into their work—or simply operating in survival mode?
- Look at your company's mission or values statement. How is it viewed in your company—cynically or as a source of practical guidance? I submit that it is one or the other.
- To what extent does your company's brand consistently live up to its promise? How high a priority is that for your company?
- Are your supplier relationships and your union relationships characterized by high or low trust and cooperation? Might behavioral integrity make a difference here?

CHAPTER THREE

BEHAVIORAL INTEGRITY
DRIVERS AND PAYOFFS
Why Small Mistakes Can
Have Big Costs

To guide thinking and research into the challenges of keeping an impeccable word, I developed the model in Figure 3.1. The figure illustrates the model in terms of a manager-subordinate relationship, but it can also be applied to others. The boxes and arrows trace how behavioral integrity is generated, as well as its broad effects. It separates managers' actual consistency from the consistency that others notice, the latter being what drives employee attitudes and behaviors that lead to profits. The model helps us notice or locate component mechanisms along the way, such as the lens of cynicism through which some employees see their managers' actions.

The model helps us make distinctions that explain how small causes can have big consequences. The general concept that drives this magnification is called an accelerating loop. One type of accelerating loop that I teach to my classes as a key element of performance management is the *success cycle*. When you set a moderately challenging goal and then accomplish it, you come to feel more confident of your capacities and think of yourself as someone who accomplishes goals. The confidence and enhanced self-concept then support you in working harder and accomplishing the next goal, which adds more juice and so on. Looping acceleration is why initial small wins are critical for any major

FIGURE 3.1. A MODEL OF BEHAVIORAL INTEGRITY DRIVERS AND PAYOFFS.

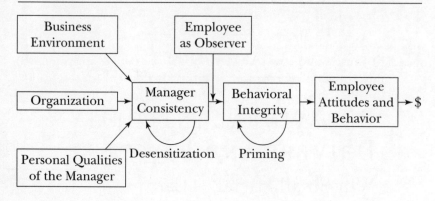

change project and why so many sports are games of momentum. Small wins can snowball into bigger ones. So can small losses. In this chapter, I explain two accelerating loops in the behavioral integrity process, each indicated in the figure by a backward-bending arrow.

The rest of this chapter takes you through the model from left to right, showing how small behavioral integrity glitches can lead to major consequences. Central to the model—and to understanding how behavioral integrity works—is the difference between *acting* consistently and being *seen as* acting consistently. I do not mean to imply any manipulative or deceptive process, because deliberate and ongoing deception rarely goes undetected under the scrutiny that employees give their managers. The model simply recognizes that while managers generate many words and many actions, it is the observer who chooses which words get paired up with which actions to represent a manager's consistency. Behavioral integrity is a subjective judgment, albeit based in part on objective information about a manager's actual consistency.

In the model, the actual manager consistency box is labeled "Manager Consistency." To its left are three factors that can drive or challenge that consistency. To its right we see the influence of the observer (in this case the employee), the resulting behavioral integrity (BI) perceptions, and further outcomes.

FACTORS THAT DRIVE
(OR CHALLENGE) CONSISTENCY

What feeds or challenges consistency? It is not easy to consistently keep promises, and it is certainly not easy to consistently embody the values to which we aspire. The model shows three broad factors: the business environment, the organization, and personal qualities of the individual manager under study.

BUSINESS ENVIRONMENT

The business environment creates challenges to consistent action. Managers in most industries face increasing levels of competition, increasing speeds of doing business and nearly constant change.[1] Technological innovation is partly to blame, as the Internet opens new channels for revenue, coordination, and competition. Instability from this and other sources sometimes pressures managers to reverse yesterday's proclamations in order to cope with today's environment. Capital markets demand accountability for results with shorter and shorter time horizons, which creates pressure for short-term, expedient actions rather than those that pay off in the long run. Management ideas go in and out of fashion, which creates pressure for managers to conform in order to seem current and thus legitimate—and so to implement policies that may be inconsistent.

ORGANIZATION

The organization introduces an additional set of challenges to consistency. These challenges emerge from the hierarchy, size, and culture of the company; from change efforts; and from the personal characteristics of the company executives. Sometimes company higher-ups countermand your personally expressed commitments to a customer or an employee. The CEO of a global services organization described to me the challenge of making commitments that stand up and make sense when they are relayed to distant offices and translated into different languages and business situations. Company cultures have something to say about whether integrity is expected or actively discouraged.

Sometimes the challenge to consistency comes in the form of well-intentioned change efforts that give rise to confusion, ambivalence, and odd mixes of jargon and policy directives. In fact, change by its nature, even when managed well, challenges the effort to act consistently just because it introduces unpredictability into the system.

Another organizational factor that shapes managers' consistency is the level of integrity they see in their boss. People who are ambitious (and most managers hope for promotion some day) tend to imitate their boss's style of doing business. One executive I interviewed noted that after twenty years of work under a company president who was known for a fiery temper, his own style came to resemble the boss's, and he had to make a conscious choice to manage his own company differently. The imitation occurred despite his witnessing how destructive the boss's behavior had been; it had crept up on him without his awareness. In surveys of thousands of employees and managers, I have found this type of influence: middle managers tend to imitate the level of integrity they see in their bosses. Those who see their boss as less than fully consistent themselves tend to behave with less than full consistency.

PERSONAL QUALITIES OF THE MANAGER

Various qualities of managers or executives themselves also affect their own levels of consistent action. How well the manager knows his own values will make a difference in how consistently he can describe and act on them. Some managers consciously place a higher value on keeping their word than others. Some are prone to distraction. Visionaries may habitually speak in terms of ideals on which they may or may not follow up. Some managers feel strongly compelled to tell people what they want to hear, or avoid telling difficult truths for fear that engaging more honestly would damage relationships.

When I discuss how to manage behavioral integrity in this book, I focus mainly on interventions related to organizational factors and the qualities of the individual. The business environment is what it is. For the purpose of change, we can do better by looking at how we as individuals operate and at how we can shape our companies to better support managers in meeting the challenges of living by their word.

HOW THE FACTORS COMBINE

The three factors of environment, organization, and manager interact to shape a manager's consistency and thus credibility. For example, in the late 1980s and the early 1990s, when merger mania was sweeping the U.S. corporate world, a friend of mine worked for an engineering-based, high-reliability manufacturer that was acquired by larger companies twice in ten years. Shortly after the second acquisition, the president of his company organized a series of off-site retreats for top and middle management to refine the organization's vision and align it with the goals of the new parent company. The process took several weeks as executives worked to articulate the long-held core values of the organization. One fact that quickly became clear during the sessions was that the employees took great pride in the company's reputation for high-quality precision products, particularly because in many cases, they were used by customers to test other products' performance in potentially life-threatening situations.

The president had come up through the ranks of the company and appeared to share the cultural value placed on product quality. Yet at the end of that quarter, when the company was on the verge of narrowly missing ambitious new shipping targets set by the new owners, the president personally intervened. To ensure that the target would be met, he waived established quality rules and allowed a shipment to be made despite evidence of defects among the items sampled by the quality assurance staff. Word quickly leaked out that under the new parent company, the president's incentive payments were tied to meeting quarterly sales and shipping targets. In fairness, I should note that when the president waived the quality rules that governed product shipments, he also sent along a quality-assurance staffer to the customer's site to complete the inspection there and remove any defective items. Nevertheless, with that event, the president lost credibility among the managers, engineers and production staff, and their perception of his integrity never fully recovered.

Consider a few important points from the story. First, note that the breach was driven by all three general factors. The influence of the business environment is seen in the repeated acquisition of the company, which put the new president under immediate performance pressure. The acquisitions came at a time when vertical integration was being pushed by capital markets. At the organizational level, the company determined the performance metrics to which the president was being held and created a climate of pressure to meet the shipping targets even at the expense of company values. Still, the president himself might have avoided the error if he had been more confident, more sensitive to his company culture, or more far-seeing.

Notice also that the president had in fact attempted to address the value of quality by sending along a quality inspector to accompany the shipment. He was attempting to integrate the conflicting demands for production and quality and thereby satisfy both, and in his mind he was acting with integrity. He must have felt betrayed and bewildered that the subtlety of his decision got lost in the retelling. But it did, as subjective interpretations of words and actions always come into play.

AN AMPLIFIER AROUND CONSISTENCY: DESENSITIZING

We turn now to the first accelerating loop in Figure 3.1: desensitization of managers about their own consistency. People typically have a need to think of themselves as fair and reasonable people, and the idea of acting consistently and keeping commitments is part of that cherished self-image. Once someone starts to act inconsistently, she creates what psychologists call cognitive dissonance— in this case, a tension between what one sees and who one thinks oneself to be. Normally, cognitive dissonance is resolved in one of two ways: change the behavior or update one's attitude to embrace the new behavior. If you think you hate custard but you have just enjoyed crème bruleé, which you subsequently learn is a kind of custard, you decide that maybe custard is not so bad. The same thing applies if you know hypocrisy is wrong but then hear managers talk in your boardroom about empowering workers while on the shop floor talking like drill sergeants. Since none of us, including you, like to think of ourselves as hypocritical, you become desensitized to the inconsistency and develop what Eileen Shapiro, in her book *Fad Surfing in the Boardroom,* calls the "split brain syndrome."[2] Where the path of least resistance to managerial success lies in verbally endorsing values that actions will seemingly contradict, many managers will accept that state of affairs and minimize awareness of any mismatch. This desensitizing makes them likely to create more and larger gaps and to act more inconsistently. They act inconsistently, then tune out awareness of the inconsistency in order to be comfortable. The loop repeats itself, and small inconsistencies give way to larger ones.

One Fortune 100 corporation listed the following statement of values in its 2001 annual report:

- Communication
- Respect
- Integrity
- Excellence

That is a respectable set of values, if a little vague, but the company was Enron. It is hard to imagine that Enron executives spent much time in contemplation of how stunningly their actions ultimately contradicted these values. Perhaps some had qualms, but these concerns would have been explained away and ultimately driven from awareness. The personal and financial consequences of dwelling on the inconsistencies would have been substantial, and most people in a position to know chose instead to desensitize themselves.

THE ROLE OF THE OBSERVER

In Figure 3.1 between "Manager Consistency" and "Behavioral Integrity," note the influence labeled "Employee as Observer." To generate the integrity dividend, it is not enough to merely live by one's word; you have to be *seen* as living by your word. The story about the unfortunate president of the high-reliability manufacturer is a lesson that the most delicate balancing act does not succeed if others do not see it as consistency between word and deed. The people working closely with you (and especially under you) are usually accurate in their perceptions of you, since they are motivated to watch you closely. But perceptions do not always align with reality, and people sometimes hear what they want to hear. It may be that when you acted in alignment with espoused value A, someone was thinking you a hypocrite because you failed to act in alignment with espoused value B. People are subjective in their judgments; it's a reality you have to deal with. But understanding their subjective biases in relation to behavioral integrity judgments gives you a jump on the difficult task. Let's look at four factors that affect what consistency cues other people will notice and how those cues will affect their judgment of your integrity:

- The fundamental attribution bias
- The perceived importance of the value
- The observer's level of cynicism
- The manager's apology or explanation

THE FUNDAMENTAL ATTRIBUTION BIAS

Your subordinates will watch you more closely than will others with whom you interact. They are motivated to figure you out because they depend on you so much. A prominent trust scholar, Rod Kramer, once described subordinates as "vigilant and intuitive auditors" of their boss's integrity.[3] They are watching you for patterns of behavior. Scarily, they also tend to blame every "bad" thing you do on who you are. It works somewhat with "good" things too, but the "bad" ones draw special attention. Subordinates figure you do what you do because you like it that way. They seldom attribute your act to circumstances or others' actions. We all tend to blame people for their actions more than they would themselves and probably more than is appropriate. This is what psychologists call the "fundamental attribution bias." Years of evidence have shown that subordinates looking at bosses are especially biased in this way.

THE PERCEIVED IMPORTANCE OF THE VALUE

A second subjective factor is the importance to the observer of the professed value that was violated. Suppose a hotel manager overbooks as a way to optimize revenues and, as a result, has to send a few weary travelers to another hotel. The manager is delicately balancing customer service with profitability as two sometimes competing values. As part of sending that weary customer walking, the manager probably provided a complimentary hotel night and tried to address the professed (and probably genuinely held) value for service in other ways as well. The employees who are most upset about the manager's overbooking decisions will be those who most value customer service. Thus, the employees who see the act as most hypocritical will be precisely those who care most about the customer. The general principle is that people are most sensitive to inconsistencies regarding values they care about. Minority and female employees are most vigilant about discrimination, especially when diversity and inclusion are professed values. Quality mavens will be most distressed about breaches of the quality ethic. If the values a manager or a company professes are truly important to the company, then their most sensitive barometers to behavioral integrity regarding those values will also be the employees who most deeply buy in to those values. That means some of your most promising employees will also be the easiest to alienate if you slip.

THE OBSERVER'S LEVEL OF CYNICISM

Observers filter what they notice about a manager's behavioral integrity according to the level of cynicism the observers bring to the task. People notice what they watch for. Some people measure and judge everyone they meet in terms of intelligence, some measure everyone in terms of physical attractiveness or fitness, and some measure in terms of integrity, hypocrisy, or character. It is a sad truth that many of the people you encounter have experienced some form of betrayal in their past. The bruises that result from those perceived betrayals lead to heightened vigilance.

When I looked at employee race in the hotel study, I found evidence that black employees might be more sensitive to managers' behavioral integrity than other employee groups. One probable reason for this difference is that black Americans as a group have been subject to a fair amount of hypocrisy over the years as various forms of discrimination have persisted despite antidiscrimination laws and professed values to the contrary.

Stories in the news about companies that lay off workers while giving large payouts to executives similarly seed cynicism. Many employees are wounded and many are cynical, and they look at your integrity through those lenses. As their manager, you need to avoid giving them any excuse to lump you in with their previous betrayers.

THE MANAGER'S APOLOGY OR EXPLANATION

The fourth factor that affects how a manager's actual inconsistencies are viewed is the explanation or apology that the manager gives. A sincere and effective apology allows the manager to be seen as maintaining high behavioral integrity despite evidence of inconsistency. The inconsistency may be attributed to circumstance, or the manager might explain that the action was aligned with another, possibly more important, stated value. Knowing how to apologize well is an extremely worthwhile skill for any manager. I discuss apologies in greater detail in Chapter Six.

A SECOND AMPLIFIER AROUND INTEGRITY PERCEPTIONS: PRIMING

This brings us in the model to behavioral integrity as a perception and the effect of priming. Like desensitization, perceptual priming is an accelerating loop. People tend to collect evidence that favors their beliefs or attitudes and to discount or ignore information that runs counter to them. This basic principle, well known to psychologists as the "confirmatory bias," is one of the reasons that prejudice is so intractable. Once people start to believe something, their minds are primed to build a case for it, and they start filtering reality to better match the belief. Naturally they do so in their behavioral integrity perceptions. Once you have tagged someone a hypocrite, it becomes very difficult for that person to regain your good integrity rating.

A problem of asymmetry increases the challenge of building and maintaining a reputation for an impeccable word. Asymmetry is inherent in how we all assign traits such as "inconsistent," "trustworthy," or "lying." How many times must a person lie in order to be a liar? One. How many times must he or she tell the truth in order to be an honest person? Lots and lots. A perception of integrity, like trust, obeys a ratchet effect: it is typically slow to build and quick to fall. A positive sense of behavioral integrity requires consistency over time and reliability. But a single violation, real or perceived, can cause that sense to plummet. A well-known trust scholar, Roy Lewicki, captures the fragility of trust by describing its attainment as being like the children's board game Chutes and Ladders.[4]

CONSEQUENCES: THE INTEGRITY DIVIDEND

We now move to the penultimate element in Figure 3.1: employee attitudes and behavior. People respond emotionally and intellectually to the level of behavioral integrity they see in their leader, and in ways that critically shape their work behavior. Here, two attitudes come into play that I introduced in Chapter Two. First, people's sense that their leaders mean what they say opens the way to trust. Behavioral integrity is not always enough—followers also need to feel that their leader cares about them and knows what she is doing—but you will not have trust without it. The second attitude regards the respect employees assign to your word— your credibility. When you have a sense that another's words can be relied on, you grant that person's word more power and take her word more seriously. That person will be better able to persuade you and to guide your actions because you do not feel a need to filter her statements to detect ulterior motives or unstated meanings. The combination of these two attitudes—employee trust and employee respect for your word—supports employees' commitment to the company and engagement in the company's task As a consequence of such a climate, employees tend to:

- Go an extra mile to serve the company
- Respond more dynamically to change initiatives
- Stick around

Those tendencies contribute to the company's bottom-line performance in ways I previewed in Chapter Two.

SUMMARY

Figure 3.1 is a visual model of the overarching theme of this book.

Behavioral integrity is shaped by forces in the business environment, such as management fashions and capital markets; forces inside the organization, such as leadership role models, management cultures, incentive systems, and other policies; and managers' personalities and self- awareness. But it is also colored by the eyes of the observers who evaluate our integrity—and make no mistake, they do. Thus, the model distinguishes a manager's actual consistency and promise keeping from the behavioral integrity that others see.

That is not to say that you can effectively deceive those who work with you on a daily basis. You cannot. Rather, the distinction is necessary because it highlights a few factors on the part of observers that color their perceptions, and, fair or not, your effectiveness depends on conveying integrity in spite of observers' biases and filters. Managing behavioral integrity means staying consistent and addressing the expectations, misunderstandings, and other factors that affect others' perceptions. For that reason (and others), it can be a daunting task.

The business environment is, for practical purposes, a given. This book focuses on managing behavioral integrity through the organization, the individual manager, and the observer. You can influence the observer through your communications, and you can shape yourself through study, practice, and discipline. Changing the company depends a lot on your rank, but change at that level is a function of policies and practices and of the behaviors you model.

There are two accelerators in the model, the feedback loops, that cause small inputs to yield large consequences:

1. Inconsistency leads to desensitization, which leads to more inconsistency.
2. Perceptions of hypocrisy lead to priming of expectations for hypocrisy, which leads to judging more ambiguous information as hypocrisy.

These two cycles magnify the impact of small inputs by setting up an oscillation that feeds on itself. They tell us, in part, why managing integrity perceptions is so challenging: small inconsistencies and blind spots can easily lead to larger blind spots, and negative labels, especially around integrity, are hard to shake.

Chapters Four to Six focus on personal challenges to managing our own behavioral integrity, looking at the values we espouse, the ways we communicate, and our personal discipline. Chapters Seven to Nine look at ways managers can enhance integrity through their organizations by appreciating the middle manager's dilemma, managing a consistent culture, and avoiding management fashions.

Into Practice

Consider

- To what extent have you become desensitized to your own inconsistencies? What have you dismissed as acceptable broken promises and acceptable value compromises? Do your subordinates see them as acceptable? Are you sure you know what they think?
- Consider the opinions you have formed about the behavioral integrity of those around you. To what extent is that judgment locked in—and to what extent can those people change it by their actions? What would it take to change those opinions?
- Are there certain areas of manager inconsistency to which you are especially sensitive and that you therefore notice? Do others notice the same inconsistencies?

PART TWO

MANAGING YOUR OWN BEHAVIORAL INTEGRITY

Building Trust and Credibility

CHAPTER FOUR

PROMISE LESS, BUT DO IT MORE OFTEN

Sky Chefs, an airline catering company, was a wholly owned subsidiary of American Airlines from the 1940s to 1986, when it was sold to private investors—just in time for three of the biggest boom years of the airline industry. The most profitable year in the company's history was 1989. In 1990, the Gulf War and a recession put the brakes on the industry, and Sky Chefs barely eked out a profit. The grim numbers continued in 1991, and there was little chance for revenue gain to improve the picture because airlines were serving less and less food.

Michael Kay had developed a reputation as a turnaround leader. He had no experience in airline catering, but the board felt that he had the right skills to save the company. The board was right. When he took the helm at Sky Chefs in 1991, the company had annual operating earnings around $7 million and a value around $50 million. The book value of the stock was around $12 a share. And Sky Chefs was in last place in its competitive set for profitability and customer satisfaction. Three years later, revenues had remained flat but earnings were at $56 million, and customer satisfaction had grown. When Kay left Sky Chefs after the sale of the company in 2001, it was in first place among airline caterers in customer satisfaction, earnings were around $200 million, the company was valued in excess of $2 billion, and the stock price was over $10,000 a share. These were extraordinary results, by any standard. How did he do it?

Michael sums up his approach to leadership with the phrase I borrowed for the title for this chapter. He does not mean that leaders should promise fewer results; to the contrary, the performance target he negotiated with the owner after two months on the job was to take the company's annual earnings from $6 million to $50 million within three years. This target was audacious, especially in a shrinking market, since the gains would need to come mostly from efficiency. Michael Kay is a firm believer in the motivational and attention-focusing power of ambitious performance targets. He is also a firm believer in laying out fewer guiding values so you can follow them and reinforce them constantly—and that is what he means when he says "promise less."

Promise Fewer Values

Promise fewer guiding values. Most leaders espouse so many that it is not clear to managers and employees how to act. As a leader, you need to develop a very few values that you will absolutely live by and then repeat them every chance you get. At Sky Chefs, Michael focused on three behavioral values. In his words, they were:

> (1) Stretch beyond what's comfortable; let's get out of this "take no chances" incremental mentality. (2) Always ask for help when you're not achieving your goals. And help other people ask for help. (3) And [recruit, develop, and retain] talent, talent, talent. And I said it *every* place I went. I never opened a talk with the boys that I didn't say it. I never talked to a manager on the telephone that I didn't say it. Within the next four, five, or six months, we built it into the performance system. You did a quarterly review with a first-line supervisor? You had to talk about those three things. You had to look for evidence of those three things. You had to score against those three things.

It became the subject of some joking among the ranks, but they knew without a doubt what Michael stood for. The key here is focus. The particular values should depend on your starting place and what you are trying to accomplish.

If you, as a leader, choose just a few values to talk about day in and day out, you stand a much better chance of actually building those values within your company and of succeeding in visibly living by them, which means reaping the integrity dividend.

A FEW CLEAR VALUES

How many is "a few"? Though tempting, any solid formula would be misleading. Psychologists have long known that most people can keep in mind somewhere between three and seven elements. But seven is a lot of values to juggle, and the more values you include, the more likely you are to lose focus. Three is simple and tight. Six is less so. As you go beyond ten, you enter a murky terrain where different followers will choose to highlight different items—and the list starts to exist more on paper than in anyone's mind and heart.

If you want people to know what you stand for as a leader or as a company, keep it simple. Bob Fox, vice president of human resources at Carlson Hotels Worldwide, stresses that for an expression of values to stick and become part of a company's daily conversation, it must be brief:

> Any credo or value system ought to be memorizable. And it ought to be able to fit on the back of a business card. If it's longer than that, it's too darn long. Now you can create stories and additional explanations that can go on for pages, but at the end of the day, you have to make a brief statement that people can remember.

Simplicity shapes an identity—a brand identity, an identity as a corporate employer, or your individual identity as a leader—that can be widely understood. Nancy Johnson, executive vice president for Carlson Hotels Worldwide, comments:

> Even talking about our brand and what we want our brand to stand for, it's got to be simple, it's got to be clean, and it's got to be clear. I always talk about the basic filters—the basic, "What are we going to fall on our swords for?" I make sure that I talk about those as frequently as I possibly can because I want everyone to understand: this is what we are all about. Simplicity and clarity are essential.

Other leadership thinkers have noted the need for simplicity in defining operational values. Jim Kouzes, coauthor of *The Leadership Challenge*, advocates

> focusing in on a few key things, which may reorder themselves later on in the future if our life circumstances change. Putting too many things on the list creates problems. We tell people five is the most that they should have. People usually can't remember more

than that, if they can remember that many. Then you take those five, and you order them in priority. You put service and innovation, service and profitability—or whatever your values may be—next to each other. And you say, "Okay, which is more important?"

Jim suggests at most five values and adds that the five should be prioritized. Prioritizing helps employees understand how to apply the values in real life, which is what you are after.

When companies or leaders espouse too many values, the list of desired values becomes a dead document. Nobody can remember it, much less live by it. One executive I interviewed told of a prior colleague who promoted ten core values and twenty top imperatives. People under him did not know what to focus on, despite the colleague's absolute conviction that he had given clear guidance. And the colleague got angry when the feedback came in that people were lost. Another executive told me of a company president who attempted to implement and track no fewer than 157 primary initiatives at the same time. Many of the initiatives were terrific ideas, but the result of the program was "anarchy. . . . People were complaining that they didn't know what they were supposed to be doing and they were just reporting on what it was that they weren't doing." Profitability went down. Turnover went up.

Too many values end up looking a lot like no values at all.

WHAT A FEW CLEAR VALUES CAN DO

Bob Fox says that if a values statement is too long, "people can't memorize it. They can't explain it. It can't become part of your ABCs, your personal Ten Commandments. People shouldn't need to go look it up. They have just got to be able to know it and embrace it."

There are many examples of simple and memorable statements of value. For example, this is the Carlson Companies credo:

Whatever you do, do with Integrity.

Wherever you go, go as a Leader.

Whomever you serve, serve with Caring.

Whenever you dream, dream with your All.

And never, ever give up.

The credo is short and memorable. It does not promise everything—and it is not supposed to. But leaders throughout the company can measure their decisions against it. I have had more than one Carlson employee recite the credo to me. It is a statement that lives in Carlson employees' hearts.

If you, as a leader, have clearly identified the very few values that are really important for your enterprise, then you can repeat your message often and find different ways of getting your point across and showing that you mean what you say. Managers often think they have conveyed their values to their followers if they have said them a few times. Stan Myers of SEMI, a well-seasoned executive, points out "that doesn't mean it was heard. Or maybe it was heard and not understood." Your followers are not dim, but when it comes to talk of values, we are all rightly skeptical. We have all seen many executives—and politicians—for whom values talk is merely window dressing. It is only by repetition and discussion *and action* that people start to consider that perhaps you actually mean what you say. You cannot create that steady repetition and reinforcement when the message is complex. Keep it simple.

The payoff of such simplicity coupled with steady repetition is that you get to shape your identity—your followers' picture of what you stand for—and make it part of people's sense of you. Just use a few themes. Joy Rothschild of Omni Hotels describes this feel or identity as a "calling card":

> In my own HR organization, you ask anyone, "What's Joy's motto?" They'll answer, "No surprises." I don't want to be surprised by anything. So even if you think an employee might call me about a problem, and they never do, I'd rather know about it. That's what I stand for: no surprises.

Rich Panico, CEO of Integrated Project Management, takes a similar approach. He says, "If we did a survey right now through the company and asked, 'What's most important to Rich?' I'd be really disappointed if everyone did not have three out of four."

Simplicity aids transparency. When you are transparent and repetitive enough in describing the key values that consistently drive your behavior, you become predictable for your followers. Strangely enough, that predictability is a good thing to create. It allows your followers to follow you even when you are not physically present because they know what you would say. Darryl Stickel, founder of Trust Unlimited, endorses this point, adding that a clear and repetitive message yields predictability, which reassures people and supports them in trusting their leader:

> You need to be extremely transparent. You want people to eventually get to the place where they go, "Oh, I don't need to ask him about this. I *know* how he's going to respond. He is going to say X, and he's going to say it's because of this value." They'll actually start quoting you to one another. . . .
>
> It's about being predictable. When I used to work at McKinsey, I worked with a set of clients for a little over six months. They got so that one of the running jokes was people would look at each other and go, "How are you doing?" Because they said that every time I would come across someone, I would ask them this. And it was so genuine and so sincere that I really wanted to know how this person was doing and that I really cared about these folks. They said, "You ask that every time. We know it's coming." They said, "But you know what? We don't want you to stop."
>
> It got so that they could predict how I was going to behave. That's extremely comforting for folks. It reduces their uncertainty. For me, that's what it's about. Behavioral integrity is about consistency, predictability; it's when I say something, I'm damn well going to do it.

Simplicity and the repetition and consistency that it permits form a basis for the predictability that engenders trust. They also allow a value to take on a powerful and resounding role in the company. Bob Wright, cofounder of the Wright Business and Leadership Institutes, suggests that key values can play the role of a "drumbeat . . . the bass drum that sets the tempo, and any of the other drums are layered on top of that." If the leader's spoken values are to take on driving power of a drumbeat, they must be simple and repetitive.

WHY DON'T MORE LEADERS PROMISE LESS?

Why do many leaders shy away from focusing on fewer promises and values? Some probably think they can accomplish more with a broader platform of values, and they fear compromising or cutting corners on the values that don't get discussed. Some might not recognize how much daily repetition is needed to move the needle on values. Michael Kay attributes lack of focus to gaps in recognition:

> There's a lack of recognition of how focused leadership investment needs to be. There's a lack of recognition about how repetitive it needs to be—in both talking the talk and role-modeling the behavior. And there's a lack of recognition of how granular the recognition for change needs to be—it's the early wins and the small wins that encourage people to take the next step.

Too complex a set of values sets up a situation that is ripe for misunderstanding as the complex message gets reinterpreted and passed along like the children's game of telephone. Each successive layer of management—indeed, each manager—adds his or her own subtle nuance to the overall picture until it becomes unrecognizable. That is true even where the values are codified and recorded: they get interpreted differently.

The larger the company is, the greater is the likelihood that different groups within it will start to develop different interpretations and emphases within the culture you try to promote. They split off. Sociologists call it cultural drift.

PUTTING SIMPLICITY INTO ACTION

How do you put this simplicity into action? What do you do? I have four basic suggestions: (1) discuss means as well as ends, (2) celebrate value victories, (3) hold managers accountable, and (4) concretize and reconcile.

DISCUSS MEANS AS WELL AS ENDS

Leaders talk a lot about results, and when they fail to get results, they are usually pushed out of the company pretty fast. But true leadership also means guiding managers about what behaviors to use in order to get those results. Otherwise followers can easily develop a "whatever it takes" mentality and culture that can lead to all kinds of ethical problems and inconsistency across managers. You have to be as explicit about behaviors as you are about results. Within your company, successful managers are those who work on both at the same time. You celebrate those folks. With that reasoning, Michael Kay at struggling Sky Chefs paired his three behavior values with three performance metrics:

> My mantra in the company during those early years was, "Here are the leadership behaviors we expect you to figure out how to practice. And here are the equally limited number of explicit results: (1) labor/productivity, (2) corporate overhead/reduction, (3) safety performance/improvement. Three and three. Never talked about anything else." In fact, when I'd walk into a kitchen and I'd get a briefing by the management team, and there'd be stuff on that briefing that wasn't in the three-and-three, I'd say, "Guys, you're working on the wrong stuff."

Michael was looking for just a few results and just a few behaviors. He talked about them all the time and asked about them all the time. He made a drumbeat—one that people could remember even when he was not in the room.

Other successful executives have used similar approaches. John Hillins, former senior director of human resources for Amgen, describes a Honeywell CEO who focused on "five whats and three hows." The CEO would randomly ask employees to recite them, and if they couldn't, he would arrange to have movies shown that laid out those priorities. John explains how simplicity helps get such simple messages through the noise of everyday work: "People have got 95 percent of their time already committed to doing the stuff they need to do every day to just survive. You can get their energy redirected only in certain areas. So keep it simple."

Both "whats" and "hows" matter. A strong focus on a few end goals without discussion of means can readily lead to ethical flexibility in the service of expediency. Bob Fox proposes that the solution to this challenge is the creation and repeated clear communication of a bright line between what's right and wrong—for example, "We are committed to making our goals. We are committed to serving our customers. But in no case will we do anything that will erode our value of integrity." You need to draw those lines, build or find stories around them, and enforce them. Then they become a reality in your company.

Rich Panico lays out clear "character elements" along with "performance elements" that are part of every performance appraisal. The character elements are absolute requirements, and an employee who fails on one of them generally is fired. To support a high standard for his company, Rich spends a lot of time thinking and talking with his employees about how to manage the inevitable trade-offs and the integration of different values. He describes his responsibility this way:

> If I give individuals a reason to compromise our values because in practice I hold other requirements more important, then I am to be held accountable for confusing the organization and creating a potentially volatile ethical environment. People need to clearly understand what is acceptable and unacceptable conduct. I'm very careful to make sure I don't create conflicting values.

When you are driving for maximum performance, the tension between means and ends can be fierce. A powerful leader who wants to safeguard her integrity will talk about both and assist followers in knowing how to reconcile them.

CELEBRATE VALUE VICTORIES

Celebrating performance is not a bad thing as long as you acknowledge the means by which the team performed. The best leaders focus their efforts by celebrating performance on a few key behaviors or performance values in order to put those behaviors squarely in the minds of subordinates. Celebrate improvements in performance to reinforce the habit of improvement and keep the focus on change—and to build your credibility and the power of your word. This is what Michael Kay did at Sky Chefs:

> We recognized that quarterly or semiannual bonus payments don't change how you feel about yourself and your work day-to-day. So every chance we got to celebrate success, no matter how small it was—on the floor, with hourly employees, with first-line supervisors, saying, "You moved the needle from here to here. That's terrific. Let's celebrate. Let's talk about what's going to happen next." I mean, all over the company—hats and T-shirts and pizza and tickets to the ball game. Because when you're trying to change the fundamental behaviors in a company, it ain't the quarterly bonus

payments that get you there. It's, "We want you to take a risk on how you work tomorrow. And if it works, we want to thank you for that, and we want to celebrate that."

We all know that effecting major changes in the way organizations do things is difficult. The key to success here is focus, which brings us back to the point about fewer values. You can celebrate and constantly reinforce only a few things, so pick them well, and then celebrate to show you mean it. Highlight the relevant successes constantly, and reinforce them in the minds of employees.

One extremely effective executive I spoke with, Allen Ibara, CEO of Phiam Corporation, described his program that not only celebrates value victories but gets employees to do so as well. He has a set of gift certificates for Starbucks, Home Depot, Barnes and Noble, and other stores in an envelope in a public place in the HR department. Everyone in the company is empowered to pick one up to give to another employee, with two rules:

1. Record who you are, to whom you are giving it, and what value you are giving it for.
2. Present it to the person in a public place, ideally with the person's supervisor and a few colleagues present.

Allen says the program is extremely successful, and his staff of a few hundred give out a couple of them a day. "It's a way to let people know that we are serious about the values and make them visible and get some attention on some of the positive things that we've done." Managers too often focus their attention on what is going wrong, and a program like this addresses that problem.

Interestingly, the program reinforces the values for the giver as well as the receiver, because the giver's action explicitly honors the value. The first time anyone gives an award to someone else, Allen usually goes out of his way to congratulate and thank the person "for doing something really cool."

HOLD MANAGERS ACCOUNTABLE

Accountability is the counterpoint to celebration. I noted that Michael Kay saw three substantial leverage points at Sky Chefs, one of which was workplace safety. When he started at Sky Chefs, workers' compensation costs were through the roof. So they set targets for reducing accidents at each of their thirty-five kitchens. Every month Michael would phone the five or six kitchen general managers who dramatically beat their targets and also the five or six who significantly failed to meet them. He would thank and reinforce the former, asking them about any innovations or practices that led to their win. And he would ask the latter, who had missed targets badly, what the barriers were and help them plan a better approach. A personal phone call from the big boss does not happen every day. It would send a jolt through those managers and let all of them see vividly what was really important. A CEO's time is limited but symbolically potent. *Promising less allows you to spend your limited time reinforcing what you say is important.* There is no better enforcement mechanism, and no better marker of integrity or its lack, than what you spend your time on.

Accountability that is "tough-minded, ubiquitous, and unremitting" sends a message through the company. Michael describes the alternative:

> Many companies that fall into decline suffer from failures of accountability. When only lip service is paid to the concept, the result is a climate of accommodation. This in turn contributes to inertia among managers who have become resigned to working far below their potential. In the turnaround, everyone should have a clear answer to the following question: "What does it take to get promoted or fired around here?" This can be achieved through well-articulated and fully and relentlessly communicated goals, supported by an accountability system that is taken seriously.[1]

Couple accountability with visible rewards for superior performance as you have defined it.

Don Delves is a top compensation consultant who described the model way he saw performance appraisal done at Sibson and Company, a compensation consulting firm where he worked earlier in his career. Sibson had a clear statement of its five most important values, its keys to success. Don recalls the values as integrity, relationships, intellectual capital, developing people—and billable hours. The firm conducted thorough performance appraisals of associates twice a year. Everyone above you met and discussed your performance on each of the five values, and the feedback was incorporated into performance coaching. A bonus could be granted based on good numbers or on good performance on some of the values. To get a raise or a promotion, you had to demonstrate them all. When Don started his own company, he chose different core values, but he kept the principle of accountability for them: "You have to practice values. You have to talk about them. You have to think about, 'Okay, what does this really mean?' And then you have to continually ask, 'Are we actually practicing our values here?'"

Embedding your stated values firmly in the performance appraisal and accountability system puts your money where your mouth is. It demonstrates integrity and translates the value from wind to reality. You cannot do that effectively with a dozen or more different values.

CONCRETIZE AND RECONCILE

A word of caution: although reinforcement and accountability are vital, a few other conditions also have to be met to empower your team to deliver on the values you propose. You cannot assume that those around you know how to translate your espoused values into recognizable reality. You must tell them how. Bringing abstract values to bear on concrete situations and actions is a genuine challenge. Everyone, including you, can gain clarity through discussions of what the values should look like in day-to-day life and which priorities rule when values and strategic directives seem to clash. Broadcasting the messages and posting them everywhere are not enough. You have to help employees see how the values you propose apply to their little corner of the company and how they in particular can contribute to the strategic tenets you lay out. If employees understand how their work and their projects relate to the greater strategy, they are happier and more effective. Their decisions will better support the direction you want to go in, and they will be better able to make sense of your decisions—and so trust you more.

Jim Kouzes says that detailed discussions are essential to effective leading with values:

> We have to go beyond just the words, and ask: "Okay, now, what's that mean to you? Give me an example. Let's make sure we're talking about the same thing here. Let's talk about some scenarios—what acting on the value looks like to you and what it looks like to me."

He is right that you cannot secure buy-in without concrete understanding. Subordinates at any level need to understand as specifically as possible what the value means in practice and then, if you want to see the value put into practice, personally and publicly commit to it.

Reconciliation is another requirement. Because life is full of trade-offs, part of communicating what the values need to look like in day-to-day decisions and behaviors is establishing priorities among the different values. Living your values and coaching your team to live by them too mean thinking about how to address those trade-offs properly in advance. It has been said that values are meaningless without priorities. Think about and discuss with your team what values should dominate others. Which one comes first? Jim explains:

> You have to have those dialogues up front, so that you don't have employees calling each time they have a values dilemma and say, "Boss, geez, I have a problem here. This customer wants to return a product. If we take it back, we've got to restock it. It's going to cost us X. However, this person's been a really good customer. What should I do?"
>
> You're thinking to yourself, Didn't we talk through this already?
>
> Well, you may have talked about it already, but if you're getting that call, the person on the other end is not clear about values preferences. That person doesn't know because you really didn't run through the scenario. This person is undoubtedly capable of making sound judgments on his own, but without clearly understanding the hierarchy of values that personal choice may not be consistent with what the organization holds dear.

Develop scenarios that test the values against each other—for example, spending money to keep a long-term customer.

Do we go for today's margin or the long gain? Do we follow safety procedures even when it means missing a production deadline? What are the priorities here? Which trade-offs are okay? Which aren't?

Talk people through the complexities of applying the few values you talk. In discussing values in concrete terms, talk through what happens when they bump up against each other. Michael Kay witnessed a powerful example of a leader showing employees how to prioritize conflicting values. He was eating with some friends at a large, well-known restaurant overlooking Boston Harbor, Anthony's Pier 4. It was run by Anthony Athanas, who owned several other famous restaurants. The place had seven hundred seats and was packed.

> At the next table was a couple who could not be satisfied, and they insisted on taking their dissatisfaction out by being abusive to the waitress. Not long into the dinner, Anthony showed up. He sized them up quickly: they were determined to be unhappy and intended to take it out on the server. Then I saw him do something that has stuck with me for years. When he came to the table, he had the check in his hand, and he tore it up. Then he said, "You know, the well-being of the people who work here at the restaurant is more important to me than the well-being of our customers. Especially when customers are treating employees unreasonably. And I'm happy to take care of your check tonight, but I would strongly suggest that this is probably not the right place for you, and that next time you should find someplace else to have dinner."

> You carve out your own value system. But the more important thing is that you act it out. Every server in that restaurant that night knew what Anthony had done. Every cook knew. Every busboy knew. He had sent a message that reinforced his value system. With powerful symbolism.

I am sure the story became a permanent part of the employee lore of Anthony's Pier 4. It demonstrated the value placed on employees in a way that words cannot by showing when that value is more important than another. There may be no more potent way to demonstrate a value than for a business owner to turn away a paying customer to preserve that value.

MAKING PROMISES IN
ONGOING OPERATIONS

Michael Kay's challenge at Sky Chefs wasn't business as usual; it was to turn the company around. As a rule, the executives I discussed the "promise less" idea with agreed that it is a potent tool for directing turnaround change. Opinions differed more on the question of how well promising less would work for ongoing operations.

Frank Guidara, CEO of Uno Chicago Grill Restaurants, argued that leadership decisions by definition need to be nuanced and responsive. He proposed starting simple when you take on a new position but giving your followers a more complex picture as they get to know you and the business. After all, you are always seeking to improve. Frank draws an analogy based on a football team:

> The first year you take over as coach, you and the team are all getting used to your plays. But what's great about veterans is you can build on what they learned in past years. So instead of having twelve defensive plays, now you can have twenty-four. Then you can have thirty-six. That's what's great about experience and longevity.

Frank's argument is reasonable and compelling. A well-seasoned team can execute more complex maneuvers or, to resume a previous analogy, can dance to more intricate drumbeats.

More compelling to me is the experience presented by Doug Brooks, president and CEO of Brinker International. Any sizable company is going to contend with ongoing turnover and the attenuation of messages that lose their clarity as they trickle down from the top to lower ranks. Over the years, Brinker has been a very successful chain of over sixteen hundred restaurants and 100,000 employees. It was not in need of a turnaround, but still it opted to simplify its values. Here is Doug's perspective on the decision:

> Southwest Airlines is the best at being simple and being really good at a few things, and they haven't changed over all these years. It's still "Have fun," but do these things great: fast, on time, the same plane. They won't even buy a second plane because they know the impact that has on maintenance, the staff, and the training. So they've been great at it.

We haven't been. We've had multiple brands. At one time we had nine restaurant concepts as part of our company. We had all these cultures at each brand, and we had this corporate team that was trying to understand it all. So a year ago, my leadership team sat down and decided to come up with some new strategies. We needed to. The ones we were doing were not relevant any more. We came up with six strategies and six behaviors. We call it "The Twelve Pack."

For us it's been incredibly invigorating. Over the past six months now, we've had small meetings to talk about The Twelve Pack: "Ask me any question you want about our company, and I will connect it to one of The Twelve Pack. Everything boils down to either one of the six strategies or one of the six behaviors. If what you're doing does not line up with one of them, then you might be doing something that's not needed or not part of where we're going. We'll do something different."

It has focused us and unleashed power. For many years, we were a company that didn't like saying no. Now that we have our Twelve Pack, we actually say, "We don't want to even spend money here in this little niche or this area. We just want to provide the basics. Here we can spend a lot more money so that we can invest in some revenue programs." We now know what it is that we are and what we want to do. And our employees know better what we want them to do than they have in twenty years.

Doug found that promising less and doing it more often gave his company clarity about what they did and did not want to be and where they did and did not want to go. I could tell from his tone that it has excited everyone around him. This reaction is not accidental: promising less made executive decisions more predictable, and hence more trustworthy, and also provided everyone a reliable road map to success in the company. Trust and clear direction are a potent combination.

SUMMARY

Pete Kline of Seneca Advisors, former CEO of Bristol Hotels and Resorts, captures the point of this chapter:

Your fundamental directives, your fundamental value systems that you're espousing to the organization have to be really short and sweet. You can't have a really broad, complicated set of priorities. By the time you get to the bulk of the staff, no one is going to have any idea what it means. You've got to have some simple premises that are paramount in your organization: "The customer is always right," or whatever it is going to be. Everyone needs to be able to understand them—whether they speak English or not, whatever level they are in the organization. And they're going to watch. If you really mean customer satisfaction is paramount, the lower-level people can't be the only ones who are expected to pull that off. They've got to see managers personally committed to customer service, talking to guests.

Promise less. Put everything you have into making those promises a reality. Talk fewer values. And then celebrate those values every waking moment. Deal in simple messages, repeated and conveyed accurately to everyone in the company and followed up with management action.

Leaders need to provide constant attention and repetition to keep an organization unified around its few key values. Rich Panico says it takes constant vigilance:

> It takes a consistent effort and clear communications to keep everyone on the same page. When I asked the question in my staff meetings about the organization's alignment and understanding of what is most important, the first response was: "Rich, do you think there's a problem?" I said, "No, we don't have to have a problem. I just want to be absolutely sure that people understand what's important to the executive team at IPM." I think too many organizations come up with that same excuse: "Well, everybody knows. Everybody knows." Well, that's not always the way it is.

Keep the drumbeat going to keep the company aligned. A good dance beat is simple: it's easier for people to hear, easier for them to recognize, and easier for you to keep true to.

This chapter leaves open the question of what few values to hold in this special way. Too broad, and they become empty bromides. Too narrow, and they become uninspiring. That is where the art of leadership comes in. Draw on your executive team for ideas.

As Allen Ibara said, "I don't think you have to say a lot of things. The things you say—they'd better be important: you'd better align behind them and you'd better stick with them." Or as Michael Kay says, "Promise less, but do it more often."

Into Practice

Consider

- What are the key values in your company? Can everyone in the company tell you what they are?
- How many values do you talk about? Too many?
- What should be most important? What are the priorities among company values?
- What key values do you promote as a leader? What simple values are your personal calling card? Do your followers know?
- How often do you talk about those values?
- How do you celebrate those values?
- How do you hold your people accountable for them?
- Do you discuss how to apply them? What to do when they clash?

Act

- Choose just a few values to promote. Many say that five is the maximum, but the fewer the better.
- Promote those values constantly.
- Celebrate values victories.
- Measure and coach performance on the values—both individual and group.
- Hold managers and employees accountable for them.
- Discuss on a regular basis how to translate the values into action: what they look like concretely and how to reconcile clashes among them.
- Explicitly use those key values to discuss strategic and day-to-day decisions.
- Check to see how well the values permeate the company. Do people know them? Do they live them?

CHAPTER FIVE

THE LANGUAGE OF LIVING BY YOUR WORD
Confronting and Committing

"Promise less" is not just about professing fewer key values. It also applies to concrete promises, as when you say a report will be complete Tuesday or that you'll meet for lunch. It applies to many small mistakes that fully well-intended executives make and how they can avoid them. Many perceived broken promises result from miscommunication.

In our efforts to maintain social harmony or simply to look good, we can unwittingly undermine our behavioral integrity. We may speak casually in a way that others misinterpret as a commitment. As members of a larger company, we may provide assurances that we cannot ourselves guarantee. We often avoid expressing unpleasant or awkward truths, and then seem inconsistent later when we act in line with an unspoken truth. Perceived violations also emerge from fuzzy requests that lead to unclear commitments.

We can address these issues of casual overpromising, unshared truths, vague requests, and vague commitments through increased precision in our language and other deliberate techniques.

AVOID CASUAL OVERPROMISING

Most communication-based risks to behavioral integrity come down to commitments we make, or that others think we make, on which we fail to follow through. For the most part, we in no way intend them as deceptions, but some recipients later consider them so. I ran into a friend and colleague some months ago and said we should have lunch together. I meant it at the time, and I remember being taken aback by the colleague's skeptical response. But the truth is that I did not take out my calendar to set a date, and months have since rolled by without a lunch date. I was speaking with genuine affection at the time, but perhaps with less than a full dedication to my word. Whatever the reason, I did not keep it. If I were not writing this book, I might not have even thought about it again. But what happened there? We have all done it. Why?

One possibility is that "we should have lunch together" is more of a ritual statement than one of genuine intent. It ends a friendly conversation with an expression of warmth. A German student in one of my classes said that in his eyes, Americans were disingenuous because we ask, "How are you?" of almost everyone, not really expecting an honest answer. In his world, the question is asked only between close friends, and the appropriate response is a genuine sharing and not our automatic, "Fine! And you?" Ritual and automatic statements warrant special attention in cross-cultural communication but carry hazards even on shared terrain. I thought I was sincere in suggesting lunch, but maybe I was speaking automatically. Regardless, the communication question is really what message was heard.

AN INSTINCTIVE RESPONSE TO NEEDS

Another possible reason for promises that often get broken is that we respond instinctively to needs or desires expressed by others, but we forget or otherwise fail to follow through. According to Darryl Stickel, founder of Trust Unlimited:

> People seem to have a tendency to overcommit, to make promises that they can't keep. This seems to be a pretty strongly ingrained part of human nature, particularly when we feel like we've either made a mistake or we see other people in distress. We want to make promises to make that go away—to make them feel better. There may even be the best intention to follow through, but we don't really think about what our capacity is.

We make promises sometimes because they feel good at the moment we make them. And we typically intend to follow through. But you might say that if we *really* intended to follow through, we would probably also have set up reminders to do so. Fortunately, thinking through the implications of a promise, and limiting oneself to those one can keep, is a skill that we can learn.

RESPECT THE WEIGHT OF YOUR WORDS

Of my casual lunch invitation, imagine how much stronger would have been its effect if I had addressed it to a subordinate. I would almost certainly never hear about having broken a promise, but my subordinate would have remembered it and felt betrayed by the lack of follow-through. Doug Brooks, president and CEO of Brinker International, notes that managers often fail to recognize the weight their words take on when they speak to subordinates.

> Remember that old television commercial, "When EF Hutton speaks, people listen?" I think young managers don't realize the power of their voice. That everyone's waiting for them to talk. Then everybody's just waiting to catch them not living up to what they said. They don't realize how their voice resonates.

Managers are often unaware that their words have been heard as a promise. Deirdre Wallace, president of the Ambrose Collection, points out that something as simple as, "I should check into that," can register in the ears of an employee as, "My boss knows about this problem and has committed to fixing it." Your chance encounter with a custodian on the way to the office may barely register in your own preoccupied head, but that custodian might remember it as his or her most significant work-related conversation that year.

ACKNOWLEDGE UNCERTAINTY

Another common source of problems with promises is our discomfort with acknowledging uncertainties and the limits of our own power inside the company. We all want to believe we have the power to promote an excellent subordinate, and the subordinate wants to believe it too. So simply adding a minor note of caution might not be enough to break through the shared fantasy: you have to make very clear what you can and cannot do. Several executives I spoke with described how broken promises had emerged from failing to acknowledge uncertainties and contingencies to themselves and others.

UNCERTAIN PROMOTIONS

A former vice president of a Fortune 500 company tells of a young engineer who was offered a better job elsewhere in the company. Not wanting to lose him, his boss promised him a promotion to the next pay band. Mentoring the young engineer, my friend told him:

> "You need to be careful about this, because I don't think your boss can make that commitment. I know how the process works, and the boss doesn't make that decision. The process counsel makes that decision. And HR makes that decision; they judge whether you meet the criteria or not. . . ." Now if his boss had said, "I'll try," then that was a different commitment, but he made a very specific commitment: "I'll get you this promotion; we'll move you to this new level; we'll give you this new work to do. Just please stay here!" I said, "I think that's beyond his control." He said, "No, I trust my boss." He sent me a note a few months later [saying], "It didn't work out. He wasn't able to do it. He blamed HR and everybody else." I said, "Well, do you remember our conversation?" He said, "Yes." I said, "So what are you going to do?" He said, "I don't want to work for this guy anymore."

By the time the promised promotion fell through, the other job opportunity was gone. If his boss had laid out the promotion process and its uncertainties, the young engineer could have weighed whether to take the risk. But the boss hadn't laid them out, and the young engineer felt deeply violated. His boss lost behavioral integrity—even though the engineer knew his boss had meant well.

Why didn't the boss discuss the uncertainty of the promotion process? It may be too harsh to suppose the manager's omission was a deliberate deception to retain the young employee. More likely, he (like most other people) wanted to appear and feel as though he had more power than he did. The friend who told me the story reflects on a point in his own career when he was surprised to learn, and loathe to accept, the limitations of his office.

> I was a VP, and there were things that I wanted to make happen that I couldn't do. I didn't have the authority. I would work hard to get the right people engaged in the processes and get approvals, and sometimes I was successful and sometimes I was not. That's a pretty common issue I see in others as well as myself: often people are not willing to admit that they can't go do something on their own.

Why would a manager be unwilling to admit depending on a larger organization to get things done? It sounds strange and unrealistic: *Of course* a corporate manager functions in a larger bureaucracy, and *of course* there are limits to individual authority. But managers' reluctance to acknowledge this truth came up often in executive considerations of how good people blow their credibility.

Ego Versus Confidence

Joy Rothschild, senior vice president of associate services for Omni Hotels, chalks the challenge up to ego and suggests it is peculiar to the hotel industry:

> You should never promise something that you don't think you can deliver. People who make this mistake *hope* they can deliver. Or they think they may be able to. But there's also a strong tendency in this very ego-driven business for people to want to be the hero and say, "I got you this." So instead of saying, "The company wants to recognize you and here's how the company will recognize you," people want to say, "I'm going to take care of you. I'm going to get you that promotion or bigger raise," so that they can come back and say, "I did it." A lot of it is ego.

The same general insight is shared by executives in other industries. Chalking the problem up to ego may sound simply like an accusation of character flaw. Americans, especially males, are raised on images of heroes and lone cowboys who miraculously save the day, and most of us harbor an irrational desire to be that hero. But there is also a logic to self-inflation: it allows us more easily to sell a subordinate on the importance of loyalty or to sell our own executive potential to higher-ups. Behind such logic is likely to be a work climate in which leaders encourage and promote braggadocio. Rich Panico, president and CEO of Integrated Project Management consulting company, describes the pressure:

> For example, I'm sitting in a meeting and an executive says, "Hey, Rich. Based on your background, it seems like you should be able to do this. What do you think?" Well, it's very easy to say, "Yeah. I can handle that." [But] the better and honest answer may be, "I don't know." If you say that you can do it, you've in effect made a promise. Whereas if you really weren't sure or you hadn't enough information, your response should be, "Based on what you're telling me, I think I can handle it, but I'd like to learn more about it so that I don't mislead you. I want to make sure that whatever expectations I create are fulfilled."

> It is easy for people to find themselves on a slippery slope, compromising integrity more and more. It's not that they were trying to be malicious. You have got to put that back on the leader who hasn't created an environment where it's okay to acknowledge uncertainty, acknowledge weakness, and not make promises unless you're absolutely confident.

Ironically, perhaps, confidence could be the antidote to ego-driven integrity problems. You have to be confident to openly acknowledge the limits to your power and ability. Ego might drive you to pretend to greater authority, but confidence allows you to share vulnerability. For a leader, supporting integrity means building one's own confidence and that of one's team.

UNCERTAINTY IN LARGER DEALS

The hazards of failing to acknowledge uncertainties extend beyond promises to subordinates. Ted Teng, former president and COO of Wyndham International, tells a story about a company selling a hotel. A large corporate customer historically booked around 20 percent of the hotel's room nights, and that customer planned to remodel some of the hotel's unused commercial space into a training center. When word got out that the hotel was for sale, the customer became concerned and conveyed that concern up through managerial channels to the CEO and the relevant committee. The answer that came back down was reassuring: the hotel would be sold only with a management contract, meaning that ownership might change, but the same people would be running the hotel, so prior negotiated plans and agreements would hold. It was true that the company was offering the hotel on those terms. What no one anticipated was that a buyer offered a much better price to buy the hotel without the management contract—and the offer was accepted. We do not know what happened to the customer. But we know that a lot of managers down the chain had made promises they did not know they could keep.

Ted sees a fine balance in the lessons he learned from his experience. He notes that the middle managers who carried the reassurance did not themselves have the authority to make and enforce the promise. Furthermore, he considers that they put their personal credibility behind the assurance they conveyed, and that credibility was damaged by the act. With the wisdom of hindsight, he suggests that they should have probed and questioned more about the message they were being asked to carry. He suggests that "when you make a promise, you ask, 'Do I have the capability, the ability, the authority, to keep it?' If I don't, then I'm making a promise hoping that those people will allow me to keep it." But caution has to be weighed against necessity because, as Ted adds:

> If you hold back on making promises, you will not be very successful in business. If you don't make promises, you don't get anything done. My [advice] is threefold: (1) Make as many promises as you can. Start out with the premise that you need to make promises. But (2) don't promise more than what you can keep. And (3) keep the promises you make.

Speak Awkward Truths

Another problematic habit of communication is a reluctance to discuss awkward truths. Awkward truths might arise, for example, when we assess people who work for us, describe the consequences of a change plan, discuss our company's performance, or discuss our own inability to meet a commitment. Common to all these situations is the likelihood that not communicating about the issue is, in the short run, easier and more peaceful than communicating about it. There is a certain strategic value in choosing when to rock the boat. The problems begin when our "choices" become automatic.

POOR PERFORMANCE

Most commonly, managers face a choice about discussing awkward truth when a subordinate has underperformed. Most people are strongly tempted to put off the difficult conversation, hoping the employee will eventually just quit. Pete Kline of Seneca Advisors, former CEO of Bristol Hotels and Resorts, tells how, early in her career, his wife, Caren, fired a secretary without conveying the awkward truth:

> Trying to make her feel better, Caren told her she was a great person and all these things. She sent a really confusing message. She tried to be so nice about it that by the end of the conversation, the secretary went to the personnel department and got it overruled. Caren wound up having to take the secretary back. It was a good lesson learned. From that point forward, Caren was always very forthright, direct, and honest. The truth is, if you force yourself to do it, don't delay it, and are honest with people, they're going to respect you more. People naturally try to take the easy way out, and frequently the easy way out gets you into that never-never land of, "Are you really living by what you say your set of rules is?"

Firing people is seldom easy, especially if you care about the people who support you. But telling the truth about bad performance is necessary for integrity, and therefore for leadership.

Telling the truth about bad performance can be even more daunting when the employee is a valued one who performs well in other ways. Guy Rigby, vice president of food and beverage America for Four Seasons Hotels and Resorts, suggests that "managers are too frightened to hurt [employees'] feelings. They don't have enough self-confidence to sit someone down and say, 'You know what? I wish you could do a better job here.'" Coaching subordinates, including telling them where they are weak and how to improve, is one of the most feared and loathed elements of leadership, but it is one of the most crucial. Too many managers shape their performance appraisals based on their level of discomfort, and that is a problem. If you choose your words based on how much you fear damaging the relationship, you will either blunder forward or hold back. Neither approach works. Guy adds, "Set and agree on expectations for the way you expect everyone to behave, and correcting poor performance becomes the easiest thing in the world."

The key lies in the relationship you establish over time. You build a relationship that appreciates subordinates' strengths, and in so doing, you build your credibility and create permission to criticize constructively. Jennifer Loving is the CEO of the nonprofit group EHC LifeBuilders. She gives this advice about how to tell an employee a difficult performance truth:

> I think that goes back to the relationship. If you have no relationship with somebody or you spend only an hour a month with them, and then you want to go tell them what they are doing wrong, you have no credibility. If you take the time when things are good to figure out what makes people tick, what they need out of their work experience, and what you need them to do as collaboration, I think you have a better shot. I don't always do that, but that is what I try for. To some folks I can very easily say, "What the hell were you thinking! We need to change that right now," and the response is, "You're right, I don't know what I was thinking. That was stupid." And we move on. I have that with the people I have stronger relationships with because there is trust. They trust that if I'm saying, "I'm not digging this right now," I'm not saying, "I'm not digging you." I'm saying, "This needs to change; help me figure out a solution."

A relationship of trust supports truth telling, which in turn supports behavioral integrity, which supports more trust. But how do you start that self-reinforcing cycle?

John Longstreet, executive vice president of human resources of ClubCorp, suggests negotiating a truthful relationship directly with employees as part of the informal employment contract. He takes this approach with subordinates, and as a result gets good work and loyalty. He gets them to agree up front. That initial agreement allows him to defuse any defensiveness that arises later in the relationship by pointing out that he is following through on his word, and so keeping behavioral integrity. He says:

> People think it's easier not to be up front and honest. One otherwise excellent company I worked for, when I started had a culture that was very much *not* up-front and honest. Managers just wouldn't address things. They wouldn't tell people how they really thought about their performance. If somebody was having performance problems, rather than address them they'd be more likely to transfer them somewhere else. They thought that was easier than confronting people and telling them that things weren't working out.
>
> One way to make it easier for you to be up front and honest with people is to establish that relationship when you first start working with them. As a rule, I sit down with all my new direct reports and say, "My style is to tell you what I'm thinking at all times as it relates to your performance. Is that something that you would like me to do, or is that something you're going to have a problem with?" And nobody ever says, "I have a problem with that." So when I actually go back and do it, and they start getting defensive like everybody does, I can say, "Well wait a minute. I thought you said you wanted me to talk to you about it." Essentially I have established an oral contract that I'm going to tell them what's on my mind about their performance, and they're going to like the fact that I'm sharing it with them.

John describes an elegant way to set up a climate for truth telling: get people to agree that they want it. Introduce it into conversation. Few people will ask to be lied to. When the decision is made in the calmness of good times, people make the choice that supports the relationship. They choose forthrightness.

TIME LINES, EFFORT, BENEFITS, AND LOSSES

In areas other than subordinate performance, managers also are often seduced away from conveying awkward truths. We succumb to wishful thinking as we project time lines and effort requirements for change projects, or as we describe how many will benefit and how many will lose as a result of a change.

Sometimes executives must manage the impressions of financial markets. Georges LeMener, former president and COO of Accor

North America, identifies a constant tension between motivating people with optimism and a darker, perhaps more realistic view:

> If you are not optimistic enough, you can have problems with the stock market or with the analysts. I think both internally and externally, you are constantly [struggling] between what you believe is a true picture of the company and the need not to be as direct and up front as you would like to be. Personally, how do I reconcile the two? I try to avoid a subject if I cannot be up front about it.

Given the excellent performance of Georges's company over the past several years, the idea that the darker news might be more realistic is up for question. But Georges is right that many executives feel pressure to share only the good news. There are different ways of doing the job, to be sure, and sometimes a bleak projection shared with conviction can be extremely motivating. The point is that as leaders, we need to concern ourselves deeply with the impact of our words, not just their truth. The integrity dividend suggests that the two do not pull in different directions as often as we might assume. But admittedly the choices are sometimes difficult.

Some managers respond to their awareness of sensitive information by taking discretion to extremes. They choose to communicate only what serves a practical purpose, and that purpose also dictates how they share. Smart young managers quickly learn to practice discretion, but they are seldom taught when not to keep quiet. Allen Ibara, CEO of Phiam Corporation, describes how the tendency comes about:

> Withholding is ingrained very early on in managers' careers. In your first management job you're going to wind up in somebody's personnel file, so you automatically know things that somebody else doesn't know. You quickly develop filters. I haven't seen anything anywhere with a policy manual that tells you how to use those filters correctly.

Thus, managers learn to be discrete with sensitive information, but they are seldom trained in the positive power of honest disclosure to build relationships or in the skills needed to pull it off.

Awkward truths are by their nature challenging to express, but the integrity dividend presents a reason to do so. Contracting employee buy-in to a philosophy of full disclosure is an elegant way to start. But that technique does not apply to many other situations involving stakeholders inside and outside the company, where there are often legal and practical reasons not to share information. Navigating between needs for trust and discretion inevitably calls for judgment and skill.

EMBRACE CONFLICT

One common barrier to addressing awkward truths, especially for women, is discomfort with conflict and confrontation. Nina Simons, co-executive director of Bioneers/Collective Heritage Institute, a highly successful nonprofit organization, says we "need to cultivate our capacity for difficult conversations":

> Many of us are raised to avoid conflict. As a woman executive, it has been my experience that women raised in this Western culture tend to be more conflict averse than men. As women, we tend to be so acculturated toward pleasing behavior that it's particularly difficult to tell somebody something that we know they are not going to want to hear—and do it in a way that's honest and forthright and where we stay centered in our own authority.

It is not just a matter of being willing to yell; there are skills to learn. You have to be willing to risk others' getting upset or angry, and you have to, as Nina says, stay centered in your own authority.

The problem arises for men also. Frank Guidara, the CEO of Uno Chicago Grill, describes the pattern in his industry:

> Most people don't want to be the bad guy; but they just don't know how to be the fair guy. So when they get into issues that they know are going to be poorly received, they either avoid them, or they promise things that, as they're saying them, they are really not sure that they are going be able to keep them—or, in fact, know that they're *not* going to be able to keep them. They just don't want to confront the issues and the people. The best managers are those who aren't afraid of confrontation, aren't afraid of holding people accountable, aren't afraid of committing.

Doug Brooks, an inspiring and well-admired leader, provides an example of a well-intentioned but ultimately disingenuous conflict dodge from his own experience as a younger restaurant chain manager:

> I remember in the 1980s sitting in quality circles, and I would hide behind the questions. The servers would say, "We want to get a raise. We don't want to make minimum wage anymore." The truth was that servers were going to have their income primarily controlled by tips at the table. And the economic model that the restaurant was built on can't take the servers' getting raises. [I needed to be] honest, saying, "Listen. That's probably not going to happen. You've got to focus on great service, taking care of your guests. Then you're going to make a lot more than a person across the street who works at a job where their hourly rate is set." Instead, being young and not being comfortable and confident in my skin, I danced around the truth. I should have said, "Listen. You're a server. You took this job. There are some realities that you have to accept."
>
> Young managers are always afraid to lay out the harsh reality. It seems like the sneaky way out is to say, "Well, I'll bring it up to somebody else," when in reality it's not going to happen.

In this situation, Doug was not exactly lying. He probably did raise the issue with his superiors, though he clearly knew what the outcome would be. But because of his lack of confidence, he side-stepped an opportunity to build a relationship based on honesty.

When people fail to acknowledge and address inevitable organizational conflict, pretense takes the driver's seat, and integrity sits in the back. In their excellent book about building trust, Robert Solomon and Fernando Flores eloquently describe the resulting state as "cordial hypocrisy."[1] Charles Feltman is an executive coach who, in his practice, draws extensively on Flores's body of work. He describes this pattern:

> If we try and pretend that there aren't conflicts in our interactions with other people, then we're relating to each other in this world of cordial hypocrisy where we don't really deal with things. Nobody lives up to their commitments, and everyone agrees to not talk about it. The whole organization can fall into cordial hypocrisy, and it's deadly. What's under the surface is resentment. The organization falls into a culture of complaint. It feeds on itself and goes downhill from there.

Where "cordial hypocrisy" takes hold, people generally sense that there are undiscussed issues on all sides, but they do not trust their colleagues enough to take a stand by making a genuine request, thus perhaps also exposing their own need and vulnerability. To talk openly, one needs to trust that a constructive response will come, but that trust is in short supply in a "culture of complaint." Lacking trust, people seek sympathy for their challenges and grievances rather than trying to fix them.

In contrast, some excellent companies develop climates that celebrate open debate and so support honest relationships and personal credibility among their people. Bob Staley, recently retired vice chairman of Emerson Electric, noted that Emerson's performance and practices earned it credit as one of *Industry Week*'s one hundred best-managed companies for five successive years. Part of Emerson's culture was, and is, a highly participative series of planning conferences where managers discuss and decide their direction. The discussions are sometimes heated. According to Bob:

> Wall Street used to say an Emerson planning conference was a contact sport. I was at a planning conference once where a young kid was probably presenting for the first time. And he was just getting beaten up one side and down the other by the chairman. And finally he says to the chairman, "You know the problem we're having is that you don't know what you're talking about." Pretty gutsy. And the chairman says, "You're right. But you're not explaining it very well. So let's go back to the beginning because I'm not a dumb guy. And I agree you know more than I do about this, but in the end we're either both going to know about it or nothing's going to happen." They went right back to the beginning of the presentation. This young kid tried to spend more time on the points that he thought we were all missing. And we got through it and decided on a plan of action and took it. The chairman and the kid had a drink together after the conference.

For most of us, telling the head of the company that he doesn't know what he's talking about seems nothing short of suicidal. But in this case, the climate was so conducive to telling awkward truths and honoring disagreement that the statement shifted the whole conversation in a constructive direction. It cut through the fog and raised the level of integrity in the room. And relationships were not damaged but strengthened.

Being the leader in such a climate calls for certain qualities. You have to be "confident and comfortable in your skin." You have to know how to stay "centered in your authority." And you have to get personally comfortable dealing with disagreement. Joe Lavin, president of Harborstone Hospitality, considers the qualities that allowed one of his former bosses to embrace constructive conflict:

> His ego obviously is under control. He is okay with people chal-lenging him and he's willing to accept that he's not always right. And that he needs to talk to people and listen to people who know what's going on in their particular area. And use that as opposed to be threatened by it.

Joe and others suggest that the key to embracing conflict is a combination of seeming opposites: confidence and humility. Together they help leaders embrace constructive conflict. To the two I would add a reminder from Chapter Two of a third essen-tial underlying factor: an underlying trust.

Many studies of ongoing work teams have shown that task-focused disagreements often spill over into personal grudges and sustained anger. I have found, in a study of seventy top manage-ment teams, that trust can prevent that spillover from occurring. Where teams lack trust, disagreements often turn sour. Where teams have trust, they can debate heartily while preserving rela-tionships and faith in everyone's goodwill. Where there is a back-log of undiscussed conflict, one needs to start the flywheel of change slowly and support it with good training and facilitation. As the backlog diminishes, trust can grow, and it becomes easier for team members to openly address disagreements without fear of their turning personal.

Demand—and Get—Clear Commitment

Fortunately Charles Feltman has succeeded in addressing "cordial hypocrisy" and "cultures of complaint." He conquers this ailment by training team members and other organizational participants in a process he calls the "cycle of commitment": training people to make very explicit requests—to ask for clear commitments—and, reciprocally, to give them. This process creates a shared lan-guage for exposing and addressing conflict.

Clear requests lend themselves to honest negotiation about whether and how the request will be fulfilled. Follow-up by both parties then creates a powerful communication dynamic that dramatically improves the parties' sense of the strength of each other's word. Asking people to do things is fundamental to any kind of management, and slowing down enough to ask effectively pays off in fewer disappointments and increased integrity all around. If you make requests clearly and fairly and, as a result, get explicit and serious commitments, getting things done becomes far easier. Of course, effective asking is easier to prescribe than to do. Here are three elements to focus on.

ASK WITH INTENTION AND CLARITY

Charles Feltman says that asking for and receiving clear commitments are essential to building integrity:

> Whatever you're asking for, request it in a way that is complete and clear to the person you're asking. Then it's up to them to respond, "yes" or "no" or "I can't do this but I can do that"—a counteroffer—and eventually you have a commitment. Behavioral integrity is about actually keeping that commitment. It is really difficult to keep a promise when it's not clear what it is.

This process of clear requests helps those around you to keep their commitments, and so also to build their behavioral integrity in your eyes. More often than we realize, we communicate vaguely and then feel betrayed when our wishes are not followed. Most of us have heard or said at some point in romantic arguments, "You should know what I want," and it seldom bodes well. Clairvoyance is not widespread. To empower others to meet our needs, we need to lay those needs out in the open. When we fail to do so, we set up others to disappoint us.

Allen Ibara says the error of assuming others know what we want is woefully common:

> The conditions of satisfaction [and] fulfillment are abysmal in most organizations. Somebody will walk away after a handshake, and I just shake my head and think, "What did you two just talk about?" There was no clue about when it is due, what is due, what the conditions of satisfaction are—what the contract is.

Allen trains his employees in communication skills that secure real agreements. In role plays, they practice phrases like, "Here is what I heard" and "Here is what you say you need." Promoting paraphrasing among employees promotes listening and engagement. Think of the different direction the conversation might go if an employee responds to the boss's request with a paraphrase (correct or incorrect) as opposed to, "I don't understand." "I don't understand" gets the boss to talk more, but it does not get the employee to stand up and take responsibility for the commitment that was supposed to come out of the conversation. How we ask the question can and should help guarantee fulfillment of the promise we extract.

Bob Wright, cofounder of the Wright Business and Leadership Institutes, illustrates this principle from his own experiences in restaurants. On doctors' advice, Bob recently put himself on a no-oil diet. As you might imagine, restaurants and their servers do not always comply with the special request:

> I can tell a waiter or waitress, "I don't want any oil. Please fix my egg whites dry and my potatoes dry." I can communicate that request with various degrees of clarity. There are times that I do not ask for it with absolute and full intent, and the food comes back cooked in oil; there are times that I ask with full intent, get apparent visual and verbal acknowledgment of understanding, and it still comes back with oil; but ultimately the responsibility is on me.

> I'm getting better and better at doing it. If I know that people may or may not do it, it's incumbent on me to ask, "*Will* your cook fix something with no oil for me?" Then I get a yes or no. They might say, "I don't know," in which case I say, "Well, would you go ask him?" And if they say no, then I'll say, "Why not?" It's taken a while to learn that if I'm at 100 percent intent, I can ask it that way.

Thus, the exchange surrounding a request makes a huge difference in setting up eventual compliance, which in turn increases trust.

The experience of one of Charles Feltman's clients, call him "Nate," further illustrates how a poor request yields poor compliance. A fairly senior manager, Nate had an ongoing problem with a peer, call him "Joe," who was supposed to supply him with information for a biweekly report. Because of some prior disagreement, Joe refused to supply the information directly and sent it through an intermediary. The intermediary was sometimes unavailable, so the information did not always get through. Nate asked his boss to fix the problem but eventually complained to Charles:

> "It's still happening. I go to the boss, I ask him to fix the problem, and he says he will, and he does nothing."
>
> Charles said, "Okay, so tell me: What specifically did you ask him?"
>
> "Well, I explained my problem, and I said, 'Go talk to Joe about it,' and he said he would."
>
> "Okay, then what happened?"
>
> "I don't know. Nothing changed."
>
> Charles said, "Okay. Let's look at what you actually asked the boss to do. You asked him to go talk to Joe. You didn't ask him to go tell Joe to send the data directly to you; you just said go talk to Joe about it." And it turned out that's exactly what the boss did: he went to Joe and said, "This is a problem. It's an ongoing problem, and it needs to be resolved." And then he left.

The boss had followed through on his word, but Nate wasn't seeing that because he wasn't getting the results that he mistakenly thought he'd requested. In fact, he had never completely and clearly requested what he wanted, but when he did not get what he wanted, he saw it as a failure of his boss's behavioral integrity.

Effective requesting can most definitely be taught. Charles describes an organizational change effort in which he trained the managers to make clear and complete requests and to wait for a commitment. He strictly ruled out what he calls the "drive-by request," in which the asker does not wait or listen. His trainees used role plays to develop their skills and discussed different settings in which to apply them. Charles says,

> It took about a year for this set of techniques to filter through this organization to the point where everyone was using it. Then they would call each other on mistakes: "Wait a minute, you're missing something in that request. You're missing a time frame, you didn't tell what time you needed it by." "ASAP is not a time frame."

GIVE PERMISSION TO SAY "NO"

Securing commitments means waiting for the people you ask to respond. The waiting allows them to make a public commitment or to decline or negotiate the commitment into one on which they can deliver. Responders must feel they have permission to say something other than "yes." As Charles says, "If you can't say no, your yes doesn't mean anything." In order for people to feel bonded by their word, they need to feel that they gave it freely. Charles tells this tale of a company where nobody could say "no."

> When I started working with them, they were slipping in their delivery of products, they were missing their deadlines right, left, and center by large margins—several months in many cases. It was a nasty situation. Their clients were beginning to leave. One of the first things we noticed was that everybody had far more work that they had committed to do than they could possibly do.
>
> And we noticed a culture of "We don't say no" that we thought was causing the overload of work. They said yes to everything. But there was also a culture of "We say yes but we don't really mean it, and everybody knows we don't really mean it."
>
> So basically what got done was whatever got yelled about the loudest. If I came to your office or your cubicle and said, "Where's my blah, blah, blah?" and put enough pressure on you, you'd start working on it, maybe finish that today, even though it was due three days ago. In the meantime, you would ignore the other twenty things that were on your list, but at least I got what I wanted. That was generally the game that they played.

People usually feel bound by agreements they believe they freely made. When they feel no permission to decline a request, their acceptance loses meaning and may not seem to them an agreement at all.

FEEDBACK AND FOLLOW-UP

In addition to asking clearly and giving permission to say no, a third practice for securing genuine commitments is using feedback and follow-up to ensure accountability. Follow-up means checking to see whether the agreement or promise was kept. The aim is not to punish but rather to raise both sides' awareness of failure or success: "I know, you know, and you know that I know." Promisers too should follow up, to say either, "Here is me keeping my promise," or, "I cannot, but here is what I can do."

Sometimes "will" dissolves into "might." After you promise to do something, new circumstances often get in the way. An important client comes in with an urgent need, the boss gives you a new project, one of your staff calls in sick, or your child gets sick. You still might be able to keep the original promise, but only if everything goes exactly right from now on. The odds are now against your keeping your word, but you hope for a miracle, wishfully pretending things are still on track.

Stop. It is worth having that difficult conversation now rather than later. It will allow the asker to make alternate arrangements if necessary, and it will preserve your reputation for living by your word.

When someone fails to meet a commitment, others interpret that person's neglect of reporting the failure as avoiding responsibility. Ted Ratcliff, senior vice president of Hilton Doubletree Operations East, describes the suspicions that rise in his own mind when employees don't report:

> When I have so many balls in the air, employees start to think
> I'm not going to be able to track all this stuff—or that I may not
> be tracking the thing that they're not doing. So they wonder
> if they can get away with it. Even if that's not their intent, that
> perception can sneak into my mind. I can perceive a simple
> thing like missing deadlines as, "Someone's trying to get away
> with something."

Strong leaders can set the tone for follow-up and accountability by inviting others to hold them accountable. Darryl Stickel suggests,

> A really powerful thing for a CEO to say through the company
> is, "Here's how I'm evaluated. Here are my commitments to you.
> I'm actually going to write them down, and I'm going to hold
> myself accountable to you," or, "I'm going to have the board hold
> me accountable." Start demonstrating that behavior at a very
> high level, and let that trickle down. "Not just me holding *you*

accountable—which is also a good thing—but also me being held accountable for my actions."

Discuss specific commitments to keep them top of mind. This extra attention after a promise has been made keeps the promise alive and helps to build a culture of commitment, accountability, and integrity.

RECOVERING FROM MISCOMMUNICATION

If there's real trust around you, you can recover from miscommunications and keep people believing in your integrity. Consider how things went on one occasion for Al Carey, the CEO of Frito-Lay:

> The Tostitos brand managers wanted to move from a bag in which you could see the product through a clear window to an opaque bag with some high-quality food photography on the package. They showed it to me, and I told them I thought it looked good. I assumed there would be further testing and discussion for so important a decision, but I never told them that—I didn't realize they were presenting it to me for final approval.
>
> Then the brand people moved fast, and the new package hit the marketplace. Customers began complaining almost immediately— many of them use Tostitos as an ingredient in cooking, and they need to inspect the product for breakage. Sales dropped dramatically. I pride myself on empowering my people, but this is a time that a bad decision was made, and it was my job to fix it.
>
> I had to go back to them and say, "Look I want the clear window again. We're going to abandon this new packaging." Oh, they were upset. I said, "Well, you guys jumped the gun a little bit, to be honest. But I'm going to take responsibility for that because I should have been clearer with you that we needed to go through more testing and discussions." I had some equity with my people because I'd been trusting with them, and I think they trusted me. I used that equity to make this decision—but it was painful, and some people weren't too happy about it.

Initially Al had failed to recognize the weight of his words and to fully communicate his expectations. And he wanted to empower the brand managers, which contributed to the misunderstanding.

But after the misstep, Al's cleanup was strong. When he talked with his team, he took responsibility for the miscommunication and laid out the unpopular decision that the clear window had to come back. But even with excellent cleanup, Al feels that the mistake drew down his "bank account" of goodwill and trust slightly. There is still a very strong relationship with his team, but there is now just a little less margin for error. He says that a few more such miscommunications would start to damage credibility.

SUMMARY

Preserving credibility and maintaining people's sense that you live by your word means avoiding casual overpromises and respecting the weight of your words. It means openly acknowledging your uncertainty, the limits to your ability, and other awkward truths. It means embracing conflict so that it does not fester silently and color everyone's views. And it means communicating clearly to give and secure concrete commitments—promises—that really mean something. Communicating this way is not automatic for most people. It has to be learned and practiced.

Into Practice

Consider

- Notice what promises you make casually and without much thought.
- Do your subordinates know fully what you think of their performance? Is that conversation part of your routine relationship? What role does your level of discomfort play in your performance appraisals?
- Do you acknowledge to subordinates the limits of your authority? When? When not?
- What conflicts have you avoided? Consider the issue strategically. Consider the impact of this unaddressed conflict on trust.

- Does your organizational climate permit constructive conflict? What might you do to improve it? Where do you see cordial hypocrisy?
- Do you and your people routinely ask for and give clear commitments that lead to follow-through? Notice whether your team makes assignments and requests in ways that maximize mutual understanding and personal commitment.

Act

- Avoid automatic or polite promises that can easily be misinterpreted. Think hard about what commitment you choose to make in a given situation. Then make a promise—or don't.
- Attend to the weight your subordinates assign to your words. The encounter that barely registers on your radar might register strongly on theirs. Be aware that your words will echo.
- When making commitments, discuss uncertainties that will affect your ability to deliver, such as limitations on your organizational power and capabilities. An escape clause like, "I'll try," is probably not enough to cut through wishful thinking that shapes how others hear you. Lay out the details of the process, and do so with confidence and humility.
- Discuss awkward truths of employees' performance and the company's performance, so people will better understand your motives and thus see your integrity. Try securing explicit buy-in for this level of honesty. Disclosure is not always the way to go, but more managers err on the side of too little disclosure.
- Embrace constructive conflict. Get issues on the table and resolve them. Undiscussed conflicts tend to fester and color people's perceptions in a way that undermines both actual and perceived integrity. People in the mode of cordial hypocrisy do not follow through reliably or recognize integrity when others do follow through.
- Communicate in a way that provides and secures clear, actionable commitments. Fuzzy commitments often undermine behavioral integrity, since people may not understand them the same way. There are three steps to this process:

  1. Ask for a commitment, specifying the conditions of fulfillment and the due date.
  2. Wait for a response. Allow the other to say yes or no. Negotiate if necessary.
  3. Follow up after the fact to remind both parties of the commitment, whether or not it was fulfilled.

CHAPTER SIX

BEHAVIORAL INTEGRITY AS A PERSONAL DISCIPLINE

Recall the book's opening story about Stan Myers's promise of severance pay to a young engineer. Stan is the chairman and CEO of SEMI, the global semiconductor manufacturers' association, and he encapsulated the point of this chapter:

> We have to really understand our self, and make sure that we are managing our self. When we do, then we get more behavioral integrity, and we get better management of the truth that we are putting out to people.

The integrity dividend is power. When you and others know that you live by your word, you become able to shape the world around you in surprising ways. People cooperate better with you, even if they do not know you well. Even more important is your own conviction that your word has weight and that by giving it, you change the world in some way. That personal conviction of power, echoed in the hearts of those around you, makes power a reality. Lee Pillsbury, CEO of Thayer Lodging and a successful entrepreneur several times over, offers that "ultimately your power is a function of 'how big are the commitments you make?' and 'how many of them do you keep?'" Power is a function of ambition and behavioral integrity.

Here is a strange but compelling idea: discipline is *exactly* the process of living by your word, even when it is costly or difficult.

Discipline is not just what it takes. It is what it *is*. Jim Kouzes offers more definition:

> The disciplined person is the follower of a way. The root of the word "discipline" comes from the Latin word for "pupil." A disciplined person—a disciple if you will—is someone who has learned a way of doing things and accepts that doctrine as the way we ought to behave. If we have a way of doing business—a clear set of values and beliefs—that have been agreed upon, I have to be disciplined in following it. I can't have integrity without discipline.

This chapter explores what you can do to strengthen your integrity discipline.

Like me, you probably look at yourself in the mirror and consider your word to be pretty good. I think I keep the big promises: I do not mess around on my wife, I make my living by honest work, and I seldom deceive anyone. Still, I have often promised, with good reason, to improve my diet and exercise regimen but have failed to do so. I did not meet all my deadlines in preparing this book. Not quite impeccable, not quite 100 percent, but better than most, which is probably good enough. Right? It might be good enough, but it is not the best any of us can do. With courage, honest social support, practice, and hard slogging, you can drive your percentage higher. Some of the practices I suggest can be put in place quickly, but real results come only by sustained effort. Unsustained, a brief flurry of integrity does little to repair and build relationships and reputations. The sustaining is the very crux of the matter; it is precisely what integrity is about. Find a way that you can keep it going—for good.

The first section of this chapter discusses an important difference between the discipline of keeping concrete promises and the discipline of demonstrating stated values. The second section discusses a number of essential elements of the personal discipline—from making oneself more aware of self-deceptions to renegotiating promises. The final section, based primarily on the work of Robert Gass, an executive coach and personal development teacher, presents a specific list of things to do, along with two assessment tools.

PROMISSORY INTEGRITY
VERSUS VALUES INTEGRITY

Behavioral integrity requires both keeping concrete promises and living by the values you profess. The two elements often blur in their consequence, as each breeds trust and violations of either may be seen as deceit. Both come down to living by your word and to others' sense that your word is your bond.

But the two must be approached somewhat differently. One hundred percent integrity with respect to promises is a tangible and achievable goal, but values integrity is more a continual striving and learning process. According to Robert Gass:

> It is possible to always either keep your word or to come back and renegotiate it proactively. I do believe that's within our power.
> I don't believe we can live our values 100 percent. One, because we're just human beings; we're not perfect. Two, because in the real world, there are competing values, and limited time and resources. And three, it's not always clear what the heck it means to live your values in a given situation.

Robert credits this insight to three years spent as president of a large consulting company. Before that time, in his work coaching executives, he often thought his clients were not sufficiently committed to their own values. Once he took on the mantle of executive leadership, his perspective changed dramatically: "All of a sudden, I was in a situation where I couldn't do anything to my own standards. There really was limited time and attention and resources, and by going all the way with one thing, I was going to *not* go all the way with another thing!" The experience taught him compassion for managers who are pursuing real-world values integrity.

Besides structure and discipline, living by the values you profess requires ongoing learning. As I noted in Chapter Four, you need to choose a few values, get really clear about what they look like, and prioritize them, but understanding how to enact a value often comes by learning from other people. Or, as Robert says, "Sometimes it is only by violating a value that you learn where the boundary was." To explain this point, he told me about his early efforts to live up to his vow to be kind to his wife. She would often ask him whether he wanted her to come along on his travels. He, who valued personal freedom deeply, would treat her as he would want to be treated, and would reply, "Whatever you want, Sweetheart." He says, "It took me ten years to realize that when I would say, 'Whatever you want,' what she would hear was, 'I don't care, and I don't love you.'" It was only by seeing that his words were causing her pain that he could better learn how to treat her with kindness. To live by our values, we must be willing to engage in an ongoing process of learning, willing to examine the results of our choices and actions and challenge our assumptions, willing to correct our course. It is always a work in progress.

Lloyd Hill, chairman of Applebee's International restaurant company, also notes how the same value can look very different when enacted by different people. As an example he mentions his company's espoused value of personal balance:

> I don't have kids at home. For me, my absolute *passion* could be that I want to be part of a team that builds a world-class, one-of-a-kind culture and organization. Since that's my love and my passion, the fact that I'm here at seven in the morning and nine at night doesn't mean I don't have balance. If that's where my fulfillment comes in and I'm having fun doing it, why should I consider myself imbalanced? As long as I'm willing to entertain a different definition for other people.

Within oneself, falling short of stated values may be inevitable any time we stretch for an ideal. That does not mean we should not stretch, but we should do so with a good dose of self-acceptance. Bob Wright, cofounder of the Wright Business and Leadership Institutes and a longtime executive coach, describes this inevitable gap between espousal and action as a "hypocrisy" that needs to be admitted and forgiven even while you strive to minimize it:

> Anybody who operates with a higher value must declare something toward which they are looking but which they cannot realize. There must always be a gap. It's an ideal toward which you live, which you declare, and you must fall short. Otherwise, it's not an ideal worth living.

Frank admission of personal gaps and even hypocrisy makes the topic of breach discussable:

> One of the things that I very much enjoy [even though] it's painful, is when you hire new staff and you've declared high values, they begin pointing [out] all your hypocrisies immediately. The real test at that point is, Are you consonant, and do you 'fess up? Do you take their coaching and continue to engage in improvement and dialogue with them?

Most people would not feel comfortable pointing out to their bosses the ways in which their boss fails to live up to stated values. It is a testament to Bob's leadership style that even his new employees do. Unspoken, those perceptions of hypocrisy would poison the employment relationship. Instead, they become learning opportunities, improving mutual understanding.

As Bob's example suggests, supporting our ability to learn how best to live our values means encouraging communication, because others' view of our actions can be our best teacher, especially when those actions, and the values we are trying to enact, affect them directly. Robert Gass speaks of creating a communication climate of respect and safety in your team to support this kind of continuous learning. You want them

> to be able to vocalize—not in a blaming way, but in a way for shared learning. "When you stepped out in that meeting . . ." "When you spoke in that way . . ." "When you didn't mention that I'd been a participant in that report, that—to me—did not feel like respect. What do you think?" Rather than screaming at each other, "You didn't respect me! You violated our values!" you enter mutual learning together.

ELEMENTS OF A PERSONAL DISCIPLINE

From my interviews emerged eight kinds of behavior that contribute to a personal discipline of integrity:

- Detecting habits of social deceit
- Delaying gratification
- Facing fear with courage

- Looking within
- Arranging social support
- Following a deliberate process for giving your word
- Keeping track and following up, and
- Apologizing and recovering

DETECTING HABITS OF SOCIAL DECEIT

In a university study, Robert Feltman and his colleagues asked people to meet and interact with a stranger for ten minutes while they were secretly videotaped. They were then asked to watch the videotape and evaluate the truthfulness of their statements. On average, each speaker lied almost once per every ten-minute interaction (.88), and when people were told in advance to convey likability or competence, goals that most managers share, the frequency of deceit more than doubled. A study by Bella DePaulo and colleagues suggests that most of us lie in 20 percent of all social interactions lasting ten minutes or more, and college students typically lie to their mothers in a whopping 50 percent of conversations.[1] To be clear, these numbers include the most innocuous type of social deceits, all the way up from "I am fine" when one is not. The point is that to develop and maintain our capacity for consistency, most of us need to learn some new social skills.

How often do we pretend to be happy or satisfied when we are not; pretend to be more or less certain than we really are; exaggerate to make a point; agree to something simply to end the conversation; or blame lateness for some other misdeed on circumstances that could easily have been foreseen and avoided? When you key your ear to small deceptions, it is alarming how many you will hear around you and coming out of your own mouth. It is safe to say that most of us lie every day, and many several times a day.

We all learned early that telling people what they want to hear was often an easy, effective way to navigate through the world. Here is an extreme example. A friend of mine was sexually abused from the age of nine, first by a caretaker and later by a family member. When she eventually told an older girl at her boarding school, the girl did not believe her and told others, who laughed at her. To cover her shame, she started making up and telling stories, so that the truth that crept into her stories would go unnoticed. She says,

> Later, I told people whatever would best get my needs met—and
> I got very good at knowing what that was. I became the queen
> of manipulation and a great story teller. I could shape-shift into
> anyone's best friend and be just what they needed.

Her social deceit was not deliberate but became automatic. As time passed, she no longer knew whether she was speaking honestly or deceptively. Years later, a caring supervisor helped her to recognize her pattern of expedient talk. First, she had to catch herself after lying, until finally she could stop herself before she spoke. Only after doing that for a while did she lose the impulse to lie in social situations. She describes the process as "winning her self back." She is now one of the most honest people I know.

Our problem is that the deceits we learned very early on are often automatic, not consciously chosen. Bob Wright traces it back:

> It all starts when you're about six months to two years old. If you're
> not accurately perceived, if your family's living too much in la-la
> land, then you don't internalize an accurate picture of yourself,
> which compromises your integrity. If you can't disagree and say the
> truth in your family, then you won't do it as an adult in a corpora-
> tion. Because we all project our family onto a corporation, and we
> operate according to early learned and unconsciously held family
> rules, myths, and beliefs.

From our family, we learn how honestly we can talk about ourselves and our perceptions. Our automatic patterns as adults reflect how we as children were told to behave around our upsets or the awkward truths we noticed and innocently reported. Robert Gass describes this process in terms of children learning to become "politicians":

> Two year-olds don't lie all that much—they are always authentic!
> But very quickly in our coming of age, we learn that certain attri-
> butes, certain expressions or behaviors, get good energy coming
> toward us, and certain things get negative energy coming toward
> us. We're quite brilliant little political practitioners when we're

young and very survival oriented and totally dependent on it. And so we start learning to play toward the approval of others and to avoid showing the things that might get us negative energy of any kind. Over the years of doing that, we start losing track of what is play and what is real.

Delaying Gratification

One of the major challenges of living consistently by your promises and values is the more immediate payoff of not doing so. Living by your word means fewer tactical options in any immediate or short-term circumstance. Reaping the integrity dividend takes the discipline of delayed gratification. To some extent, all grown-ups have learned to work and wait until payday, but Jim Kouzes argues that a profound ability to defer gratification is in short supply among today's managers and leaders:

> Many are unwilling or unable to do something that's good for the corporation in the long term, but not necessarily good for them in the short term. They know they are likely to get punished if they look Wall Street in the eye and say, "Sorry, but we have to invest in new product development if we're going to be competitive five years from now, and it's going to affect our quarterly returns." Doing what is in the long-term interests of the business may also mean that we don't get what we want in the short term. We often have to make great sacrifices to stay committed to the company's and our own values.

Kevin Dunn, an executive coach and former division president for McDonalds Corporation, noted the two-edged sword of financial accountability: it helps many companies become more competitive because they are forced to measure themselves against their rivals. However, he adds, "This weekly or daily or monthly analysis of companies is not helping us. We're building brands too quickly and under the microscope, so we're not willing to look long term at building the brand." Executives focus on short-term gains because that is what financial markets too often reward.

In the wake of 9/11, many hotel companies lost money because of very low occupancy, and most of those laid people off.

Not Omni Hotels. It chose deliberately not to lay anyone off. Richard Maxfield, a regional vice president of operations for Omni, explains that

> we really felt like that was an opportunity to send a strong message to our associates and our customers that this little blip in the world is not going to change our long-term vision of what we're trying to create—satisfied customers and satisfied associates.

Omni's willingness to sacrifice the expediency of layoffs to take a stand for its values—its willingness in hard times—shows a genuine discipline in values. "You never really understand what integrity is until it costs you," Rich Panico says:

> When I ask individuals about integrity—when we're recruiting and interviewing—I ask them when has defending their value really cost them. If it never cost them, it is unfair for them to say, "I'm a person of integrity." It's got to be tested and proven.

Values define priorities. If integrity or any other value, is important then it is worth some sacrifice.

FACING FEAR WITH COURAGE

Integrity calls for the courage to admit weaknesses, to say things people might not want to hear, to ask others how they see your conduct. It calls for the courage to stake your career, your marriage, your future on what you judge the worthwhile course. Many women think of themselves as lacking courage because they feel low on physical courage, but what I am talking about here does not depend on adrenaline or testosterone. It is a quieter, moral courage of conviction that is ultimately greater according to the writings of Field-Marshal Sir William Slim, passed on to me by a former English marine:

> I have known many men who had marked physical courage, but lacked moral courage. Some of them were in high positions, but they failed to be great in themselves because they lacked it. On the other hand, I have seen men who undoubtedly possessed moral courage and were very cautious about physical risks. But I have

never met a man with moral courage who would not, when it was really necessary, face bodily danger. Moral courage is a higher and a rarer virtue.[2]

Moral courage is needed because the most honest thing you could say is seldom the safest, as I explained when discussing the fearfulness of vulnerability in Chapter Two. If your word is your bond, then you are predictable, which is not a good thing insofar as you fear others working against you. Ask any boxer or martial artist. The worst thing you can do in combat is to broadcast where you will be. Ironically, broadcasting of your intention is the best thing you can do in building relationships. Rich Panico believes "it takes much more confidence and inner strength to trust in business than not to trust."

Aneil Mishra, a scholar and consultant who focuses on trust issues, argues that "you have to be both very humble and very courageous if you're going to be a high integrity person. It takes humility to recognize your faults, the things you do not know. And it takes courage to admit them to others."

Despite the scariness of it, Rob Goffee and Gareth Jones, in their insightful and well-titled book, *Why Should Anyone Be Led by You?* point out that vulnerability, selectively shared, is critical for establishing trust and a sense of authenticity that allows followers to connect with you and to engage their hearts.[3] I think it does more. Acknowledging vulnerability also allows you to make more reliable promises. If you can admit your limitations, you can have a conversation about what you can and cannot commit to. If you want to appear superhuman, you will be constantly tempted to overcommit. And every time your subordinates notice a weak spot—and they will—the weak spot becomes evidence of hypocrisy and so undermines trust. Don't set yourself up to blow trust by pretending to be perfect.

It also takes moral courage to demand accountability and confront people when they fail to live up to their commitments. None of us likes to hear we have blown their word. Establishing norms that hold people accountable, including yourself, entails a series of difficult conversations. Do not plow into those conversations thoughtlessly. But do not allow your fear to keep you from having them.

LOOKING WITHIN

The better you are at introspection—looking inside yourself—the easier it will be to build and keep integrity. The better you know yourself and your guiding principles, the better equipped you are to tell others reliably what to expect from you, because you yourself know what to expect.

Self-Knowledge, Self-Acceptance, and Self-Presentation

In attempting to see ourselves clearly, we are always playing catch-up with people around us. Those who work with us every day, especially subordinates, often see us more clearly than we see ourselves. Because they depend on us, they watch us closely, trying hard to figure us out. Overall it is easier to hide some parts of ourselves from ourselves than to hide them from other people. Stan Rowe is a corporate vice president for Edwards Lifesciences, a major medical device manufacturer. As he puts it,

> As a manager you are a pane of glass. If you think you can hide things from people, you're fooling yourself, because your subordinates see through you very readily. If you don't realize that, you are self-destructive. Part of the honesty here is to know as a manager what your own strengths and weaknesses are. If I know what those are, then the people who work for me also know what those are, and there are ways I can deal with that as a manager. But if I ignore it and think no one else knows it, then there is a deceit involved in that—and a huge weakness.

How well you see, share, and deal with your strengths and weaknesses is pivotal to good leadership and good management. For one thing, as Stan says, it also allows you to assign the most capable team members to the appropriate tasks:

> We are not all things to all people. None of us is a perfect manager. You can be organizationally challenged, or you may not be as technically proficient. But understanding [your] strengths [and weaknesses] and being able to use the people who work under you to help bolster them, and to hire people who have complementary strengths is a cornerstone to [managing].

When you know yourself well, you can also make it easier for others to figure out how to work with you, which makes you more effective. Michael Kay is a former CEO of LSG Sky Chefs. He recalls the fluoroscopic X-ray machines that were in shoe stores when he was a child:

> If I could invent a management-recruiting fluoroscope machine that would allow me to look for a manager's sense of himself—What do I believe in? How do I use what I believe in? How do I work? What do I value?—if I could fluoroscope for that and find the ones who are far along the scale, it would make hiring easy. Managers who have a highly developed sense of themselves do the best job in bringing that out in others. When you're clear about who you are, it is easier for the people who work for you to decide how most effectively to work with you. And that's what trust is all about.

The need for self-knowledge extends beyond recognizing strengths and weaknesses; it includes knowing your personal style and values in order to be able to act on and share them. When the values we claim do not line up with our actions, the problem may lie not in the actions but in a pretense about the values. Heather Allen, an organizational transformation consultant in the United Kingdom, finds that the vast majority of her clients say their family is their first priority, yet many fail to find time for family events and routines. When she points out the discrepancy, some shift their behavior to line up better with their stated values, sometimes even changing jobs. Others do not change behavior and typically either pretend there is no inconsistency or learn that their true priorities differ from those they like to present.

The way you want to present yourself is also often the way you want to think of yourself. We have a tremendous capacity to kid ourselves, and this pull to present and think of ourselves in a way that does not reflect our true priorities relates back to the ego issues I mentioned in Chapter Five. Deirdre Wallace, president of the Ambrose Group, a green hotel company, says she is

> trying, every day, to live up to my expectations of not only who I want to be but who I want my company to be, or to become. There's ego involved, and ego and integrity don't always line up. People want the glory but do not want the work to get the glory.

I want to be a great hotelier, and I want to be known as a green hotelier, but where do my actions fall short? Yes, I want to be known for that and appreciate it and value it—now that's my ego—but I still have to do all the work and keep my integrity to get to that place.

The behavioral integrity problem of ego is the temptation to unwittingly represent yourself in line with your aspirations rather than your reality. The ego problem worsens when managers resist any notion that they have real integrity problems and proceed to blame failures on subordinates. We all have integrity problems, in the sense that we all need to work continuously to live up to the values we claim. Where we claim values that we wish we had, rather than values we truly hold, we make that challenge far worse. Pronouncing or otherwise presenting values to your team is not the place for stretch goals; it is the place for naked honesty. When a leader is able to honestly present his or her values in a way that is personal, followers typically become engaged. Stan Rowe considers this ability to reveal oneself to be a key element of the emotional side of leadership:

> You have to be able to talk about your true values. What is it that you really believe in? This is something that we long for in presidential candidates. We want people who stand up and say, "These are my values. This is what I really believe in." When I stand up in front of a group and say, "We are all doing this for patients," it's one thing. It's another to stand up and say, "Let me tell you about something that happened with our new products and a patient and how important it is." When you walk them through it and reveal how important it is to you emotionally, you communicate something much more important.

Self-Knowledge and Commitments

How well you know yourself affects not only how accurately you can present yourself but also how reliably you can keep your commitments. Robert Gass describes how most people experience terrific ambivalence and tension between various internal forces:

> When there's a lack of internal alignment and a lack of internal integrity, there's no way you can have integrity with other people. If you have several people inhabiting your body and

any one of them can step forward any given time and take control of your mouth and your limbs, you know you can't depend on yourself.

How consistently we are able to live by our word in the outside world is a function of our internal consistency. If we are ambivalent in large or small ways, then our actions and our words will naturally be inconsistent because they express different, isolated parts of ourselves. The necessary challenge is to break down the internal walls so we can unite and focus the various elements within ourselves.

Robert discusses this alignment problem with a metaphor of arrows:

> People give their word casually, and they don't think it through. They don't necessarily have personal integrity even as they're committing to a thing in the first place. Many people are fragmented. So this part is going to say one thing, but they're not fully aligned inside themselves. They're out of touch with themselves; they're not integrated internally. Without having internal integrity, it's hard to have integrity for other people.

> It's like there's one big arrow pointing in the direction you say you want to go, but inside that, there're lots of little arrows. Suppose you've been offered a job position. One arrow says, "Hey, it pays better!" [Another says,] "Hey, it's an advance on my career." But [other arrows say,] "Gee, but I feel really comfortable where I am. I like the people who I am working with now; I really don't like the boss very much in the new position." "I can't tell how secure this whole new operation is that they want to transfer me to."

Most people, he suggests, make a decision to act as soon as they find a 51 percent majority of their internal arrows pointing in a given direction. He recommends a more deliberate internal process that is akin to consensus decision making in groups: explore and reconcile the different internal pulls until, at the point of action,

> 100 percent of your being—every part of your heart, your spirit, your mind, everything—is moving in that way. I would call that personal integrity, the integrity of your body, of your being, your whole. All of you is moving together. There's no inner conflict,

no ambivalence. And when acting from that place, one tends to have integrity with the external world.

We all have inner conflicts that undermine our focus and our ability to present a consistent message to the world: conflicts between what we think we ought to value and what we actually value, between the value we place on our personal lives versus our careers, between the desire to become more effective and the desire for comfort, and others. The more we can see those conflicts and address them explicitly, the better we will be able to offer our word and mean it with every fiber of our being.

Maximizing your ability to live by your word includes taking a moment of reflection before you make any commitment. Listen hard to your inner voice; look for ambivalences, cautionary notes, competing commitments, or anything else that might get in the way of 100 percent commitment to getting it done. Lee Pillsbury, CEO of Thayer Lodging Group and a successful entrepreneur several times over, proposes that this moment of keen reflection needs to be supported by courage in looking at yourself and in responding honestly to the person who made the request:

> You ask me to do something. At that moment, deep down I know whether I'm going to do it. Am I comfortable enough with myself to confront that truth? And then am I comfortable enough with myself in the world to say to you, "I'm not going to do that"? It may be that I "should" do that. The world is full of "shoulds." There may be all sorts of consequences to not doing it, and some of them may not be pleasant. But if you are really true to yourself, if you really know yourself, if you are really honest with yourself in the moment, you know whether you're going to do it. "Yeah, well, I'd like to do it. I should do it. I know it's important to you that I do it. And I'm not going to do it."

Our ability to listen to ourselves closely, and to accept and act on what we see, is critical to making commitments we can live up to.

When you fail to reflect for that moment before committing, you risk your credibility. You might prefer to avoid possible conflict with the asker, or you might not want to disappoint them. You might be rushed and simply hoping to end the conversation. Any number of pulls might distract you from this critical moment of reflection. What can happen in the rush of getting through your day is saying "yes" but not fully meaning it. As Robert Gass notes, "The birth of things has a lot to do with how they end up, so if the 'yes' is halfhearted at the beginning, that person is not going to deliver impeccable-grade results." The irony, of course, is that the halfhearted "yes" that was said in order to avoid confrontation ends up creating far more difficulty down the road than a timelier, wholehearted "no".

Building Self-Concept for Integrity

How do you define and describe yourself *to yourself*? Our self-concept or internal image of ourselves guides much of our action. It is as broad and complex as we are, and parts of it lie hidden in the shadows of our mind, driving our actions in ways that we are often unaware of. We may have a stubborn insistence left over from childhood that we are fat, or good at math, or bad at math. Whatever the notion, we tend to bend the reality around us to conform to it. If we think ourselves inept at something, we tend to sabotage our own efforts at it, as though to "prove" our contention.

This form of self-fulfilling prophesy differs from a simple blind spot (or selective perception), wherein we block ourselves from noticing something that runs counter to our cherished notions. I think of the self-fulfilling prophesy as a more interesting twin of the blind spot because it actually shapes or reshapes the outside world to fit the inner one. As an illustration, consider a problem that gymnasts have when mentally rehearsing a balance bar routine. If the movie they run through their mind shows a fall and other missteps, they are likely to overcorrect in actual performance and thereby make a different mistake. The advice that coaches give their gymnasts is to imagine—in their mind's eye and their mind's "body"—doing the routine flawlessly. That strategy is far more likely to produce a clean performance.

I tell you this because it makes a difference how you think of your own integrity: how much you personally respect the power of your own word. Those broken New Year's resolutions, those promises we have made to ourselves and not fulfilled, degrade our image of ourselves as people of our word. Speaking for myself, I have often committed to losing a few pounds or to working out more regularly and then failed to follow through. These broken promises have degraded my personal power by downgrading my conviction of the power of my word.

Lloyd Hill speaks about self-esteem as an agent of personal power that is nourished or weakened in what might otherwise seem like trivial dishonesties:

> Say you are undercharged at the store, or you go get some change at the bank, and the bank gives you an extra hundred dollar bill or a two dollar bill, and you count it there and you give it back to the cashier. Tellers, young people of today, are shocked senseless that someone would give them back fifty cents, or a dollar, or ten dollars. Every time you make a tough decision in favor of honesty and integrity, you build the wall of self-esteem. Every time you make that little decision not to return the quarter, or the thousand dollars, or whatever it is, you remove a brick from self-esteem. And self-esteem is one of the very few attributes shared by nearly all financially, emotionally, and personally successful people.

We build our self-concept as we witness our own actions. We have blind spots, but we have some idea of how often we act in line with our words. A realistic conviction that we live by our word is a pillar on which our spirit can stand tall, and that supports our continued action with integrity.

Paul Hortobagyi is a general manager at Le Merigot Hotel, a Marriott flagship. He has been extremely successful and one gets the sense that his employees love him deeply. As general manager, he is the senior executive on site. He talks about how he manages his to-do list and how it makes him feel:

> Managers often push themselves to the limit because they made that promise to themselves about what they want to accomplish. I made a list for myself yesterday, and I've got to finish that list. My boss hasn't made that list. I did. I know what I have to do. The accomplishment feels great. Once you've finished, there's nobody to say, "Look, I've made my list!" I cannot show it to anybody, but I did it.

Social support and external pressure are useful tools for enforcing integrity, as I will discuss, but at some point, one's internal sense must carry the day. We strengthen our sense of our integrity by living up to our commitments to ourselves, and that sense, in turn, increases our ability to live by our word in general.

Robert Gass nicely summarizes the problem of promises made to oneself:

> When we don't keep these promises, we diminish our trust in ourselves. We start to discount our own word. We commit, but the little voice in the head says, "Yeah, right!"

> What's required? The same mindfulness we practice toward others: slowing down and really reflecting before giving our word; consulting our inner knowing; and practicing the three Cs of skillful commitments:

> - Clarity: Understand the implications of our commitment—what we will actually have to do to fulfill it.
> - Context: Carefully consider this choice in the light of existing commitments, our purpose, and our personal ecology.
> - Choice: Check for inner alignment and that we are operating from "choose to" rather than "have to."

Most of us tend to treat the promises we make only to ourselves in a more cavalier manner than we do the promises we make to others. The irony is that the long-term consequences of breaking those self-promises is in some ways more severe. Not only do we lose out on the benefits of whatever we were promising—health or personal growth or career development perhaps—we also undermine our own credibility with ourselves. A trainer in a Landmark Forum workshop once illustrated the extraordinary power of believing in one's own word. He described how he absolutely hates working out, but he knows that regular exercise is necessary to allow him to meet his strenuous job demands. He says he works out at least three times a week. "Why? Because I said so." The extent to which we know in our bones that we are people of our word is powerful. Is willpower really as simple as believing and maintaining one's word to oneself?

Arranging Social Support

The work of improving your integrity can be terrifying, slamming you into your personal demons. It will at times be far more comfortable to drop the whole effort. With social support, you will be far more likely to persist. Other people can help you increase your integrity, especially changing your everyday mode of relating to people. Confidants privy to your efforts can keep you on track as you wrestle with fears or problematic skills. A confidant can be a peer, a close friend, a coach, or a mentor. Create a circle or find an accountability partner with whom you can talk about the struggle on a regular basis. Ideally your confidants are embarked on a similar challenge. They can simply ask you routinely how you are doing at clarifying or living your personal mission, cleaning up your outstanding commitments, monitoring your promise making, or whatever you are up to in the process. Above all, they must be honest in their feedback to you, not unconditionally approving. They must hold you accountable when you lapse and let you know when you fool yourself.

Other people can support you by adding social pressure when you make a public promise. Public commitments are good because they are sticky. Failing to live up to a promise you have made in front of others creates consequences, and you may work harder in order to avoid shame, embarrassment, or just plain looking bad. As I reveal here my own challenge to exercise more and lose a little weight, I set myself up: I fully expect people who have read this book to ask me how I am doing with those commitments. If I can't report success, I will be weakening my personal credibility and thus also my effectiveness in promoting the concept of behavioral integrity. So I had *better* lose that weight!

Bob Wright tells a tale of two tribes that paddle out to do battle on a deserted island. Which one will win? The one that burns their canoes when they arrive: "We paddle home in the enemy's canoes or not at all." A public commitment is one form of burning your canoes.

FOLLOWING A DELIBERATE PROCESS FOR GIVING YOUR WORD

When we promise casually or automatically, we get in trouble. Specifically, we put our credibility at risk because we make promises that we do not wholeheartedly want to deliver on or that we are unable to deliver on. The answer to both of these pitfalls is the willingness to say no, coupled with acute mindfulness and self-questioning at the moment of making a promise.

Why do we make promises we do not want to deliver on? A few reasons: one is that we do not often consider our full set of priorities and desires. We talk with someone who wants something from us; the request seems reasonable, and making the promise seems the best way to handle the situation. So we make it. Studies have shown that most executives spend ten minutes or less on each task they face in a day.[4] Most managerial work is more about putting out fires than deliberate, careful action. Leaders feel they can do only what seems best in the moment, often on an emotional impulse that overrides their cooler thought. Darryl Stickel, founder of Trust Unlimited, a consulting firm that specializes in trust management, points out that such automatic promise making is especially likely when we see someone in distress or when we believe we have made a mistake. "We want to make promises to make the distress or the mistake go away," he says. "That tendency can really bite us." A third reason is ambivalence: we often ignore or are unaware of personal ambivalence.

One simple process to counter that problem is to ask yourself two basic questions before making any promise or commitment:

"Do I really want to fulfill this promise?"
"Am I able to guarantee its delivery?"

Robert Gass describes these questions as principles of alignment and sobriety. The process begins with alignment:

First you have to make sure, "Do I really want this? Is all of me behind this?" And then, on a second level [sobriety], "Can I deliver on this, even if I wanted to?" "Do I have the capacity, do I have the experience, do I have the time?" People get in delusionary states where they feel they'd like to do this, or they'd like to please, so they say yes, but they're not looking at how many hours they have in a day, they're not looking at the commitments around the table. Are you being sober? Are you being realistic? Can you do the thing?

Robert trains executives to think about these two issues before they commit and to get better at the necessary reflection. If the answer to either one is "no," then the negotiation must continue before you make a promise that puts your word at risk.

The willingness to say "no," and to continue negotiating when you do not want to make the promise that is on the table, is the necessary follow-up to the two questions that precede any promise. If you ask the questions but do not say "no" when you have to, then you are not protecting the value of your word. Lee Pillsbury described his long-time business partner as a man of absolutely impeccable integrity, a man who "will do anything to avoid breaking a commitment." He makes a tremendous number of promises to many very important people, and he delivers, like gravity:

> He is one of the few people I deal with who'll turn down my requests. I might say to him, for example, "Would you call so and so, one of our investors?"
>
> "Why? What would I tell him?"
>
> "Well because . . . whatever the story is."
>
> Then he makes an assessment, and if he doesn't think he wants to—if he isn't going to do that—he says right then and there, "I decline your request. I'm not going to do it."
>
> He says yes a whole lot. What he says yes to, he's religious about keeping track of, writing down, and doing. And he's also very good at saying no.

Safeguarding and building the power of your word requires asking hard questions before you commit and being willing to act on whatever answer comes back. Say yes, and make 100 percent sure to deliver and follow up. Or say no and keep negotiating, or handle whatever consequences follow.

KEEPING TRACK AND FOLLOWING UP

After mindfully giving our word, we need to take the same seemingly obvious steps that we sometimes also neglect in our communications, as described in Chapter Five: write it down, keep track of it, and follow up with the person you made the promise to. Especially follow up when you fail to keep your word, even though that is the time when you least want to talk to the person you failed. Don't overrely on your memory, which will play tricks on you.

Part of the problem is sometimes rank. No one likes to admit it, but we tend to take the promises we make to our bosses more seriously than those we make to people over whom we have power. Yet subordinates take our promises very seriously. Unless you have an unusually open relationship with them, they probably won't tell you about the promises you have broken. After all, you are their boss, and the conversation might go badly. But they do notice, and as often as not, those broken promises stick around to poison the relationship. Your memory may serve to keep track of the big promises made to your boss, but it won't likely keep track of these seemingly small ones to subordinates. Remember they may not be small to someone else. Write them down.

Lee Pillsbury's partner, the guy with impeccable integrity, writes everything down on 8-1/2 by 11-inch pads that he carries around to manage himself. Others use their digital organizer or a computerized to-do list. Don't use scraps of paper; they tend to get lost. Use something that is with you almost all the time and is easy to update. Recording your commitments, large and small, is a simple but critical element in any program to maximize and preserve the power of your word.

APOLOGIZING AND RECOVERING

Another element of personal discipline is apologizing and otherwise restoring and repairing damage to the power of your word. Most people are reluctant to apologize; for example, my five-year-old son sometimes has the hardest time simply keeping eye contact during an apology. We usually do not like to think of our failures as "ours," and we fear that they reflect badly on our personal competence and worth. But apologies are necessary in the personal discipline of integrity. There are three steps to apologizing and recovering:

1. Acknowledge that you made a promise and failed to deliver.
2. Renegotiate proactively if you see a deadline not on track or a promise you won't be able to keep.

3. Fix any harm done by the initial breach, and work hard to keep it from recurring.

Acknowledge the Promise and Your Failure to Deliver

Too often we try to sweep a broken promise under the rug. We do not mention it and hope that others do not notice. Of course, they do notice, whether or not they say so. Acknowledging the situation is the first step in cleaning it up. It establishes a shared reality and a basis for further conversation. Bruce Hodes, a Chicago-based management consultant, described this process as "honoring your word. You honor that you said it, that it means something, that you need to revisit it, and that you need to clean it up. 'Hey, I said this, but I did this.'" In this way, you affirm that you value your own word and that you will work to restore it.

Explanations usually do not help restore credibility, a point I sometimes forget because I often buy into my own explanations. Sometimes circumstances do get in the way of keeping one's word, but explaining does not help, especially when your credibility is already shaky.

Lee Pillsbury says of his long-time business partner, "If he is five minutes late on a phone call, the first words out of his mouth are, 'I'm sorry. I apologize.' And never an excuse. Never a reason. Simply, 'I screwed you up. I mistreated you. I apologize.'" This style of apology seems to fly in the face of normal social expectations, as so many people provide excuses for everything. But it is remarkably clean and is more effective at restoring integrity than is an explanation or an excuse.

> An excuse is just a way to avoid taking responsibility. Responsibility begins with recognizing that you are at cause and being willing to say, "I'm the reason I'm late." It isn't the policeman, it isn't the dog, it isn't the kid. It's me. And responsibility is not the burden or the fault or the guilt. Those are all just judgments. They are not responsibility.

It is infuriating when you personally believe that outside circumstances or explanations really drove the breach, and it can go against long-standing patterns to simply allow the egg on your face. But choose the more effective course: to apologize effectively, accept responsibility.

Ted Teng, former president and COO of Wyndham International, also advises against excuses.

> You don't get anywhere in rebuilding trust without a sincere apology, not one of these sort of watered-down type of, "Well, to the extent that the federal government fell short, I take responsibility." If you just came out and said, "We fell short. We disappointed you. We let you down. And for that, I'm sorry. And I will do better"—that type of apology is much stronger than the politically correct, "Well, we didn't know" type stuff. Leaders have to own their failures to get past them.

> In the American culture, we're not quick to accept responsibility. Politically, and in big companies and all that, we come up with a lot of [mitigating] circumstances. In Japanese society, when something doesn't go right, the chairman resigns and accepts full responsibility—even though that person may not have anything to do with that particular incident. "Because it happened on my watch, I will step down."

I have mixed feelings about scapegoating the boss, but the apparent American fascination with mitigating circumstances does not serve the cause of integrity and trust. Mitigating, hedging, and splitting hairs work counter to rebuilding trust and reestablishing integrity. What works is the direct acceptance of having failed. As life comes up and challenges you, you will fall short sometimes. Integrity means being willing to look at where you fell short and to adjust course. The quality of that looking, both internally and in its social conveyance, is defined by whether it is simple ownership or some form of responsibility dodge.

Bob Wright talks about what happens when your habitual response to failure is to make excuses.

> You just become an undependable excuse machine. There is a big difference between irresponsible apologizing and actually taking responsibility. If it's blame, shame, or excuses, the system stays the same and you lose integrity immediately because the apology is irresponsible.

Blame is saying someone else did it. Excuses say that circumstances did it. But isn't shame a way of saying, "My bad. I am sorry"? Yes and no. It is an admission of the failure—but then, says Bob, it takes a different direction:

> Shame is not responsible because it's often manipulative, egging people to feel sorry for you; it actually keeps people from learning. *Apology* comes from the Greek *apologos,* to uphold the word, and so you acknowledge what's true. But if you then move to shame, you've moved from responsible honesty to a negative event around your self. And frequently shame is an aggressive act toward your self that is driven by repressed anger toward someone else.

The drama of shame often ends up pulling the focus away from the people who have been hurt. It is a self-indulgence that does not help the victim and does not increase your own ability to keep integrity. Done right, an apology is not dramatic. It acknowledges the original commitment, the breach, and any harm that was done; owns the failure; and expresses or renews a commitment to make it right. The simpler the better. Ted Teng offered a template: "Hey, we screwed up. And we will do better. We can explain the circumstances and whatever, but at the end of the day, we didn't have the result that we wanted."

We all make mistakes. The discipline comes in allowing ourselves to recognize when we have done so, and then to take it public. Rich Teerlink is the former chairman of Harley-Davidson, where he presided over a dramatic turnaround and built a culture of trust and engagement. He is an extraordinary leader—and he makes mistakes. But he supports his people in pointing them out to him, and then he owns up:

> I launched into a little tirade to a group of sixty leaders because they weren't doing what I thought we should be doing. They were working very hard and just weren't getting the outcome I wanted, so I fought. I had one of them come up to me on Monday morning right after a three-day meeting. She knew I had gotten in early, and she was there. She said, "Rich, I'd like to talk to you." "Sure." I had an open door policy. She says, "You know, that meeting included the greatest speeches we've ever had. [Then] you got up at the

end [with that tirade]. You took a pin and stuck it in the balloon of enthusiasm that was in the room."

As she was saying it, I said, "Oh, crap. I did that." I meant well, but I did the wrong thing. I wasn't practicing any values. I need to be respectful.

And so I had to swallow hard and tell everyone, "Hey, I'm sorry. But ego got in the way." I didn't like saying, "Hey, folks, my ego got in the way," but the keys to a good apology are first to admit to people you're wrong and tell them why you think you're wrong; and second change your behavior.

Because apologies are necessary for managing trust and preserving the power of your word, you may want to create a climate in which people feel safe pointing out your mistakes. You also have to listen to them, show you have listened to them, and learn from them. Otherwise your apology is not worth much.

As a leader, you will sometimes need to apologize for someone else's error or misunderstanding. That process can be galling, but less so if you can see and appreciate how you yourself might have foreseen and prevented the problem in the first place. As a leader, that is what you *should* have done—and clearly you didn't. Don't beat yourself up about it, but you do need to apologize. A few years ago, Bruce Hodes initiated a profit-sharing plan for his consulting company whereby he would divide 6 percent of the company profits between his two employees. He laid out the plan in a meeting, without documentation, and both employees believed that he had promised them 6 percent of the company profits *each*:

> So they've got this expectation of the money, and I've got this expectation of the money, and they're very different amounts. They were very upset, and they thought I broke my word and I'm a liar. I had to acknowledge what had happened—acknowledge that there was a mistake, apologize for it, get real clear on exactly what profit sharing was going to happen, work hard to have them see how it could be misconstrued. I think one of them got there; one of them didn't. What I didn't do was say, "I didn't say that." I said, "You heard that—and I meant what I said—but we aren't paying out 6 percent each"—and it was all right on the table.

One employee accepted the apology, and one did not. That is one of the scary things about apologies. None of us likes to look bad or empower others to judge us—even though they do so all the time. CEOs and other highly successful executives often like to think of themselves a bit like superheroes. They are extremely competent, and their extraordinary confidence helps them take on some huge challenges and make big decisions that paralyze others. But a superhuman self-image sometimes gets in the way of seeing mistakes and owning up to them.

Bruce calls apologizing a part of "completing your failure" so you can move on. He says that even though in his profit-sharing tale the failure could be seen as other people's misunderstanding,

> I should have known better, after twenty-five years in business. When you deal with stuff like that, you need to be real clear; it needs to be in writing. And I did it from my desk, sort of shooting from my hip. It wasn't nailed down, and it was misconstrued. It was a stupid mistake. I have to be willing to live with that.

'Fessing up helps manage the damage. Bruce delivered on his intended promise, and he has reestablished trust in his workplace. It took some follow-up after the apology, and even then it did not work with everyone. But when people feel you broke your word, apologizing is your most constructive first response.

Renegotiate Proactively

Sometimes you see your failure coming. You agreed to a deadline, and now you see the project is behind schedule. Or you make a promise and then have wiser thoughts. The temptation is to bury the problem and hope nobody comes after you for it. That is your inner five-year-old talking. As Robert Gass says:

> What do you do when you've made a commitment that you don't want to or can't live by? What most people do is they "dance"; they try to put up the smokescreen or just hope the person won't notice rather than actually going back and dealing very directly and proactively.

Instead of trying to bury it, Robert suggests another approach:

> If you've committed to having something done by Wednesday, do not wait until the following Friday to deal with the fact that it hasn't come in and he hasn't noticed. On the Monday before it is due, say, "Hey, I committed to have it to you by Wednesday and I'm having difficulties at commitment. Can I renegotiate and give it to you on Friday?" You have to be forthright to deal with your commitments cleanly. The target is to always either do what you said you would do or renegotiate it in a clean way, proactively, before you have to deliver.

Acknowledging pending failure before the deadline shows consideration for the person who depended on you and a willingness to manage the consequent damage.

Fix It

Apologies are not a substitute for delivering on your word, and your subsequent actions will show people whether your apology was sincere. Even if you believed the apology deeply at the time, if the offending action continues or recurs often, the apology will further undermine credibility rather than restore it. Carl Camden is the CEO of Kelly Services, a global staffing agency. He sums it up well in the context of rebuilding a client relationship after a perceived failure, saying that fixing the problem or the damage— not merely promising to fix it—is more important than figuring out who is right: "Apology plus action has to be ten times more powerful than an apology."

MAKING THE COMMITMENT TO HONOR YOUR COMMITMENTS

In this chapter we have seen lots of challenges to being or becoming a person whose word is as solid as steel and as good as gold. It goes against habits most of us have learned since childhood. It means sacrificing some short-term gains for a long-term payoff that might be uncertain. It is unnerving. It calls for building self-knowledge and a conviction that your word shapes reality. It calls for social support and developing new skills around making promises, keeping track of them, and apologizing.

In the light of all that, surely you must ask yourself, "Is it worth it?" If your answer is "yes," then just do it. Take on the exercises, the coaching, and the journey of building the power of your word. If your answer is less than certain, now might not be the time. But I argue that it is worthwhile because it is fundamental to excellent leadership. Just do it.

Amy Lyman is the cofounder and chair of the Great Place to Work Institute which produces the 100 Best Companies to Work For lists in over twenty-nine countries around the world. She offers that

> the notion of being consistent between what you say and do is something leaders in great workplaces understand more deeply than leaders in other workplaces. The leaders in great workplaces understand that it is important to the success of the company, and they challenge themselves to walk that talk, to uphold their promises.

Some people recognize the importance of behavioral integrity and take on the challenge of personal discipline. Some do not. Lloyd Hill believes the awareness is bone-deep and, like tendencies to dodge, may also come from childhood:

> We all have our fundamental beliefs, don't we? Our anchors. In difficult times you go back to those anchors. I think that some people understand the importance of integrity, that it's the nucleus of leadership. And I think that other people don't have a clue that that's all that important.

Whether the awareness is developed through growing up, introduced through a workshop or mentor, or sparked by a book that hammers on this simple point, capturing the integrity dividend requires discipline. You need to think about it in almost every interaction, every communication, every task you take on. Carl Camden sees the integration of integrity into the daily, hourly fabric of getting the job done as fundamental to capturing the integrity dividend:

> All of the major value propositions that companies need to engage in are positioned initially as a discipline. Quality is one. You've got to pay attention to it. You've got to have people always focused on

it. And you've got to have special events around it. But where did that discipline truly take hold at companies? It actually came from the companies where it wasn't held out as a separate discipline, but was part of the day-to-day standard operating processes of the company. The same would be true of integrity.

Integrity cannot be limited to annual performance reviews or 360-degree surveys or employee feedback, though those are all good things. It cannot be the thing you work on when you are not doing other work. To the contrary, it must suffuse everything you do. Otherwise it is not integrity. Otherwise, it is pretense.

As you work at it, it gets easier. New habits form, and new skills and muscles develop. You start to notice the payoff of being surrounded by trusting relationships, and that makes the short-term sacrifices easier. Robert Gass offered this perspective on the development process:

> As people start developing more habits—of impeccability, of authenticity, of integrity—it's like working out in the gym; you start building the muscles. A lot of contemporary research talks about neural pathways and forming new habits. It definitely gets easier. It starts becoming more habitual. You're building up neural pathways; you start building up a positive experience base, and when you do it, it feels better. It's harder to fear it when it pays off in the long run. There may still come a time when you feel like you're walking off a cliff. It's not necessarily that fear goes away but that you become more willing and more experienced at navigating the fear.

Learning to operate in the world with greater integrity than before is incredibly awkward, even when the improvements are small ones. But it gets easier with practice. There will be scary times along the path, and likely scary times will keep coming up now and then. But with conviction and support, you can navigate those times in a way that builds and preserves the power of your word.

SUMMARY

The integrity dividend does not offer an easy answer. There are serious challenges entailed in capturing it, and conquering them calls for sustained effort, vigilance, and discipline. Habits of social deceit must be detected and replaced with skillful honesty. Quick and easy solutions to problems must sometimes be forgone in favor of approaches that yield more sustainable results. You have to be willing to engage with people in ways that may at first be uncomfortable and awkward. You have to become intimately familiar with the ambivalences and the quiet wisdom in your gut. This chapter offers a few tools for addressing these challenges and so developing your capacity for integrity. Arrange social support that gently but firmly holds you accountable for your commitments. Be very deliberate in the process of giving your word, and then keep scrupulous track. And develop your willingness to apologize skillfully and without excuses. Building habits of integrity is a challenge. I invite you to take it on, because it pays a dividend.

Into Practice

Consider

- How often do you reflect on your espoused values as a guide to your behavior?
- Notice any deceit that slips into your social interaction, especially to smooth it. How might you accomplish a similar goal without deceit?
- How good are you at delaying gratification? Do you sufficiently consider actions that will have long-term payoffs?
- How uncomfortable are you about confronting your own or others' broken promises?
- How good are you at detecting your own ambivalences?
- How deliberate are you about the process of making commitments?
- How well do you keep track of *all* your commitments?
- Notice the social norms of people at home and at work around the issue of impeccably keeping promises. Notice how they talk about promises. Do they keep their word? Do they expect others to do so? Do they raise the issue when agreements are broken? Are they careful to make agreements specific and clear up front? Can they say "no" to a request? Do they apologize cleanly or with excuses? Notice the impact on trust and on effectiveness of these norms.

Act

The following recommendations draw heavily on the work of Robert Gass, who shared with me several daily assignments he gives people to help them develop their promise-keeping muscles. Practice these disciplines for a few weeks, and watch how they affect your state of mind and your relationships:

- Choose an accountability partner. During the first few weeks or months of exercising your integrity muscle, find someone to briefly report to every day or two. It should not be your boss, and probably not a subordinate either. Ideally it should be someone who is working on the same exercises. Check in with this person regularly and say honestly how you are doing with focusing on key values, compiling your commitment list, cleaning up old commitments, checking feasibility before committing, and keeping commitments. Your partner's job is to listen without judgment and to help you get back on track when you fail.
- Develop a single sentence that sums up your key values and purpose as a leader. Think it through carefully. The phrase should resonate deeply in your heart and may remind you of your life mission beyond the workplace. Improve or modify the sentence as new ideas and insights come to you.
- For several weeks, contemplate the sentence for a full minute before every scheduled meeting, every phone call, every substantive e-mail, every significant task you engage as a leader. Ask yourself how the action you are about to take relates to the values and purpose you describe. Strive to make this reflection an automatic, ongoing habit.
- Examine in detail how you spend your time and your money. Is this allocation in line with the values you claim? If not, consider whether a shift in your words or your actions might be warranted.
- At the end of each day, ask yourself what you have done to enact the values you claim to hold dear. Don't beat yourself up about shortfalls, but strive to be able to say you have done everything you could to support your claimed values. Do this inventory every day until it becomes second nature.
- Set your intention to notice every time you give your word and to keep every commitment. You want to achieve and sustain a level of 100 percent follow-through. Remind yourself daily of this intention. There is great personal power in the gap between 90 and 100 percent—and even more when the gap is bigger.
- Complete the self-assessment survey about promise keeping in Exercise 6.1. Retake the survey periodically to track your progress.

EXERCISE 6.1. SELF-SURVEY ABOUT THE IMPECCABILITY
OF YOUR PROMISE KEEPING

Circle the number that best reflects your honest assessment.

1. I take time to reflect and weigh carefully other priorities
   before committing.

   Never   Always
   1   2   3   4   5   6   7   8   9   10

2. I make sure to really evaluate my ability to deliver 100 percent
   on my commitments before saying yes.

   Never   Always
   1   2   3   4   5   6   7   8   9   10

3. I come from "choose to" rather than "have to" in making
   commitments.

   Never   Always
   1   2   3   4   5   6   7   8   9   10

4. I am comfortable and easy in saying "no" to commitments
   I don't want to make.

   Never   Always
   1   2   3   4   5   6   7   8   9   10

5. When making commitments, I make sure that both of us are
   really clear on the timing and exact expectations.

   Never   Always
   1   2   3   4   5   6   7   8   9   10

6. I deliver on my work commitments impeccably to others
   within the promised time frame.

   Never   Always
   1   2   3   4   5   6   7   8   9   10

7. I deliver on my commitments to my family impeccably within
   the promised time frame.

   Never   Always
   1   2   3   4   5   6   7   8   9   10

8. I deliver on my commitments to myself impeccably within the promised time frame.

Never   Always
1   2   3   4   5   6   7   8   9   10

9. My system for tracking commitments really supports my keeping my commitments.

Never   Always
1   2   3   4   5   6   7   8   9   10

10. When I am having difficulty keeping a commitment, I deal with the other party in a proactive and direct way.

Never   Always
1   2   3   4   5   6   7   8   9   10

11. Other people see me as someone who is impeccable in keeping their agreements.

Never   Always
1   2   3   4   5   6   7   8   9   10

12. I hold others accountable to the commitments they make to me.

Never   Always
1   2   3   4   5   6   7   8   9   10

13. I manage my agreements and commitments so I can comfortably meet them in a sustainable way.

Never   Always
1   2   3   4   5   6   7   8   9   10

Your reflections:

- Deal with your backlog of agreements. Make a single list of your outstanding commitments or promises: at work, to friends, to family, to yourself. Put it in a form that you can carry around in your daily routine. Combine the items from your work to-do list with your memory and your personal digital assistant and any scraps of paper you might have written on. You might even have to go around and ask people what they are owed. Pull together a single list. Assign a due date to each agreement.

- Review your whole list, daunting though it may be. Think about each item realistically and soberly, and consider whether you can keep the commitment in the light of your overall load. Mark each item into one of four categories:

  C for committed: I will do this on time.
  R for renegotiate: I will renegotiate with whomever I made the promise to, seeking a promise I can commit to or a release from the promise.
  A for ambivalent: I am choosing to remain unclear.
  I for ignore: Notice that ignoring a promise does not make it go away, and it often generates ill will among the people you made the promise to.

- Revisit the list often, with the intention of moving every item into the "C" category or renegotiating in good faith to get released from it. Your goal is to have all the commitments fulfilled or on track to get fulfilled. Clear out the pipeline. Feel the growing power of your word.

- Consider whether you owe any apologies for your broken word. Give those apologies without drama or explanation. Make a new commitment to those people to clean up your mess. Be sure it is a commitment on which you will deliver.

- For a few days, pay special attention to taking time before you give your word. You might need only a momentary pause, or you might want to ask for fifteen minutes or a few hours to think about the commitment in private. Use this time to think through exactly what the commitment would entail, how well it fits with your existing schedule and other large or small commitments, and whether you really want to make this commitment. Try imagining yourself literally walking through the accomplishment of your various commitments. Your body will tell you if you are setting yourself up for overload or failure. Give your word only when you are 100 percent committed to delivering on it.

- Write down every commitment you make immediately. Cross it off as you complete it.
- When you fail to deliver on a promise (and it will happen sometime):

  1. Acknowledge it to the person you made the promise to—in advance if possible.
  2. Renegotiate in good faith what you can deliver.
  3. Do not waste energy berating yourself.
  4. Use your energy to start keeping your word every time, starting *now*.

- Most of us consistently underestimate how long it will take to accomplish tasks. This form of kidding ourselves serves us in some ways, but it also sets us up to miss deadlines and so break promises. Figure out, from your track record, how badly you typically underestimate: 25 percent? 40 percent? 50 percent? More? Don't beat yourself up about it. Adjust accordingly, so you can make realistic promises. Simply make your best estimate, then add your correction.
- After you have worked on these issues for a while—and when you feel ready for a new perspective—set up a time to interview a close business associate, a close friend, or your life partner about your promise keeping. Use the questions in Exercise 6.2. The interview can be by telephone or in person. This challenging exercise will provide you with new information. It will also create social support for your growing commitment to integrity.

EXERCISE 6.2. INTERVIEW FORM FOR OTHERS ABOUT THE
IMPECCABILITY OF YOUR PROMISE KEEPING

Please tell me the number that best reflects your honest experience
of me.

1. When I commit to something, you feel completely confident
   that I will do what I say within the time that I say.

   Never   Always
   1   2   3   4   5   6   7   8   9   10

   Comments [anything they wish to say about why they gave you
   this number]:

2. I appear to be comfortable and skillful in saying no to you
   regarding commitments I don't want to make.

   Never   Always
   1   2   3   4   5   6   7   8   9   10

   Comments:

3. When making commitments, I make sure that both of us are
   really clear about our exact expectations.

   Never   Always
   1   2   3   4   5   6   7   8   9   10

   Comments:

4. When I am having difficulty keeping a commitment, I bring
   this to your attention in a timely and responsible way.

   Never   Always
   1   2   3   4   5   6   7   8   9   10

   Comments:

5. I appear to manage my agreements and commitments so I can comfortably meet them in a sustainable way.

Never   Always
1   2   3   4   5   6   7   8   9   10

Comments:

6. I hold you accountable to the commitments you make to me.

Never   Always
1   2   3   4   5   6   7   8   9   10

Comments:

7. I appear to keep my commitments to myself impeccably within the promised time frame.

Never   Always
1   2   3   4   5   6   7   8   9   10

Comments:

8. Any other feedback for me regarding commitments and accountability:

Your reflections:

PART THREE

BEHAVIORAL INTEGRITY AND THE RIPPLE EFFECT

Building and Sustaining a Leadership Culture of Integrity

CHAPTER SEVEN

EASING THE MIDDLE MANAGER'S DILEMMA

One awkward reality of corporate life is that middle managers are sometimes asked to implement and champion policies with which they disagree. It was striking how strongly this unpleasant integrity issue resonated with the corporate executives with whom I spoke: Almost every one of them had experienced it. Some had been asked to implement personnel policies they knew would cause hardship and ill will. Others were told to use and teach sales approaches they thought would not work; to make menu changes that seemed to make no sense; to follow military orders they knew to be based on flawed intelligence; to follow consultants' advice they knew to be misleading, strategies they suspected were haphazard or erroneous, policies they believed endangered their charges; and so on.

It is a part of corporate life that aspiring middle managers are sometimes asked to suppress their concerns and toe the party line. Many are reconciled to it. But they don't like it. Where it happens often or in a major way, the best middle managers—those who really care—get broken. Spirits flag. And those best managers stop bringing to the office the judgment and inspiration that can drive corporate excellence. Instead, they operate to survive.

This chapter makes suggestions to middle managers about how to handle this unavoidable dilemma. It also advises senior managers about how to minimize its negative impact on subordinates. I confess I have no easy answers for the middle manager. It comes down to choosing your battles, getting humble, deciding how much you trust your bosses, and knowing what lines you're not willing to cross. There may well be costs to pay, and the final outcomes often do not resemble what we think of as fair. For senior managers, my advice largely resembles classic recommendations about maximizing subordinates' buy-in.

But whether you are in the middle or senior position, the behavioral integrity framework makes it easier to understand and anticipate the inherent challenges.

THE BASIC DILEMMA

A friend of mine, a nurse, was a middle manager at a major managed care company. She supervised a team of nurses who helped people with complex illnesses to find appropriate care. At one point, a mandate was passed down that her team should guide patients to purchase medications exclusively through a specific contracted pharmacy. My friend and her team were distressed at the mandate, because the contracted pharmacy was expensive. In many cases, the patients would have paid less through a local pharmacy; in other cases, in which the medication was available through the physician's office, the patient would have had to pay only an office visit copayment for the drug.

This policy went against the key value that drove my manager friend and her team to excel: patient care. It also imposed both personal and organizational costs. It placed her and the nurses she supervised in the position of providing advice they knew was not in their patients' best interests. They would continue to care, of course, because caring tends to run deep in nurses. But inevitably they would also become a little callous as they compromised their principles to profit their employer. They would care just a little less, love their work a little less, try a little less hard, and put less of their heart into their work. The level of service the company provided would be a little lower, and so would employee loyalty.

You might well say that your own company has no such bureaucratic customer-harming policies. That may be. And it may be that the decision to contract had justifications that my friend was not aware of. Still, consider how it feels when any caring person is expected to enact a policy that seems to make no sense, and how it feels to ask others to do so.

What effect does a values-compromising policy have on people's caring for the mission of a company? What kind of middle managers does such strain weed out? And what kind of manager does it develop and leave in place?

The situation is a dilemma: in the view of the middle manager who faces it, the proposed policy often seems to be at odds with the espoused purpose of the company and seems unlikely to work in the long run. Yet she is required by her job to put on a brave face, act in a way that she thinks nonsensical or even destructive, and get her followers to cheerfully do the same. How does the dilemma typically affect her?

- She feels her own consistency is challenged as she is asked to act contrary to the principles and missions she has embraced and espoused.
- Her experience makes her question the behavioral integrity of her superiors, who are handing down policies at odds with their espoused values.
- Her ambivalence generates mixed messages that drive trust down. Her subordinates notice inconsistencies between her own behaviors and espousals as she is torn between loyalty to company hierarchy and loyalty to her own concept of the job and the company's mission.

BUT THE BOSS IS BOSS

There's no denying the basic fact that middle managers are not in charge of the company. Upper-level executives clearly agree with R. J. Dourney, president of Hearthstone Associates, former vice president of operations of Au Bon Pain, and former senior operating executive of Applebee's International and Brinker International, who says, "Once everybody says what they have to say and the door opens and they walk out the door, middle managers, like all management, should be the champions of whatever the company's policy is."

Larry Reinstein, president and CEO of Fresh City restaurants, agrees:

> People are not going to agree with every decision that comes from the boss. But ultimately, the reason he is the boss is that's his job. You need to support the boss, to move ahead and do what's required for the company. You need to sell it, just like it was your

own idea. I believe that if there's an ethical problem, the [subordinate] should go work for somebody else. Beyond that, I think it's really incumbent upon the person to just take it and go for it.

The senior executives I interviewed strongly emphasized their expectation that middle managers support their superiors' decisions in front of their subordinates. It is fine to express concerns to your superiors—in fact, it is probably your obligation to do so—but at the end of the day, to quote one executive, "we come out of the room with one message and that is what goes out into the world." Ed Evans, executive vice president for human resources and organizational development at Allied Waste Industries, says he has spent a lot of time counseling managers who disagree with policies. He phrased the challenge this way: "I'm part of the company, and ultimately it's the company's policy, and it's not a matter of whether I agree or not. It's a matter of whether I understand it, and then I have a decision to make to apply the policy—or not to let the door hit me in the behind."

WHO IS AT FAULT?

Since the boss *is* the boss, it may seem easy to simply blame the dilemma on senior management, but Doug Brooks, president and CEO of Brinker International, a restaurant company with over $4 billion in annual revenue, takes pains to point out that the dilemma is not entirely higher management's doing. Both higher and subordinate managers can be enlarging the problem:

> There are two people at fault there. There's the head manager, who probably hasn't made sure that there's buy-in or agreement by the middle manager. And there's the middle manager who, assuming the boss isn't an ogre, needs to try to have some dialogue with the boss [by saying, for example,] "I'm not comfortable with that. Is there another way we can package that? Is there another way I can say that? Can you give me some help?"

> I know traditionally the middle manager isn't comfortable challenging the boss, or asking the boss why he or she is making the manager do this. But if you don't agree with what management has to say, you have to let them know that, ask them about it, question them about it—or leave.

No one pretends that the leverage is equally distributed, but Doug is right that there are choices to be made on either side and enough responsibility to go around. On one side is the senior manager who did not secure buy-in from subordinates, and on the other is the middle manager who did not get his or her concerns addressed sufficiently. It is the tension between the two responsibilities that increases the dilemma.

Dick Axelrod, a management consultant and author of *Terms of Engagement* and *You Don't Have to Do It Alone*,[1] comments on these dual, conflicting roles and expectations:

> Do you have the courage to speak the truth? Because there is always the assumption, "If I speak my truth, I'll get fired." And, on the other hand, you've got leaders [complaining], "I'm not getting the truth." You have got to look at the way the dynamic becomes self-fulfilling. I think your role [as a middle manager] is to be as open and forthright as you think you can in this given situation. We're always asking the leader above to take the risk, but you've got to be willing to take some risk too. It's really within that team or group to create that [risk-sharing] culture.

On that note, let's consider separately what middle managers can do to cope with the challenge and what senior managers can do to prevent it.

WHAT THE MIDDLE MANAGER CAN DO

As a middle manager, your best options usually come down to expressing your concerns to superiors and seeking to understand justifications. In those ways, you may be able to change the policy or, if not, come to peace with it and equip yourself to sell it to subordinates. When the justifications for the change are not forthcoming, the challenge comes down to trusting your leaders. These approaches can be useful where the request is not for something you consider unethical. In cases of ethics, your challenge is to know what line you are unwilling to cross, and equip yourself to pay the cost, if any, of your ethical position. In all of these dilemmas, the essence of your challenge is to find a way in which you can be genuine in supporting the policy to your subordinates. Most likely they will see through anything else.

VOICE CONCERNS AND ASK QUESTIONS

It seems clear that middle managers have access to critical information that top managers need in making and refining decisions and that a middle manager's discomfort with a decision may stem from that special knowledge. Most executives I spoke with said the middle manager is absolutely obligated to share concerns upward. This is what Skip Sack, CEO and founder of Classic Restaurant Concepts and former executive vice president of Applebee's International, has to say:

> If you're a lieutenant colonel and the general says to you, "Tony, here's what I want you to do," I think you have an obligation to say, "General, I think we're making a mistake, and these are the reasons why."

Regardless of whether the "general" agrees, such a conversation allows the decision to be made in an informed way. It should also allow the middle manager to learn about justifications that might not be apparent to her. Scott Brodows, COO of SynXis Corporation, a global distribution technology company, also stresses the need for middle managers to communicate:

> There may be cases where the senior guys can effect change and solve a problem if they know about it. Sometimes middle management doesn't like to engage in those discussions, so they don't. In some cases, a senior manager may not want to hear about it. As a middle manager, you need to use your judgment: Is it a big issue that needs to be fixed? Or maybe the middle manager just needs assistance with communication. The middle manager can say, "Look I hear what you're telling me. I'll do it. But how do I get this message across? Here's what my employees are going to say: 'It's not aligned with my goals.' They are going to push back. They're not going to work as hard. How am I going to resolve this?" As a senior manager, I want to hear these things. I want to understand where I can help out. Middle managers need to feel comfortable having those conversations.

As Scott suggests, you need to recognize your boss's style and tailor your approach to it. You might need to choose your battles. He acknowledges that

> middle managers are in a tough position. They don't have the bandwidth, the ability to effect the change. But they're in a powerful position in that they know what the rank-and-file employees need. And they also know what the next person up the chain is needing and thinking. So they really need to be that effective conduit.

Linking the top to the line is part of the job.

You need the courage to speak your truth. As Dick Axelrod noted above, many middle managers fear that speaking their truth will get them fired. Ironically, where that fear is prevalent, senior managers often complain that nobody tells them the truth. There is a social feedback loop here that can end up with both sides getting their bad expectations confirmed. The ultimate goal is to change the culture of the company, or at least your relationship with your superior.

Where does the needed courage come from? It seems to derive from personal confidence, a positive awareness of one's employability elsewhere, and the presence of a boss who supports it. Rich Panico, president and CEO of Integrated Project Management, describes his own confidence level:

> I was with Johnson and Johnson for fifteen years. People ask me what led to my success there and what I was most proud of. The answer is simple. I never felt threatened—never—in presenting what I believed was right, regardless of the politics, because it didn't matter to me. I was confident enough that I could get a job anywhere. Ironically enough, I was always predisposed to what I thought was best for the company, but I also stayed aligned to my personal values. I can remember talking to one vice president who was frustrated with a position I had taken on an issue. I believe his greatest frustration was that he realized his position did not influence my position on the matter. I would rather be true to myself and what I thought was best for the company than change my mind for fear of retaliation. I'm very blessed to have this confidence and encourage my people to do what they absolutely believe is best and what they can live with for the rest of their lives.

Rich's commitment to be true to himself, to what he believed was best for the company, and to promoting that level of integrity in his people probably helped his consulting company, Integrated Project Management, win the 2005 Better Business Bureau's International Torch Award for Marketplace Ethics. When a middle manager is convinced that a superior's policy or decision is bad for the company, Rich suggests, she should speak up—with well-constructed logic.

USE YOUR LEVERAGE—SELECTIVELY

In general, once higher management has set a course, the middle manager's job is to buy in fully. But if the decision compromises the company's or middle manager's fundamental values or ethics, there are times when the middle manager may successfully buck the system, with productive results.

Recall the middle management nurse whose situation I described at the start of this chapter. The company had passed down a mandate for her and her team of nurses to guide their patients to purchase medications only through a specific contracted pharmacy. Because this policy went against the key value (patient care) that drove her and her team to excel, she and the team decided to systematically disobey the mandate and guide patients toward lower-cost pharmacy options. And they prevailed. After realizing the referrals were not coming into the contracted pharmacy at the anticipated volume, the company reexamined its pharmacy policies and negotiated with the contracted pharmacy to create a price-competitive option.

A decision to resist company policy can never be taken lightly, even when it seems clear that upper management has not weighed the trade-offs thoughtfully and complying with the policy will ultimately have more negative than positive effects. In pursuing her course, the nursing manager was careful to take into account the amount of power she and her team had to step out of line. She was not unrealistic about how much power she wielded, and she chose her battles carefully. When the company mandated an increase in the workweek from 37-1/2 to 40 hours with no additional compensation, she saw little sense in resisting or complaining; higher management knew there would be push-back in her department and everywhere else. When her boss did not allow flextime for several working mothers on her team, my friend chose to resist only in a quiet manner: allowing her team members to take the time they needed as she herself took up the slack by working the required odd hours. Her boss knew about the minor subversion but allowed it because of the extraordinary performance and loyalty my friend elicited from her team.

Carefully choosing her battles, taking winnable, principled stands, and resisting in nonconfrontational ways, my friend carved out an environment that supported a highly motivated team inside a larger bureaucracy that seemed almost hell-bent on undermining it.

Keep in mind that some battles are not worth fighting. As Scott Brodows notes,

> I may debate it or seek to understand. But at some point, my personal strategy is that you've got to accept it and move on. If you fight with your boss on everything, you're not going to have much of a career.

Trust in Your Leaders

Beyond the justifications, and in the rare cases where justifications cannot be shared either for confidentiality reasons or because an organization is very large, middle managers need to consider their background faith in their superiors as they react to a decision. Greg Oxton, executive director for the Consortium for Service Innovation, was a manager at IBM for fifteen years. He draws an analogy to onions: if, deep inside, the middle manager believes in the purpose and values that the company holds, then the onion is solid; experiences of minor disagreement are merely outer layers that can be peeled away without ruining the onion. Middle managers' "ability to deal with differences is directly related to their level of respect for higher level management's values."

R. J. Dourney describes how trust in his manager carried him through one decision with which he disagreed earlier in his career:

> Years and years ago I started with Chili's. We had 21 locations. When I left we had 680. In the early days, the only things we had on

the menu were a hamburger, a cheeseburger, a bowl of chili, and French fries. That was it. Five years into this role, Norman Brinker [the CEO] went down to Mexico and saw fajitas. He thought they were brilliant. So we decided to roll out fajitas in all of our restaurants. We didn't have broilers, so we had to widen our hoods and bring in broilers. Well, a certain percentage of the leadership team in the organization thought this was the end of the company. Some actually quit over it. Very few people bought in. I myself didn't have the ability to see what Norman saw, but I knew that Norman really believed that this was the right thing to do, and I trusted him. That's what I could hang my hat on: I had confidence in my leader. If you lack that confidence *and* you disagree with his idea, you'll never sell it to your people.

In the long run, higher management must earn respect for its judgment. But that respect is also colored by a middle manager's humility or lack of it. Kerry Miller is an executive search consultant and former vice president for People Development for Bertucci's Brick Oven Restaurants. To the overly self-important, he says,

Guess what? You work in business. You aren't the end-all, be-all. At least not if you're working for a great organization. There are other folks out there who have great thoughts, and they just may not line up with your business thoughts. As long as, at the end of the day, it's not going to be a fatal decision for your business, you've got to get behind it and drive it.

KNOW YOUR BRIGHT LINE

Your "bright line" is the ethical border or boundary you are unwilling to cross. One of the people I interviewed, let's call him Jim, told a story about his work as a senior human resource executive in a Fortune 500 company where a middle manager's dilemma challenged his ethical boundaries. The company's board had retained a consulting team to recommend how to restructure and streamline operations. Jim became curious when the consultants' recommendations did not match up with the best practices he had encountered in his considerable reading on the subject. Each of the recommendations included references to other reputable and successful companies that were using the recommended processes and practices—revised spans of control and the like. So in order to better educate himself, he figured he would have his team contact people at the companies the consultants described. He found to his surprise that the references were false: the consultants' recommendations were not in fact put in practice at the described sites. He suspected that the board might not respond well to the information he had gathered, as they seemed to like the consultant's approach very much. So he prepared his wife and family, and his team, for some potential upheaval. Three days after he submitted a formal report of his data and findings, he was informed that his role would be eliminated. He requested and received a substantial payment in return for his silence, and he moved on.

Jim's willingness to walk away allowed him to do the right thing—at least, by his own lights. He knew what he was not willing to do, the line he was not willing to cross. Was it a smart decision in other respects? When versions of the story circulated through the organization, the message that managers took from them was that no one should question the higher-ups: if you know something, it could cost you your job. That perception also suggests that Jim was wise to leave.

Some business coaches advise all executive to keep a pool of "walking-away money" (sometimes called "f - - - you money") to use in such emergencies. Some values are worth it. So is being able to live with yourself.

SELL WITH AUTHENTICITY

It is not just a matter of shutting up and doing your job; you have to help others feel good about implementing the policy as well. Saying you believe in the policy when you don't is tricky. Most of us are more transparent than we realize, and often our ambivalence betrays us and we end up sending mixed messages. But blaming the higher-ups for the decision risks their ire and your own credibility as a manager. Here is how Marlene Foster, vice president of financial services organization at Kaiser Permanente, has handled the challenge earlier in her career:

> I discuss a situation with my management and/or my leadership team about what should be done. If I strongly disagree with the

direction of a decision, I might even bring it up a few times. But once a decision is made about a course of action, regardless of whether I agree with it, I need to walk out of the room and execute on that decision to the best of my ability—without any grumbling on my part. If I display any negativity about the decision, if I complain about it or try to distance myself from it, I risk losing the trust of both employees and management.

The key seems to be to try to walk a middle path: find something you can believe in about the decision, even if it just comes down to faith in the decision makers or identification with the team, and emphasize that aspect. Share the rationale for the decision if you can. And hope your bosses are right in their judgment.

Skip Sack, whose military analogy I quoted earlier, warns against passing on blame:

> Some middle managers cop out by saying, "I don't agree with this, but George told me to do it, and that's what we're going to do." Passing the buck on the person who made the decision is cowardly. A better way is to say, "We discussed the various concerns, and a decision has been made. Our job is to implement it and make it work." Then you go out and put 100 percent into making it work.

If you can say the decision is reasonable and explain its justifications, do so. If you trust the decision makers, then say so. If you remain utterly convinced that the decision was wrong, then it is better to say less about it and focus on how to make the implementation work. You are walking a fine line between blowing credibility by lying about your feelings, which people will detect, and blowing credibility by complaining about top management.

WHAT THE SENIOR MANAGER CAN DO

It is not news that any good implementation requires the buy-in of the people who will be executing the decision, but it is striking how often senior managers assume that buy-in by middle managers can be faked or the process of securing it short-cut. People can usually tell when their middle management boss is toeing the party line as opposed to truly endorsing a decision, yet many senior executives say they consider any expression of less-than-full support to be a betrayal. That attitude is a problem and an invitation to less-than-full integrity. How can senior management create a better climate for buy-in—one that supports middle managers' integrity and allows them to capture the integrity dividend? How can senior managers ease the middle manager's dilemma? Broadly, they can discuss commitment, share the rationale, invite input, welcome dissent, and work at creating trusting relationships.

DISCUSS COMMITMENT

Whenever commitment may pose a dilemma to middle managers, senior managers should consider the commitment they are asking and discuss it with the middle managers. Consultant Dick Axelrod tells a story about one of his clients, whom I will call Mike, who was an executive tasked with repairing badly damaged morale at Boeing in 2000 after its first major engineers' strike. Mike wanted to hire Dick as a consultant, and he absolutely wanted his team's buy-in for this arrangement. According to Dick, Mike laid it out, making the issue explicit:

> He said to his group, "I don't care whether we use his methodology or not, but, this thing is too important—I can't afford to have people walking out of this meeting not being 100 percent behind me. So if we need to use some different methodologies that we can all support, then we will do that. This can't be one of those things where you are just halfheartedly for it. We've got to find a solution that we can all work with here. It might not be the ideal—there might be a more perfect solution out there—but if I don't have this group behind me, we are never going to get the solution implemented."

Such a direct request for commitment is rare. It gave permission to Mike's people to disagree or offer alternatives, but it also said that their buy-in was paramount—more important even than hiring Dick. In this way, Mike asked for, and got, his team's whole-hearted buy-in. His subsequent work with the engineering team at Boeing stands as one of the best examples of leadership and conflict management anywhere, as you will see in Chapter Ten.

SHARE THE RATIONALE

Promoting open discussion and debate around policy decisions is not just an exercise to make middle managers feel good. Done well, it also deepens their understanding of the decision and equips them to deal with the push-back they might face. Middle managers—or any other employees, for that matter—need to understand how decisions make sense in terms of the company's goals and values. Understanding that larger context helps them trust their leadership and helps them to see their leaders' integrity. R. J. Dourney described how he recently managed a dilemma for his subordinates:

> We did some layoffs recently, and I had senior executives who felt that we were compromising the organization by the action. Yet they had to go out and march to that. A big part of why we were successful is we spent a lot of time discussing why the layoff wasn't contrary to our position. I don't think the executives have to be convinced. But I do think they have to understand why we're doing what we're doing, and that it won't compromise their integrity. They don't necessarily have to agree.

Business decisions can be really complex. It is tempting for any senior executive to dismiss challenges from below as uninformed. "Having to explain oneself" has become a phrase of degradation, but it should not be.

I mentioned earlier that Mike, the Boeing executive, worked hard (and successfully) to improve labor relations after an extremely acrimonious engineer's strike. Boeing sells 75 to 80 percent of its planes outside the United States. Selling airplanes to other countries often requires a show of good-faith "partnership," meaning that the foreign government will help you get the contract if you agree to pay some of the money back into its economy by hiring its nationals as workers. The engineering union saw these actions as simple overseas outsourcing. Mike describes his position at the time:

> I was always the one who was being asked to explain, "Now why did you put a thousand engineers in Moscow. A thousand!" And SPEEA (the union) looked at that as "a thousand of our jobs that you took

away from us. We could have a thousand more people employed here." And I would explain to them *again,* and again and again, the strategy behind that. It got to the point where they didn't agree, but they understood. They thought there were other ways to get this accomplished, but we stayed steadfast to purpose.

Explanations are not merely an inconvenience or, worse, a humiliation. Providing clear explanations of why a policy makes sense and how it fits with agreed-on values is part of good leadership because it helps people get on board. And it helps them to believe in you and what you are doing.

Invite Input

A large body of evidence shows that people tend to embrace final decisions more fully, even when they still disagree, if they feel they have had a chance to raise concerns and get them genuinely considered. The technical term for this process is *voice,* as in, "Did you have a chance to voice concerns?" It is a good idea for you as a senior manager to ask the team what they think about a major decision before the decision is final. If the team is good (and I hope it is), it might even be able to teach you something. I am not saying to abdicate your responsibility, or to hold off on deciding until you can get everyone to agree. As a senior executive, you are going to have to make the final decision, and you won't always be able to get everyone to agree. The key challenge is to invite discussion and dissent while preserving your authority and stressing the need for buy-in. You do not want dissenters to see the process as false participation whose only aim is to generate buy-in. People need to feel genuinely heard and considered.

Larry Reinstein notes the importance of a team environment. Within it, he often begins the discussion with words like these:

> The environment is such that we're going to work on things together. I want everybody's input in this thing. Ultimately, you may or may not be happy with the decision that is made. We're hoping everybody is going to buy in. Invariably, some people are going to think some ways, some people are going to think other ways, but we come out of the room with one message, and that's what goes out to the world.

He asks for input and collaboration without implying the decision must be unanimous or even consensual. He openly discusses buy-in, acknowledging that it cannot be commanded. But he makes clear that external communication about the decision needs to be unified.

More needs to be said about the authority behind the final decision and how to prepare dissenters to support it. The key is to make sure people understand that you are ultimately making the decision, that you are carefully considering what they have to say, and that, fundamentally, middle managers must trust their senior managers. John Longstreet, executive vice president of people strategy for ClubCorp, discusses how to end debate:

> There have been times when I've allowed the debate to go on as long as I thought was acceptable and then I've had to say, "I hear what you're all saying and appreciate the fact that you all have an opinion, but in the end this isn't a democracy. I need to make the decision on it, and you're going to have to trust me on this one." When managers don't say that and just go off and make the decision, the team members say, "Why did he ask me for my opinions if he was going to do it [his way] anyway?" You're always going to get some of that, but if you're up front and honest about what the process is going to yield, you minimize it. Saying these words is probably key: "This is not a democracy, and I ultimately have to make the decision. It doesn't mean that your opinions haven't helped to shape my decision. It might just not be what you want to hear me say."

WELCOME DISSENT

Voicing disagreement with a boss—openly questioning his judgment, or simply probing for justifications—is scary because it is realistically risky. The manager's percentage play is often to keep his or her mouth shut. For this reason it is not enough for senior management merely to invite open discussion. Embrace the disagreement as a gift. Joe Lavin, president of Harborstone Hospitality, has successfully held several executive positions with Marriott International and Choice Hotels. He describes

how his manager at Marriott actively promoted debate and disagreement:

> My last boss was the head of North America for Marriott. We got
> in an argument once. I was trying to initiate a new program in
> Execustay [temporary housing] that he didn't like. He was asking
> all kinds of tough questions, and I basically said, "Well, goddamn
> it, you're not right about that. You've got to trust me on this. And
> we've got to do it, and I'll pull it through. And I want you to help
> me." It was in front of a lot of people, and he's a big guy, but we
> sat there and argued. It was civil. It wasn't nasty. He called me up
> afterward and said, "I'm glad you did that, because it shows you
> really believe in what you're trying to do. When you show pas-
> sion for something, I know you'll be able to get it done. Don't
> ever retreat from that kind of discussion with me." You know
> how much respect I have for that guy. That's the kind you want
> as a boss.

Joe acknowledges that a leader who can embrace disagreement is rare. It requires a degree of self-knowledge and humility
and an appreciation of the expertise around you. Joe strives to
model this approach. He prides himself on being open to debate
all comers about his policies. He asks his subordinates to "rein
him in" on occasion, and follows their advice enough so they
know the request is genuine. People seem to really like working
for him.

A second way to welcome dissent is to address the social pressures that stifle it by using a nonconfrontational technique to get
the discussion going. Allen Ibara is the CEO of Phiam Corporation. He swears by a process he calls the "3M sticky note exercise,"
which he has used for fifteen years:

> Everyone is equipped with a pen and two colors of [sticky notes].
> On one color I try to collect positives; on the other color I collect
> issues and opportunities. On the positive side, I usually start with
> something like, "What is the best thing about this new policy"?
> On the negative side, I usually start with something like, "What is
> the one thing that can derail this policy?" "What is the worst thing
> that can happen with this policy?" Or "What is the one objection
> we can expect?"

The rules are that only one brief thought or word can be written on each note, and you can use as many notes as time permits. Usually a few minutes per question are fine. The notes are collected after each question and are grouped by theme to get a quick glimpse at group thought. It is important to make sure the group understands the majority issues as well as the thoughts on the fringe. Quite often with some patience and the information visually in front of the group, some additional thoughts appear. If time permits, I often include a level or two of management and supervision in these meetings. I think inclusion is good, and I often get better and more feedback from the different ranks than I would with a single level. I am positive we all have a chance to walk away with a more common understanding.

I have always found the above useful, but the real gem is that it brings out inputs unfiltered. The senior manager's or the loudest or the quickest verbal response often influences the rest of the room. This exercise does a better job of getting equal inputs from all present. We all know what happens when executives announce, "Here's what I think! Any questions?" Yet we all wonder why there are so few questions.

One final observation. If you get no questions, the audience is likely to have not understood anything, is so anxious to leave that they do not care, or is afraid. I usually have at least one or two "worst-case items" on my own list. If someone does not ask or identify them in the exercise, I bring them up to the team as a "What if?" and see how they respond.

Allen's exercise gets the arguments out onto the table, gives managers a sense of voice, and expresses the leader's genuine interest in collaboration. It welcomes dissent without demanding that middle managers press too far beyond their comfort zones. As such, it might be one of the quickest tools available for stimulating this kind of discussion and resultant buy-in.

Note that the discussion of dissent must be framed in such a way that dissenting managers will not feel betrayed if the decision does not go their way. If you do not frame it this way, your middle managers may well question *your* integrity, though they aren't likely to tell you they do.

CREATE TRUSTING RELATIONSHIPS

When all is said and done, middle managers will sometimes see a policy issue differently than you do. You can encourage debate and dissent and share your rationales, but some still won't be convinced. That is when you have to draw on what might be called your bank account of trust. But prior to that, of course, you have to work to build up the account.

John Longstreet tells a story about how he learned about that bank account and how to use it. His boss had cancelled an incentive program for salespeople who met their goals, and John had argued strongly against doing so. John was never convinced until well after the fact, but at some point, his boss simply said, "You have to trust me on this." John says:

> You've got to have that relationship with your people where once in a while, even though they disagree with you, they'll get side by side with you and take it forward. But you first have to set up an environment where they're comfortable coming in your office and if need be yelling and screaming at you. If I hadn't disagreed with Steve on that point and felt comfortable enough arguing with him over it, I never would have pushed him to the point of saying that sometimes I'd just have to give him the benefit of the doubt. That was an important part of our relationship that he probably should have set up earlier on. But it doesn't matter. It got set up. And I said, "Okay, now I understand the ground rules. Sometimes I have to give you the benefit of the doubt. Okay, fine. I get it now."

Mark Lomanno, president of Smith Travel Research, tells another story about preserving trust while implementing a challenging policy. The company had been generating monthly reports for years and had just started to generate weekly reports. Mark made the decision that getting the weekly reports out precisely on schedule should be given priority over the monthly reports. He reasoned that a day's delay on the monthly was less of a problem than on the weekly. Some of the managers pushed back hard and went so far as to approach Mark's boss about the issue. The boss talked it over with Mark and ended up agreeing with him. There were some bad feelings all around, and line employees were hearing about it. Mark says,

> I brought the managers in and said, "Look. This is how we're doing it. I'm sorry you don't feel that way. I'm telling you that it's one of those things where you have to trust me. I'm in this job. If I don't do it well, Randy will get rid of me. Trust in that. Trust in something, but this is what we're doing."

Although Mark felt betrayed by their approaching his boss and angered that they had argued their case against his decision to subordinates, he took pains not to penalize the dissenters financially. Perhaps he felt that financial penalties would undermine the trust that he was asking for.

SUMMARY

The middle manager's dilemma is a bear that senior executives too easily forget. Most I spoke with said that middle managers are obliged to voice absolute endorsement of policy decisions in front of subordinates. It was only on deeper questioning that they allowed for more nuanced presentations that permit middle managers to avoid lying. And these senior executives were already well attuned to the importance of integrity and trust.

In most organizations, the incentives point toward middle managers' (1) accepting their boss's policy decisions without voicing dissent or substantive questioning and (2) expressing unqualified support of those decisions to subordinates. There are several problems with this pattern:

- It suppresses debate that can be both constructive and instructive.
- The subordinates are seldom fooled, and they learn to trust their managers less.
- The middle managers who are most distressed by this pattern are those who care the most about the company and about integrity.

Addressing the challenge is not easy, but there are constructive approaches available from both the middle manager and the senior manager perspectives.

Into Practice

Consider

- When have you experienced the middle manager's dilemma? What did you do?
- What will you do next time you experience it?
- How do you feel about subordinates disagreeing with you? What do you do? Is your response constructive?
- Do you share the justifications for your decisions? If not, why not?
- Do your subordinates trust you enough to move ahead despite any serious reservations?

Act

What to do about the middle manager's dilemma depends on where you sit.

- Middle Managers
  - Voice concerns and ask questions. Give your boss a chance to win you over.
  - Trust in your leaders. If you still cannot see how a decision makes sense, allow that they might have deeper insight.
  - Know your bright line. Know what ethical lines you will not cross, and know what those lines are worth to you.
  - Sell with authenticity. Find ways you can support the policy without deceit.
- Senior Managers
  - Discuss commitment. Discuss its importance, and ask for it, with awareness that it can only be given voluntarily.
  - Share your rationale. Explaining your thinking helps everyone understand the policy so they can implement better and also so they can see the integrity of the decision. Say how it fits with espoused values.
  - Invite input. You need not give away your authority, but asking your middle managers for input will make your decisions better while also improving buy-in.
  - Welcome dissent. Subordinates who will speak truth to power are a blessing that should be nurtured. Consider the sticky note exercise for stirring the pot while maintaining managers' sense of safety.
  - Create trusting relationships. Sometimes people will still not agree even after all the above have been done and done well. The fallback is "trust me," which works only if they already trust you.

CHAPTER EIGHT

CREATING A CULTURE OF ACCOUNTABILITY

Georges LeMener, former president and COO of Accor North America, says that if he were allowed to use only one management tool, his choice "without one second of hesitation" would be performance appraisal systems. That is a heck of an endorsement coming from a top executive of a company of 170,000 employees.

Of course, leadership is far too complex to rely on any single device, but performance appraisals can powerfully shape the conduct of executives, managers, and line employees toward the company's ideals when they are integrated with a system of supporting activities. They are also probably the best opportunity for employers to demonstrate their own behavioral integrity and commitment to professed values and put their money where their mouth is. Done right, it builds credibility.

Yet JoAnne Kruse, executive vice president of human resources for Travelport (formerly Cendant Travel Distribution Services), says, "Most people tell me they feel sick to their stomach when they have to do appraisals, even if the news is good." And she's right. Most managers procrastinate and face them, finally, with dread and loathing.

WHAT MAKES PERFORMANCE APPRAISALS SO CHALLENGING?

Let's get this straight: we are looking at what is arguably the most potent leadership tool for affirming one's own integrity, building trust and all that goes with it, and shaping the behaviors of those who report to you. Yet the prospect of using that tool makes many managers want to hide, or at least quiver.

Why? They fear the need to say awkward things and the conflict that saying them may provoke. They worry that criticism will undermine employees' motivation and that what they do or do not say may have bad legal consequences.

Managers often feel uncomfortable with the fuzziness of the performance measures on which the appraisal rests. And where they try to impose precise criteria, resulting scores sometimes align only poorly with the manager's personal sense of how well the employee has performed. In the end, there is often little alignment between what the evaluation says and the reward or punishment that follows. Managers also dislike appraising performance because the discussion is treated as an extraordinary event rather than as part of an ongoing employee development process. Behind these negative reactions lies the problem that managers and their companies too often have failed to lay the groundwork that effective performance evaluation requires.

Kevin Dunn is an executive coach and former president of McDonalds Great Lakes Division with responsibility for over twenty-six hundred restaurants. He sees lack of systems as the source of managerial phobias about performance appraisal:

> Without the tools of accountability, of a culture that has clearly defined roles and responsibilities and goals, you really don't have the platform to say, "Here's your performance." Creating that culture takes discipline, focus, and the systems within the organization to constantly be doing it. Laying that groundwork can seem boring and mundane. But performance appraisal is absolutely critical, and it can be fun. People need a culture or system that gives them a forum to discuss performance on a regular basis. Not just the bad things, but a combination of building on your strengths and opportunities.

Kevin argues for an integrated, aligned system of feedback, accountability, and coaching. Whether that system causes employees to flourish or leave, they will see that you and the company have the courage of your convictions.

Alignment is the essence of behavioral integrity. Since most companies and leaders have not invested in the underpinnings of a well-aligned system, their managers feel naked or unsupported in their assessment tasks. This chapter lays out ways to align and prepare for performance evaluations so that, rather than dread them, managers can use them to full effect in improving both company performance and behavioral integrity on the job. Behavioral integrity is fundamental for trust, and several studies have shown that performance appraisal practices strongly affect employee trust in management.[1]

This chapter examines three requirements for effective performance appraisals: balanced frankness, a clear definition of excellence, and a credible system of accountability.

STRAIGHT TALK IN PERFORMANCE APPRAISALS

Many managers feel they must motivate individuals by praising their good performances without criticizing poor performances. Scott Brodows, COO of SynXis corporation, says he too on occasion falls into this trap.

> Managers think of performance reviews as an opportunity to motivate employees, and they are very happy to point out the good, congratulate their employees, and thank them for their efforts. But when it comes to pointing out problems and getting into what could be a contentious conversation, managers avoid it. The frequent result is that reviews are not a fair reflection of performance. And then, when time comes for the manager to give the raise or other compensation that's tied to the review, that compensation is not perfectly aligned with the feedback.

Employees often feel betrayed when what they understood from the conversation doesn't square with subsequent behavior on the manager's part in terms of, for example, the size of a raise or bonus. The manager's feedback was more positive than the behavior, and the employee processes the difference as hypocrisy. But it is not about lying; it is about incomplete communication.

Rick Federico is CEO of P. F. Chang's Restaurants, a national chain with roughly $1 billion in annual revenue. He describes the dilemma facing him as he reviewed his team's recent performance:

> My business is more challenged today than it's ever been. And we have now gone through eighteen to twenty-four months when

our support team has not generated any annual incentive compensation based on the performance of the company. I've had to be very forthright in terms of "here are the issues, here are the challenges," but also be able to paint a picture of recovery: "This is how we get out of this." If you're not careful, people will miss the first part and focus on what they want to hear, which is that "everything's fine." You have to really make sure there is balance. You want people to understand the reality of the circumstance and their role in it. But you also have to be able to portray your confidence in the team's ability to work through this. If you can't do both, you're probably the wrong person for the role. If you do not deliver a vision for how the team will get out of this or any situation like this, they won't want to line up and bust their rear ends to help you get through it.

Rick argues further that your employees require the same level of honesty that you would give to the board because giving an unrealistic picture sets you up for disappointment and them for a sense of betrayal.

Regarding the conflict you are likely to encounter when you deliver the negative side of a review, R. J. Dourney, president of Hearthstone Associates and former vice president of operations for Au Bon Pain Restaurants, says:

> What's the worst you can do to me, as my direct report, if I gave you negative feedback? Hit me? You get upset. Maybe you disagree. But the likelihood is that you're going to digest it, and grow, and move on. Very rarely will people quit over that type of feedback if it's honest and given in good faith. But what if I don't give you that feedback, and I don't tell you what you need to work on? That's where a schism forms. In the absence of information, people start coming up with their own theories. All too often they're wrong.

When you do not give straight feedback, people will guess about what you are thinking. And whether they are right or wrong, you have passed up a chance to lead by letting employees know exactly how they are doing, in a way that gets positive results.

How can you tell the full truth in performance reviews and not damage employees' morale? There is a skill to giving honest and direct feedback in ways that others can hear and act on.

JoAnne Kruse notes how many managers are untrained in this process, feel inept at it, and so avoid it:

> A lot of managers will be too coy in their communications instead of just sitting the person down and saying, "Here's what's not working for me." Most will not do that unless they're angry or extremely disappointed. It has to be pretty serious for them to come out and say what's wrong. And often they don't do it right because it's too emotional.

Unfortunately, avoiding the difficult message results in late and often poor-quality feedback. Because it does not let the receiver address the problem early on, it can even amount to bad faith. When you don't tell people what you need, you set them up for failure.

A PECULIARLY AMERICAN PROBLEM?

American managers may be particularly susceptible to giving lopsidedly positive feedback. Georges LeMener grew up in France where Accor, the multinational company in which he worked, is based. He is sensitive to the need to be optimistic and motivational while also conveying the hard truths. In this regard, he sees a marked contrast between his U.S. managers and his French managers:

> In the U.S. I have found that the system is based on positive talk vis-à-vis the employee. It starts like that at school. In France, it's exactly the opposite. In school you are told what you do wrong, not what you do well. It is a system of negative talk.

> At Accor North America now we have found a balance, for example, when we do the appraisal review and we talk to the employee, between the positive and the negative. But I have found that it is very difficult for my American colleagues to give negative talk. I have had to teach them how to give negative feedback when necessary. Vice-versa, I have learned how to be more positive.

> When I started to work in the U.S., I was very frustrated with your appraisal review system, which in my opinion didn't respect the reality. Everybody was happy about it, but everybody was giving good grades. Six months later, somebody was fired, and of course my first reaction was, "Give me the appraisal review. I want to see

what was said by his boss." Of course, the appraisal review was absolutely positive from A to Z. For me, that's not being straight and up front. It's not how you build trust.

It is interesting that managers might err on different sides of that balance depending on the country where they grew up. Many managers have to wrestle with themselves in order to share the negative side. Some are not good at sharing the positive. But both positive and negative are absolutely necessary to direct and motivate people and preserve integrity perceptions.

STRESS ON THE EMPLOYEE SIDE

Straight talk is doubly hard because both parties are ambivalent about criticisms expressed in a performance review: the manager who soft-pedals the message and the employee who does not want to hear it. From both sides the odds are stacked against communication. Scott Brodows describes how his feedback is sometimes misunderstood:

> You want to give constructive criticism, but that ends up being too often just, "You're good at these three things." Then you either gloss over the challenges, or you don't mention them at all. Or you don't explain them in a way that the employee understands. That's something that's happened to me recently. I've had conversations with employees where I felt like I was being clear: "Here are some things to work on. If you do these things, you will be rewarded. If you don't, there will be consequences." Down the road, we have the follow-up conversation, and I say, "You didn't do these things." And the employee says, "What do you mean? I didn't understand that I had to do them. You never talked to me about that."
>
> Whether it's [poor] communication from my end or the employee hearing what he or she wants to hear, I'm not sure. Certainly employees walk away feeling frustrated. They feel like, "Heck, I didn't know what to do and I'm being punished. I don't understand why."

Here is one reason that employees may not hear well. Getting criticized in a performance appraisal is stressful for anyone who depends on a paycheck. The human body's reaction to stress, evolved over millennia, is to send blood to the large muscles to prepare for fight or flight. That means less blood to the brain.

No matter how smart your employees are, they drop a few points in IQ the moment they enter the room. You have to be extra clear in communicating criticism. You need to ask employees to rephrase it back to you to check their understanding. If they do not understand, they will tend to blame you, though not necessarily to your face.

LEGAL IMPLICATIONS

Behind the reluctance to criticize a person under review are also legal concerns. It is important that what goes into the record include factual support for conclusions and judgments, but managers often think twice about recording "facts" because of potential legal complications. From this concern, some avoid saying anything negative. JoAnne Kruse comments:

> We're such a litigious environment that what you get is very watered-down written feedback. On some level, it is just not worth the fight. [And therefore later on] you wind up with the most bizarre claims, charges, and accusations. Rather than take a chance and put something down that might be controversial, or that a person's going to get all bent out of shape about because it's in their record, [the manager] will write it down but soften it up. They'll use a euphemism for what's really the issue.

Many managers fear that any written negative feedback will open the door to legal hassles if the receiver takes umbrage. Such fears are sometimes warranted, and there are clearly times when discretion is the better part of valor. But such discretion can fracture the honesty that undergirds any effective leadership, and managers should be careful as they weigh discretion versus fuller truthfulness. JoAnne notes that often the verbal exchange carries far more truth than does the legally permissible written record. That difference is certainly not ideal, but it might be the best the circumstance permits.

FALSE PRECISION, FEAR, AND TRUST

Often managers try to evade conflict by imposing an artificial precision onto a review. Numbers can seem more objective than words, and using a formula may help forestall or dampen an employee's protest against a low appraisal. Objective measures can be wonderful, but employees know when the objectivity is a sham. I once worked for a hospital where the performance appraisal forms tallied scores from around sixty questions, many of which were irrelevant to our jobs or trivial and unobservable. There was enough "fluff" in the evaluation to allow any manager to tilt it hard toward his or her intuited assessment. I, and other employees, recognized the process as disguised subjectivity. The process did not engender trust.

Charles Bofferding is former executive director of SPEEA, a union that represents roughly twenty-four thousand aerospace professionals. A senior manager at Boeing (driven by the experience of a couple of discrimination lawsuits) asked him for a performance review algorithm that would turn objective input into a single numerical score for an employee's overall performance. Bofferding's reaction?

> False precision drives me nuts. I think we live in an imprecise world, and at some point somebody has to stand up and say it. I do think we need measurable goals, because I'm a big believer in feedback loops and accountability. Sometimes it's motivating to have goals and check them off as you are doing them. However, when you start getting into this false precision, you are off integrity.

> To me, [the success of performance appraisal] depends on what people are using them for. What's in their heart? What is the principle they are trying to honor? Performance appraisals should be focused on an individual having the best career possible, so that an employing organization can have the best outcome possible for its mission.

There is an unavoidable element of subjectivity in any performance review, as everyone involved knows. Honesty requires acknowledging the subjectivity and making it acceptable by creating a context of trust and goodwill. If it is clear that the manager has the subordinate's interests at heart—not exclusively, but as one clear consideration—then false objectivity becomes unnecessary. JoAnne Kruse makes a similar observation:

> I love when people say, "I want an objective performance appraisal." I'll say, "This is about you. It's not objective. It's completely personal

and is subjective. It's my opinion of your performance. I'll make it subjective. The thing is, my opinion really matters."

When I make an inference about someone, I need to acknowledge that it is an inference. If I state the same judgment as fact, I have let the truth slip away. The same goes for emotional reactions: letting them color my understanding without owning them also slides away from truth. Recipients of my feedback typically read my feelings and judgments for what they are. If I fail to own up to them, they know I am trying to make the feedback sound more objective than it is.

I said earlier that evaluators become anxious at the thought of evaluating performance, and without trust, evaluees are scared too. No wonder performance reviews are so often an exercise in false precision, tempered truth, and misunderstanding: they are a message conveyed from one terrified person to another. But the presence of trust makes a world of difference.

Trust is both a facilitator and consequence of effective performance reviews. Trust makes it safe to give and receive honest feedback. As Charles Bofferding suggests above, the perceived intent and values behind the review make all the difference in how it is received. When the context is trustful, there is more room for truth, and truth builds more trust. Doug Brooks, president and CEO of Brinker International, takes the point further:

> I think performance reviews are actually fun—if you get into them and you build trust with the person who reports to you. If they truly believe that your goal on the other side of the table is to help them get better, it's not a scary experience. It's something that they really should want. But the boss has to create an environment of trust. Then it doesn't hurt quite so much to hear from the boss what they have to work on.

A context of trust makes performance reviews less scary for both parties. Trust allows the powerful combination of honesty, concern, and accountability that works really well in performance appraisal. It builds performance and relationships. Rick Federico described his early career experiences with industry legend Norman Brinker, who founded Steak and Ale and was the CEO of Chili's Restaurants and Brinker International:

> Norman Brinker was the first person I worked with, and there isn't anybody more forthright and genuine and honest than Norman.

There's also nobody who will hold you more accountable than Norman. You end up knowing what your role is and how you're going to help participate in creating the solution to the challenge. But clear and honest and candid feedback is something [one] earns the right to deliver. And if it is delivered in a way that is constructive around the activity but not personalized, people genuinely appreciate it and the fact that you're taking the time to help guide them through whatever the issue must be.

DEFINING EXCELLENCE

To say that there is a large subjective component in any performance evaluation is not to exclude an objective component. Subjective judgments need to be matched by some form of clear and transparent measurement of excellence linked to accountability. Tell people what they will be evaluated on, and give them examples of what excellent behavior looks like; then evaluate against that standard. Then there are no surprises, no inferred hidden agendas, no caprice. Darryl Stickel, principal of Trust Unlimited and a former McKinsey consultant, says McKinsey excelled at defining and measuring employee performance against an ideal standard. By contrast,

> Most other companies do a very poor job of defining excellence—then they pay for it. If they were more transparent and consistent about applying metrics, so it didn't feel like things were done either on a whim or for political reasons, it would boost trust hugely.

It would boost trust because employees would see behavioral integrity. No gap between word and behavior: "Here are my standards, and here am I rewarding you based on those standards."

Two practices can help define excellence companywide: display values metrics publicly and positively, and then link behavioral values metrics to financial metrics.

THE POSITIVE, PUBLIC DISPLAY OF VALUES METRICS

Where standards and metrics are visible, consistency and trust can percolate through everyday life. Allen Ibara, CEO of Phiam Corporation, discusses how he measures company values and displays the metrics publicly. One of his company's key values is fun at work:

> Everything on the value list for a company has to be measurable somehow. I graph all these on a metrics board for the whole company and put them up someplace very public. But how do you measure fun? The metric is participation. If we have a company event, say a picnic, 25 percent [participation] would be below standard, 50 percent would be good, and 75 percent would be off the charts. The other thing we tend to do with all metrics is to make them positive. For example, HR is always keeping track of employee turnover—but turnover focuses on the folks who've left, just as quality defects focuses on the things you did wrong. I flip that around. For the public metrics, I measure perfection, like how many things we did right, instead of defects; or retention, like how many people stayed, instead of turnover. You still have to know who left and how many defects you made—but in terms of the public metric, it is "retention" for turnover and "perfection" for quality. It is very important to have positive metrics naked and visible, and to talk about it every day, every week.

Publicly posting metrics is a way to extend their use beyond the performance appraisal itself. For one thing, it lets them become a constant resource for coaching. Posting metrics also supports people's efforts to continually monitor and improve their own performance and that of their teams. Jim Kouzes offers that "the best kind of feedback is one where I can keep my own score. I see it on the dashboard—how fast I'm driving. I see it on the golf course—how many strokes it takes to sink a putt."

Above, Allen Ibara described using metrics of communal performance to publicly define excellence. He puts the metrics board on wheels and brings it to brief departmental meetings. Management can also combine metrics into well-integrated sets of individual performance goals. Stan Myers has implemented Management By Objectives at SEMI, the global association of the micro- and nanoscale industry. In his organization, every employee develops performance goals based on the performance goals of his or her higher-up, and all those goals are budgeted for and linked into a strategic plan. All employee, manager, and executive goals are viewable online by any employee, so anyone in the company can see the goals of anyone else. Actual performance to those goals is not posted. The program is still new, but Stan's sense is that it helps promote mutual accountability—and thus behavioral integrity.

Enterprise Rent-A-Car takes transparent accountability to a whole new level. All of its eighty operating groups rank all of their internal area managers, city managers, branch managers, and assistant managers on a full spread of performance metrics, and the groups post these rankings on the Web. According to Tom Chelew, vice president of fleet services, the groups then substantially reward top performers in just about every category. Tom warns, however, that the practice "creates a very competitive environment. You've got to be careful what you measure, because you will get results." Without Enterprise's well-established culture of service, employee development, and opportunity, this system of transparent accountability could generate toxic competition among employees, but the depth with which these values permeate Enterprise Rent-A-Car operations keeps the competition largely constructive.

The more public you make the metrics, putting them in front of people every day, the more critical become your choices of what to measure and how well you present them.

LINKING BEHAVIORAL VALUES METRICS TO FINANCIAL METRICS

Above, Allen Ibara advises phrasing metrics in positive language. Tom Chelew mentioned that the measures must focus on desired behaviors and results. Carl Camden, CEO of Kelly Services, the global temp agency, adds that quality metrics—those linked explicitly to your operating values—need to be integrated with financial numbers. Otherwise you risk that a substantial portion of your workforce will dismiss quality and focus on dollars, perhaps at the expense of the other elements. Carl says:

> At most companies, everybody has their P&L [profit and loss] metrics. Then they turn the page and say, "Now let's look at our quality metrics." That does not work in the long run. It works as long as the CEO or somebody is stopping by the office every quarter and saying, "Did we do our quality metrics?" like, "Did you take your medicine today?"

Carl thinks a better practice would incorporate the quality metrics in among the financial metrics rather than holding quality apart:

> It's all financial performance. Financial performance is linked intrinsically to the quality measures. So if cost of service was 14 percent of sales, then I want the 14 percent broken out in what was [attributable] to staffing assignments and being early or late to deliver and people having to be replaced, re-recruiting having to be done, and all that—so it's not sitting on another page. It's a line item in the P&L report. The cost of poor quality is measured, and it's right there with the cost of advertising, with the cost of rent, with the cost of electricity.

In other words, it is not enough to measure and report the right stuff. You need to present it in a way that conveys its importance and tempers people's natural tendency to focus solely on the financials. The items on the scorecard must be truly balanced and integrated in order for the card to reliably affirm company values and so enhance behavioral integrity.

CREDIBILITY, ACCOUNTABILITY, AND ENFORCEMENT OF STANDARDS

Credibility requires standing behind your standards—setting them and then enforcing them by holding people accountable. In turn, in order to convey integrity, a manager must couple accountability with support. Accountability without support looks like (and is) a setup. John Longstreet, senior vice president of people strategy for ClubCorp, relates a conversation he had with a subordinate executive in which he spelled out both support and accountability:

> [The subordinate] had been in the position eighteen months, and the previous year was definitely a rebuilding year. He had replaced most of his executive team, because they needed to be replaced. I sat down with him, and I said, "Look, Joe, you've done a tremendous job this year in retooling the place for success. That said, this year your property is going to be the single biggest miss in the entire company: you missed GOP [gross operating profits], you missed plans. You've done a good job in the year getting set for

success, [but] patience is short now. If we can't hit our plan over the next six months, then I'm not so sure that we're still going to be able to continue the relationship. I just want you to know that now. And I want you to know that I'm here to do everything I can do to help you do that. I'll be here anytime you ask me to help. I'll help run interference with the home office. I'll be your biggest advocate. But we have to be on plan six months from now."

John acknowledged Joe's challenges, recognized how far he had come, offered himself as a resource, but also conveyed a message of absolute accountability: "We hit plan in six months, or we are done." Do you think Joe thought less of John after the conversation? John did not think so. He says, "I think he appreciated it." I would guess John is right. He was acting with unmistakable integrity: transparency, honesty, support, and clear accountability.

ATTACHING REWARDS

Standards must be explicit, clear, and also enforced positively and negatively. One outcome of a positive performance appraisal needs to be reward, generally in the form of salary, bonus, promotion, or some combination of these. For good performers, reward is the action that has to align with the words. Too often it does not.

For example, the Boeing executive we are calling Mike presided over the rebuilding that happened after the engineers' strike in 2000. He decided that low morale was impeding his units' performance, so he insisted that managers develop plans for improving morale, and he integrated measures of worker morale into managers' performance appraisal. He wanted to move from exhortation to concrete consequence. He says, "You can go out and do motherhood and apple pie all you want, but if you don't make it real somehow, nothing's going to happen, right?" The process worked remarkably well: morale went up, and his organization underran its annual budget by around $200 million a year. The next year the budget was reduced, and the organization underran it again. Mike attributed the savings to his work on morale and convinced Boeing leadership to implement the program throughout the company.

Mike had one recalcitrant manager who fought the program tooth and nail. This manager had his own, somewhat brutal style that worked for him, and he didn't truck with having his performance review based on his subordinates' battered feelings. The manager used various means to avoid any financial penalty the first year of the program. Mike comments that he himself lost some credibility during that year because he did not rein in this manager who was obviously rejecting the new focus on morale. In the second year, the manager was penalized a third of his bonus due to poor morale in his group. Mike says the effect was quick and strong:

> I learned a long time ago that you can't manage what people believe, but you can try to manage their behavior. So I was trying to manage his behavior in the workplace. You know what? He suddenly got people on his leadership team to start taking this seriously. He realized that the next year he was going to get the same result if he didn't do something. He didn't believe in what we were doing. He didn't really value people. But he did value his money enough to try to get his team to improve morale in his organization. Finally, it started to come up.

I wish I could say that the manager changed his beliefs about management; he didn't, and ultimately he left the company. But if Mike had not attached clear consequences to the manager's failure to embrace his key business values—at least in practice, if not in his heart—he would not have changed the manager's behavior even a little. And he would have lost ever more credibility with his other followers.

KEEPING THE FEEDBACK FLOWING

Whether your intent is to shift cultural values or to better engage the members of your team, make feedback and coaching frequent. People need to know what you think of their work as they do it. Speed and frequency allow followers to adjust and improve their behavior, and it also lets them see you as a constant, consistent, principled force.

In Chapter Four, I described how Michael Kay used frequent celebrations of success to help drive the turnaround at Sky Chefs. He created a constant stream of "hats and T-shirts and pizza and tickets to the ball game" in response to small, targeted improvements. It is the day-in, day-out recognition that shifts fundamental performance. It shifts how people talk with each other and how they respond to the ongoing challenges. If a challenge comes up almost every day, feedback that comes only a few times a year gets drowned out in the hubbub.

Constant feedback is better at bringing about wholesale change, and it is also better at developing people. Perhaps more so now than ever before, developing people is key to engaging their hearts because they know you are helping them to grow. Consider the recent experience of Stuart Waugh, managing director of TD Capital Private Equity Investors, who oversees a thirty-person team that manages over $2 billion in assets:

> It doesn't take much to get somebody to go that extra mile. Part of that comes from starting with a shared trust and shared values. But it also comes from even the minor hints of appreciation or sense of acknowledgment of contribution. I don't know whether it's a generational thing or not, but I find the younger people we have working with us are very anxious for a quick feedback loop and a sense of how they're doing. It's not insecurity but wanting to do well, to succeed, and to know on a much shorter cycle time than I was accustomed to when I started. They want to hear back about what's working, what's not working, and then get an opportunity to give feedback themselves.

Ambitious employees crave feedback. In our digital age, the younger ones want it fast. More seasoned employees have learned to make do with the tidbits most managers dole out on rare occasions. But giving feedback often creates energy and supports a climate of engagement and continuous learning.

Rick Federico describes how performance appraisal and constant coaching should be related:

> If you believe that once a year sitting down and doing a performance appraisal is demonstrating the power of feedback, you're mistaken. A performance assessment, the formalized "let's sit down and write it up and talk through it," had better be an accumulation of all the other feedback opportunities or coaching moments that you've had along the way. If there are surprises in a performance evaluation, you probably haven't done a particularly good job of mentoring along the way.

Several other executives I interviewed also noted that performance appraisal must be integrated with constant coaching: "no

surprises." If they don't seem to integrate, you are probably discussing issues differently in your day-to-day interactions than you
do in formal appraisal meetings. Or you may simply be failing to
acknowledge performance in your routine interactions. Either
way, your inconsistency weakens your credibility.

Michael Kay suggests that performance appraisal and coaching should combine objective performance feedback with behavioral feedback on the so-called soft skills of management:

> I don't want to minimize the value of having a structured perfor-
> mance appraisal. But my experience is that the best kind of rein-
> forcing feedback is the kind that happens randomly and regularly.
> If you have clear, measurable performance objectives, you don't
> need to go have a meeting with your boss to know how you're
> doing. Why you do need to meet with your boss is to know how
> you're *behaving*.

Michael distinguishes clearly between measurable, objective performance information and behavioral feedback. Most of
the objective performance information is easy to collect. The
behavioral information—about leadership and teamwork and
communication—is harder to collect. But, he argues, behavioral
feedback is critical for development, and it needs to arrive more
often than once a year so that managers can act on it.

Giving more frequent feedback seems to make sense in principle, but executives are busy. Where can they find the time?
Michael proposes short conversations:

> I was talking to a regional vice president, who had monthly meet-
> ings with the twelve or thirteen kitchen general managers who work
> for him. I said, "Charlie, you meet with your guys every month,
> right? You spend two days around the same table, managing perfor-
> mance, right? There's something you could tell every one of those
> guys at the end of the two days about how they behaved. How they
> acted. You know, two minutes' worth. [For example, you can say,]
> 'You know, Dave, I didn't think you were terribly productive this
> time around. Here's what I saw going on. Why don't you go think
> about that?'
>
> I'm not even talking about a note. I'm talking about saying, "Look,
> we're going to take the last hour before we break up and all go

home. I'm going to spend three or four minutes with each of you
individually. I'm going to give you some feedback on how I thought
you did this month. Not how your performance was this month;
not what your results were. That's what we just spent that last two
days doing. I'm going to give you some feedback on how you
behaved."

Michael conducted brief sessions of individual, behavioral
feedback after his own team's monthly day-and-a-half leadership
meetings. He did not always meet with someone if he had nothing
to say, but he gave lots of feedback related to the behaviors he had
described as performance objectives at the beginning of the year.
He says, "We were every bit as clear about the leadership behaviors as we were about the numbers." That practice is part of how
Michael achieved his extraordinary results with Sky Chefs.

If you as a leader really want to shape the conduct of your
team and maximize behavioral integrity and credibility as you do
it, you'll need to give frequent feedback and coaching. JoAnne
Kruse says the format isn't important:

> The system itself is irrelevant. I always tell people, "Put it on a sticky
> note, I don't care." What you write down is not the thing that's
> most important. At the end of the day, what's most important is
> that you're consistently holding them accountable and recognizing
> them for the things they do well—and holding them accountable
> for the things that they don't do well. And you don't just tell *them.*
> You tell everybody in the group. When you do that, then the form
> that you use and how many boxes you check—that's [just] a nice
> thing that makes you feel good for the ten minutes you're in that
> room. Then when you walk out, it's all about the other four thou-
> sand interactions I've had with you in the other 364 days.

But beyond giving feedback there's another step: follow-up.

FOLLOW-UP

Follow-up makes feedback stick. It conveys that you really mean
your words, and that helps people to inch their skills forward.

Developing people has become a key performance factor in
most industries. You build stronger, more consistent management
talent for the future, and you engage your people more fully today.

The problem is, this notion has become a bromide—something leaders often espouse, then fail to invest the required time and resources for follow through. As John Longstreet notes, sporadic developmental attention without follow-up is a recipe for cynicism: "You start the flywheel when you tell that individual that this is important, but then you fail to follow up. The net result is [a sense of] betrayal: 'My boss says that he cares about me, but he really doesn't. He just wants me to go in and do a job.'"

The same pattern shows up on a larger scale. R. J. Dourney tells of a time he broadcast a focus on employee development.

> My partner and I own a number of restaurants in Boston. They're called Cosi. They're fast casual. When we bought these restaurants, one of the first things we did was spend time with our managers. We said, "We are going to build three more units over the next six to twelve months. We want to be able to promote from within. We need to make sure everybody knows that. We need to start talking about their development."
>
> So one of the first things we did was an internal career day. We invited any employee who wanted to talk about their opportunities to grow to come and meet with us. Virtually 90 percent of our employees showed up at this meeting, raised their hands, and said, "Hey, whether it means I can be a manager, or a general manager, or something, I want to grow."
>
> Great! Now the onus was on the restaurant managers to follow up with these folks, doing a performance review on them and telling them how they did. Well, as no surprise, our better general manager [at our Federal Street location] sat down with his people, revved their engines, and told them what they needed to work on; told them what opportunities were there for them; put them on a development game plan.
>
> The next time we met with them, our Federal Street employees were bouncing off the walls, they were so excited. Not all of them had been told that they were going to be general managers tomorrow. Rather they had been given very constructive feedback. But they felt that their boss cared about them, was being honest with them, and was helping them grow.
>
> Conversely, we had a weaker general manager who didn't do that, didn't have those honest conversations. I had started the flywheel,

[but] by the time [his employees] came to the next meeting, instead of being motivated and excited that we were moving ahead, they were suspicious. They no longer bought in. They looked at it and said, "Yes, you're telling me that this stuff is important."

The manager who failed to follow up generated cynicism and lower morale in his workforce and poor financial performance in his restaurant. In fact, morale and performance would likely have been better if there had been no internal career day to get hopes up. When follow-up doesn't follow promises, employees become cynical. You lose their hearts and engagement for whatever initiatives you plan.

RANKING, ENFORCING, AND WEEDING

Of course, explicit standards must also be enforced. Not all people live up to reasonable expectations, and rewards don't always work. At some point, you may need to weed out those who won't maintain performance in a supportive, accountable work environment. Rich Panico describes his position about enforcing standards—in this case, his company's stringent standards of honesty. In doing so, he reminds us also of the manager's responsibility:

> I made a presentation to a graduate class last year and said that we fire people for lying. A student said, "That's not very Christian of you." I thought that was an interesting comment. My response was, "We're very up front about our absolute requirements. The individual chooses to accept those rules when he or she joins us. The violation is a conscious choice. If, however, I give individuals a reason to compromise our values because in practice I hold other requirements more important, then I am to be held accountable for confusing the organization and creating a potentially volatile ethical environment. People need to clearly understand what is acceptable and unacceptable conduct." I'm very careful to make sure I don't create conflicting values.

If you fail to enforce the standards you set, you do not really mean what you say and you profoundly undermine your message of what is acceptable and what is not. Part of what is striking about Rich's position is his taking personal responsibility for the climate he creates. He recognizes the possibility that he might unwittingly create incentives for compromise in the form of conflicting values and remains vigilant to the danger.

Although Enterprise Rent-A-Car has used forced performance rankings to positive effect, there are pitfalls in this approach. Jack Welch, former CEO of General Electric, in his best-selling business books promoted the idea that the bottom 10 percent of any employee group should be forced out and rewards lavished on the top 20 percent.[2] It is true that such a system rattles the cages of complacency that can so easily settle on bureaucracies, and that is a good thing. The problem, and perhaps it is one of implementation rather than concept, is that the competition built into the system can undermine collaboration and trust among the people ranked. Allen Ibara of Phiam Corporation shares this concern:

> Some very high-level organizations in [Silicon Valley] here pride themselves on getting rid of the bottom 5, 10, 15 percent every year. Certainly weeding is necessary, but in my mind, to have it as a goal doesn't speak very well. These are the same organizations that have teamwork as a number one value. [The problem is that] when you sense you're nearing that lower end of the spectrum—the bottom half—it is awfully tempting to roll a grenade into somebody else's project—certainly to not go out of your way to help.

People will do ruthless stuff if they think their livelihood is in jeopardy. If teamwork is professed as a value, then team-oriented rankings and rewards might be more appropriate than rankings of individuals. But that in itself does not do away with a need for weeding. Many team-oriented company cultures become tolerant of marginal contributors, and weak or unengaged players can drain resources and undermine the passion of the rest of a team. Managers need to be able to recognize and address poor and especially chronic performance. Standards should be high, because people are often capable of doing more and better when they are pushed. Just as a great athletic coach demands more of people than they may have given previously, a great leader must demand more.

Maybe Welch's formula of "10 percent out" ratchets up performance standards through a large organization. But the fact that it is a formula sometimes sends a message that is at odds with its intent, especially where collaboration is a key value. A better approach, where it can be managed, is clear, consistent, transparent assessment of performance, coupled with willingness to acknowledge and address extremes of bad or good.

Bruce Hodes is a consultant who often supports companies in their efforts to better adapt to growth. To build company integrity, he addresses their enforcement of standards. In doing so, he has given considerable thought to rankings and enforcement:

> I'll sit with a leadership group, and we'll read their direct reports. We'll classify all the employees in one of three ways. An A player is somebody who is great at the job and promotable: they could take on another department or become a manager and leader. A B employee is somebody who is also great—they aren't going anywhere, but they are a really solid citizen. A C player is somebody who is marginal and, if they told you they were leaving, you would be thrilled because you think you could do better. We work with cultures so they get rid of the C players. If you're a culture in which you put up with D's and F's, there is no hope for you. But lots of cultures will have C players, who are really deadweights.
>
> When you know somebody is a C player, you have two months to turn it around. And you have three options: you can put them in a new role where they can be a B, you can coach them to be a B in their role, or you can move them out. And part of all of it is coming to them and saying, "Here's the deal." A lot of times we find that employees who are C players have no idea.

Bruce argues that feedback is essential, especially in change situations. Done right, it empowers people to improve and shows them how to do so. Enforcing clear and explicit standards, assuming you have equipped your people to meet them, is an act of integrity. Too often managers are lured away from that simple alignment by inertia, compassion, or other considerations.

MODELING AND TRICKLE-DOWN

To create a culture of accountability and integrity, you must also model the conduct that you want to see. In their efforts to duplicate your success, your direct reports will tend to imitate your management style, including the level of integrity they see in you. I have demonstrated this pattern of trickle-down in a survey of about fifteen hundred hotel employees and managers. To change the integrity level of those around you, you must change your own first. This means, among other things, holding yourself accountable. According to Darryl Stickel,

> A really powerful thing for a CEO to say is: "Here's how I'm evaluated. Here are my commitments to you. I'm actually going to write them down and I'm going to hold myself accountable to you." Or, "I'm going to have the board hold me accountable." Start demonstrating that behavior at a very high level and have that trickle down. Not just me holding you accountable, which is also a good thing, but also me being held accountable for my actions.

Allen Ibara shares his personal performance metrics with his team and finds the practice helps to motivate them. It not only allows employees to see how their work fits into a larger picture; it also puts the senior executive on similar, accountable footing. By demonstrating the behavior you espouse, you preserve your credibility, and you shape the company around you. Actually your behavior will shape the company around you anyway, so it is a good idea to behave deliberately toward this end. Pete Kline of Seneca Advisors, former president and CEO of Bristol Hotels, describes the need for CEOs to "live by the rules":

> I've seen it in small businesses as well as large. If you have a small business where the owner of the company is stealing from the IRS, which happens a lot, how can that person be shocked by employees who steal from him? The culture is created from the very top. And if everybody is watching somebody show low integrity at the very top, it doesn't breed an environment where people feel integrity is all that important.

That idea of modeling does not just apply to ethical values like, "Don't steal." It applies as much to less weighty values like, "Be on time." Allen Ibara describes the integrity behind small actions: "If you're serious about timeliness, time management, and great service, and you say you're going to start something on time, it's a personal integrity issue. It's a promise." As an everyday example of his company's values, Allen makes a point of starting and ending his meetings on time because "you're asking customer service to be on time, you're asking your product people to be on time.

If you can't start a meeting on time and end it on time I think you have a gap." Allen offers a tip for ending meetings punctually: plan to end them fifteen minutes early. The way you handle your daily tasks and your direct reports will trickle down through your organization. Creating a culture of integrity has to start with a long look in the mirror.

THE PAYOFF

Well-developed systems of evaluation, coaching, and accountability support an environment of trust, engagement, and continual learning. They strengthen your leadership pool. Importantly, they also reinforce consistency of leadership style across the ranks of middle managers. Especially in times of growth or upheaval, consistency of style across managers gives subordinates a reason to trust the behavioral integrity of the company.

Frank Guidara, CEO of Uno Chicago Grill, sees such systems as especially important for consistency when you are promoting people within the hierarchy. He says that higher management takes its time choosing who will fill the top open spot, but the choices often become more hurried as the backfilling trickles down the organization. The result is a lot of new managers, all at the same time, who do not know their jobs very well. This, says Frank, is a time for intensive coaching, goal setting, and feedback. A 360-degree survey might be in order to help new managers see how they present themselves. The consequence of systematic coaching is greater competence and greater trust up and down the line. In Frank's words, "It supports consistent leadership for the hourly employee who is in fact interacting with the guest, so that they're not [taking orders from] one leader who's going to the right and one who's going to the left." Where employees know what to expect from leaders, they trust them more.

Systems of ongoing feedback and accountability also help perpetuate a learning environment in which collaborative information flows freely in all directions. Rick Federico describes the workplace he aims to build:

> I want an environment where if something is wrong in the organization or if something is out of whack, people feel comfortable

walking through my door and sitting down and saying, "I've got a problem with this," or "I've messed this up." I don't want them to feel like that's a career-threatening exercise. The door can be open, but if the mind isn't, people aren't going to be willing to come and share their wins and their losses. We work hard as an organization to make sure that people aren't cosmetically trying to mask their challenges. We would prefer to deal with them up front. As a result, we get better thought and better action plans from our people. And candidly, the collective resource is better than the individual.

When you lead with consistency and openness, built on a genuine caring for the growth of your people, you support a relationship of mutual honesty and sincere efforts to contribute. Your subordinates will tend to emulate the level of integrity you display, and that shapes how they will approach their subordinates and how they will approach you. The kind of relationship Rick describes does a lot to support the performance of his company and is part of what makes him so highly respected in his industry.

SUMMARY

Performance appraisals, a key leadership tool, are so deeply loathed and feared by so many executives that they are often done poorly. Nevertheless, when they are combined with honest talk, defined excellence, and accountable rewards, they are powerful demonstrations of behavioral integrity.

Managers at all levels face many barriers to straight and direct feedback. They worry about creating conflict and demotivating people. They sometimes give in to false precision or wait too long so that their emotions overtake their focused desire to help a subordinate develop. Subordinates often resist hearing and understanding the feedback, and legal concerns sometimes affect what can be put on paper. Still, you must get your message through, or you put your own credibility at risk when appraisals and rewards or punishments fail to align.

Excellence should be publicly defined and measures of it publicly displayed. Behavioral values metrics should be linked to financial metrics. Accountability needs to be known and practiced, and whatever standards the company sets must also be enforced.

Even the best feedback and coaching will be undermined if the top executives fail to demonstrate the values they are trying to instill, but behavioral integrity on the part of top management begets behavioral integrity further down. Demonstrate the values you are talking about, including integrity. Look for ways to enact those values even in small ways, like starting and ending meetings exactly on time, so that they become part of the company's fabric of everyday life.

Into Practice

Consider

- Do all your direct reports know exactly where they stand with you?
- To what extent do you openly acknowledge and discuss your subjective performance judgments of your reports? To what extent are your views open to new information?
- How clearly can your direct reports see what excellence should look like? How might you measure excellent performance on the values you promote?
- How can you make group performance public?
- How well do consequences line up with performance in your organization? How can you align them better?
- How often do you give performance feedback? How well do you follow up on development plans and goals? How can you make these conversations more frequent?
- How consistently do you model the behavior you desire in others? Where do you see opportunities to do it better?

Act

- Address communication barriers to make sure that your full and honest feedback is understood. Give both behavior and performance feedback. Take the time to have a two-way conversation, and ask to hear the other person's understanding.
- Do not try to disguise your subjective judgments as objective facts. They are valid and important. Own them.
- Define and collect transparent, objective measures of group and individual performance in alignment with espoused values. Let people know what they

are. Consider making the measured results widely available. Discuss and celebrate them often.

- Attach positive and negative consequences to behaviors and performance.
- Trimming poor performers is necessary to maintain credibility, but avoid formulas.
- Do all the above constantly. Frequent feedback and celebration has far more impact than the occasional type.
- Follow up to preserve accountability and credibility.
- Model the behavior you want to see throughout the organization.

CHAPTER NINE

MANAGEMENT FASHIONS AND THE FLAVOR-OF-THE-MONTH CLUB

When John Longstreet, executive vice president of human resources for ClubCorp, first met with regional managers and club managers, they asked why he joined ClubCorp. When he responded that he came partly because of the rich company culture, they laughed. Perplexed, he asked, "I'm sorry. Why are you laughing?" One of them replied with a grin, "ClubCorp doesn't have a culture." Longstreet disagreed and here explains what he saw as the ClubCorp culture that had emerged from a long and storied history:

> In fact, we were both right. Because over the years the company had gotten so into the most recent concept of leadership or the most recent book on ethics and integrity or whatever it was, that they just kept piling on new, good ideas on top of the old culture message. So we made up a little wallet card of our essential beliefs at ClubCorp. Except there were about twenty essentials, the type was tiny, and the real message got lost.

ClubCorp management had been continually experimenting with new management ideas, which seems like a good thing. However, in the process, they had lost sight of their core values. They had buried them under a pile of new terms and new ideas and had lost the ability to convey them powerfully to new employees and managers. They could no longer describe, in simple terms, the ClubCorp priorities. Furthermore, they had diminished their managers' ability to respond to any genuinely new directives. New initiatives were understood as the latest in a long string of overhyped ideas and were treated accordingly.

The inevitable question is, "Why isn't the integrity dividend simply another one of these management fashions?" The short answer is that any idea, treated like a transient fashion, can be destructive. Treating ideas like transient fashions creates contradictions, which undermine behavioral integrity. Casually implementing a focus on integrity and then supplanting that focus with another idea shortly after would likely create destructive cynicism precisely because integrity is central to the problem of management fashions, as this chapter explains. Integrity is an abiding principle that warrants abiding attention.

As we've all seen, whether they follow the latest management guru or the latest set of strategic priorities, some leaders blow their credibility by changing things too often. Often their intent is to build a climate of exploration and innovation, of flexibility and learning, but the result is employees and managers gripped by cold and rigid cynicism.

THE COSTS OF REPEATED INNOVATION

This comment comes from John Hillins, former vice president at Honeywell and former senior director of compensation and benefits at Amgen:

> "Here comes another one from corporate." How many times did I hear that? "Here comes another frickin' program from corporate. Okay. I'll play." The Fad-of-the-Month Club, they used to call it. People look for signals on these things: "Is this, in essence, a major organizational change? Or is this the flavor of the month?" In any of the successful change models, one of the things you have to do is convince people that it's a permanent change, which is tough to do.

Credibility matters. Once employees understand an organizational change effort as being the favor-of-the-month, that effort is doomed to failure because everyone "knows" that there will be little, if any, follow-up. And change experts appreciate that follow-up may be more critical to change than rollouts. What kind of person creates a flavor-of-the-month club for management ideas? Unfortunately, the desire to make a difference with limited time for learning makes most of us vulnerable to this error. JoAnne Kruse, executive vice president for human resources at Travelport (formerly Cendant Travel Division), describes the mistake and the common response:

> You get managers who read a book and they decide that that's how we should do things. The problem is, they generally don't understand it at the level of depth they need to be a true disciple. Then they read another book the next quarter and want to change everything. Normal people don't reference gurus. When you meet someone who does, it's generally an indicator of where they're coming from, and I find most employees pretty quickly discount these people. When the person changes gears quickly like that, the employees and their own managers—everybody—just understands that they read a book, and they've got this new idea—they sort of laugh about it—then they just don't do anything that the person brings up unless forced. The executive thinks that they're enlightened and they're enlightening others, and in fact, they're not affecting anything at all. The employees just become very cynical.

The more things change, the more they stay the same. By the third or fourth new initiative within a few years, the employees and managers you hope to influence have learned to tune out the new stuff in the interest of getting their jobs done. This problem is all about behavioral integrity: the fit or misfit they see between your words and your actions. Each of these new management approaches or strategic imperatives contains stated and implied values and promises. When, a few months later, the wind shifts again, people see those values as having been violated, the promises as broken. And as the list of partially implemented approaches in a given workplace grows, so grows the collection of jargon, espoused values, and policies. As these lists grow longer, there is more and more opportunity for you and other managers to behave inconsistently with them because there are simply more principles for you to violate. Furthermore, the elements in the collection stop fitting together; they stop reinforcing each other and start to contradict each other. Gaps between word and action become almost inevitable.

The intentions were good; there was no malice here, and each idea or philosophy may have been perfectly sound. They just don't necessarily fit together, and they definitely do not fit together without somebody working to make them fit. At issue is the employee perception that emerges from constant change. Behavioral integrity is the perceived pattern of alignment between your words and actions. It is in the eye of the beholder. Employees start to see a pattern of gaps. They figure it is because of who you and the other managers in this place *are*. They come to think of you as having lower behavioral integrity, and they start to figure that your words do not mean quite as much as they used to.

There is an irony here: this problem is driven partly by scholars and authors like me, by readers like you, and by books or articles like the one you are reading. There are literally thousands of books on leadership instantly available on the Web, and more coming out daily. Seminar flyers fill our mailboxes. New M.B.A. graduates come to the workplace and seek to justify their considerable investment by trotting out the latest and greatest management practice. Frequent changes of direction create real problems in the workplace. The irony is that our efforts to improve leadership have become an instrument of its destruction.

Thinking hard about the process of leading and managing is a good thing. Frequently changing the way you talk about it is not. Kerry Miller, executive search consultant and former vice president of People Development at Bertucci's Restaurants, describes the pattern:

> A lot of leaders today rely on analysts and what the guys across the street are doing to make their decisions. And they've got what I call "focus ADD" [attention deficit disorder]. They see somebody across the street doing something successfully. They don't stay true to their core business, and they start doing things like the guys across the street or what the analysts tell them they should be doing. Genuine leaders are those folks who really understand their business and don't flip in the wind and make decisions based on pressures from across the street or from your analyst.

Kerry argues that where what he calls focus ADD takes root, it tends to apply across areas, from management approaches to strategic initiatives: "If the company's disease is focus ADD, it pretty much runs through everything they do. If their philosophies are jumping around, it means they've probably got pretty unsound product rollouts." Furthermore, he submits, employees will be unclear about the key values and priorities of the company: "You take people's focus off the business when you've got them jumping around like that."

There is value in experimenting, exploring, and learning as individuals and as a company. You certainly have to adapt to changing circumstances. It is usually a good thing to look at old problems with new lenses. And you have to update your tools now and then because sometimes a better mousetrap really does become available. The question is how to do it while minimizing the downside costs.

The market of management ideas has become so vigorous that it undermines good management practice. To adopt and promote any management approach and then forget about it a few months later creates fundamental credibility problems and reduces your capacity to lead your employees. That includes the approach I'm advocating in this book—especially so because the relevance and power of the behavioral integrity framework can rapidly raise hopes among employees. I hope this chapter will accomplish two things: help your organization lessen any tendency toward flavor of the month and encourage you to treat the ideas of behavioral integrity as something more permanent and organic.

Combating Flavor of the Month

The executives I interviewed offered a few approaches that seem promising:

- Slow down. Think it through, talk it through, and be selective in the changes you implement.
- Choose carefully what few programs to implement by looking for the themes that carry across management gurus or philosophies.
- Balance change with continuity. Talk about both.
- When you choose to implement a change, *commit* and follow through.
- If the change or effort is temporary or tentative, let people know that, and tell them why.
- Allow humor into the change process.

SLOW DOWN

Larry Reinstein, president and CEO of Fresh City, has an upbeat but selective attitude: "There are so many wonderful ideas out there. The thing we all have to be careful about is to go slow on those wonderful ideas. Pick one." Larry goes on to compare the situation to going to a conference that offers many different workshops:

> You have fifty things that are great education. Now pick one
> that you can do something with. If you stick with that one thing,
> and you work it really really hard, and keep staying on top of that,
> chances are you'll make a lot of progress. If you keep picking a
> different thing, chances are you won't get too far with anything.

It is true that most business environments are picking up pace. And there is a lot of talk about speed—being nimble, adaptable, learning fast. But it is also true that you lose velocity when you change direction. Ask any race car driver. You won't move very fast if you take every turn and travel down every side road.

Quick, responsive action makes sense with certain product introductions, where being first to market carries a big premium. But it does not work when it comes to managing masses of people. Think the shift through before you bring it to your team. And talk it over with your team before you decide to roll it out to the company. Your team members are good at what they do, and they will look at the challenge and the solution you propose from different angles. When the engineers plan a moon rocket trip, they map out every turn before lift-off. That way, they can make the best use of their momentum and waste as little fuel as possible. There is a cost to changing course after you launch, so the more glitches you can anticipate and prevent, the better. John Lazar, an executive coach, puts it this way:

> I think decision makers need to look deeper in terms of why they're
> choosing to go this way or that. They need to do their homework.
> "Is there a demonstrated value?" And they need to stay the course,
> with an understanding of what zigging and zagging does.

CHOOSE CAREFULLY

How do you choose the programs to put into place? One approach, as you learn about different ideas, is to seek common threads that run through multiple management approaches. These common threads are likely to point you toward enduring and proven practices for leading people. Brian Young, vice president of operations for Sea Island Resorts, comments:

> I played golf a lot when I was a kid. And then I stopped for several years and picked it up again when I was about thirty and really loved it again. Then I read every how-to book I could, devoured every single golf magazine, and became one of those people you love to hate. I was so passionate about it I would read absolutely everything. At some point I got to the realization that they're all saying the same thing, and it may be the next new fad, but it really is the basics that count. We're talking about human behavior here, and I venture to say that some of the challenges in human behavior have not changed. You read Shakespeare or Homer, and they are talking about the same stuff we're talking about.

This approach does not say to quit reading or taking seminars or whatever you do to broaden your thinking. Many of the management ideas you encounter may bill themselves as the ultimate answer, and the excitement generated by an energized crowd may draw you toward that conclusion. It is true that new ideas can be energizing. New tools! New levers to pull! It is also true that transformative new ideas are rare, says Phil Kiester, general manager of the Farmington Country Club: "Whether it's a diet or a management fad, we all want to think there's this one set of ideas that's going to change our life forever, and I just am hard pressed to think of many times when that's turned out to be true."

So study your maps, and plan your route. If a new road opens up, consider whether it connects well with the route you're already on. You can afford to be selective. There are many branching ideas out there. Preserve your consistency because consistency breeds trust and inconsistency undermines it.

BALANCE CHANGE WITH CONTINUITY—AND TALK ABOUT BOTH

To stay out of the flavor-of-the-month club, balance your change efforts with things that you will keep constant. Also let people know that is how you operate. As in walking, you need to keep one foot planted firmly on the ground if you are to move the other. You

have to keep something that employees and customers can recognize as your identity—something that can earn their loyalty. An
effective identity must be more than your company name and your
line of business. You need to know what aspects of your business
are available for change and what aspects are not. And you need to
communicate about the unchanging as well as the changing. For
example, Larry Reinstein says,

> One of the hardest things in our organization, and virtually in every
> other organization, is to stay constant and to stay on the program.
> It's all about focus. It's about consistency. It's staying with it. Again,
> not easy. There are a lot of smart philosophies out there. I've read an
> awful lot of books, heard an awful lot of speakers, learned an awful
> lot. It doesn't mean that you can just jump from one thing to the
> next thing. It's not just management philosophy; it's also changes in
> direction. Change is a good thing and a bad thing. The companies
> that have done the best work in the past have changed in certain ways
> and have stayed consistently the same in others. One of our goals
> is to be innovative in terms of things that might be noticed by the
> guests. But we try to be consistent in terms of how we operate things.

John Longstreet turns to Southwest Airlines to illustrate invio-
late principles of a company's identity:

> Southwest Airlines definitely has [inviolate principles]. They've
> decided there are certain things they're doing to do, and they're
> going to be the best at those. There are other things they're
> *not* going to do, not going to try to do. You know, they're the best
> airline that doesn't assign seats. And that drives some people crazy.
> I'm sure they have debates every other month. "Should we start
> assigning seats?" Five or six people say, "We absolutely should," and
> one person says, "Wait a minute, that's not what we're about. We're
> the airline that doesn't assign seats."
>
> I think they've been really good at that, but it doesn't mean that they
> don't try new things to market their product, new things to make it a
> better place to work so the employees will be even more friendly than
> they are now, new ways to empower employees to do crazy things.
> Because they know that's part of their culture. The key is there are
> things we're not going to disturb without an act of Congress.

Note that John does not say to stop experimenting and exploring
but to distinguish the elements of the company's strategy and culture that form its identity—as a brand and as an employer.

Kevin Dunn, an executive coach and former Great Lakes Division president of McDonalds, echoes the notion that the most effective companies maintain their core values and occasionally shed those that no longer serve them. He notes that new leaders are sometimes unaware of which elements belong in which category, and that amid the chaos of daily operations, they may struggle to keep the two straight. Also, "a lot of times when a new leader comes in, he wants to distance himself from the current situation." New managers often feel pressure to make their mark and try to change things around just so they can say they made a difference. Efforts to have such an impact, in a "loud" environment and with insufficient reflection, can lead to false starts that erode credibility and lose momentum. New managers are well advised to take the time to learn the company's working core of culture or identity because it reveals what is open to change and what is not. It will be time well spent.

JoAnne Kruse emphasizes the need to link new bits of knowledge or new approaches with what one already knows and practices. It is wonderful, she says, for managers to learn and explore,

> as long as they keep it consistent with the framework of how they look at their organization and their people, and they help people bridge the gap. So when there is a new management idea, the person needs to ask, "Why is that relevant to everything else we talk about? Is it a change, or is it another way of looking at the same problem? How do we add to the tool set or create another solution that we can add to our box of goodies when we have to solve a similar problem next time?"

Alison Smith, director of organizational effectiveness for Carlson Hotels Worldwide, says, "We used to get accused of [flavor of the month] all the time. And I think we were prone to go from one thing to another. What we now realize is that a lot of these things are not mutually exclusive." She goes on to say that explorations are a positive part of Carlson's culture:

> We often take new models, new learnings, whatever, and hold them up against what we already know to be true in our business. And we say, "How does this fit in? And where might what this is telling us be something that we already know, and where might it be different?"

Alison also strongly endorses explaining to employees and other stakeholders the reasoning behind different change efforts over time and the results they have generated. Provide people with a history that makes sense of the pattern of change. From her company's conscious efforts to integrate its various learnings and its clear and consistent communication about its history of change, it has found that "people aren't so accusatory anymore." When you help people make sense of change, they are less likely to lapse into the cynical stance that accuses executives of change for its own sake.

Nancy Johnson, executive vice president for full-service hotels at Carlson International, makes a point of helping workers to see the thread that joins the new to the old: "You really need to say, 'This isn't anything that we haven't discussed before.' This is just a new way of looking at it, and maybe a more fun way of looking at it." Nancy says you really can create a climate that continually explores new ideas without developing the flavor-of-the-month syndrome. She believes Carlson has done that by communicating clearly about what fundamental style issues stay the same and what change.

The need to highlight continuity in communications with workers applies even in major turnaround efforts, and perhaps especially so. John Longstreet described how he and his team communicated about their abiding, professed values at a time when their conduct appeared to go against those values. He and his team came to ClubCorp when the company was deep in the red, and they had to act quickly to cut costs. At the same time, they were espousing the service-profit chain, which says happy employees lead to happy customers, which leads to profit. He provided his employees a way to make sense of the executives' behavior without considering it to be hypocritical, which it wasn't:

> If we didn't cut costs, we might not have a company left to be able to focus on the service-profit chain. So we said, "Look, we understand the service-profit chain. We believe in it. But we're going to have to suspend it, kind of like martial law, for the next year. We're not going to be any less caring about employee partners or members, but we're going to talk, totally, this year about how we're going to get the company back to a profitable picture. Some of that's going to involve cutting overhead. But we're going to cut our overhead in a very humane way, a very fair way, and we're going

to make sure that anybody who becomes a victim of that feels that they were well taken care of."

By helping employees to make sense of management's changing behavior in the light of the values that management professed, John was able to avoid employee perceptions of hypocrisy. He was able to provide a sense that executives' driving values stayed the same, even though their behavior was forced to change. The point here is to help the employees see the common thread. Help them understand how executive actions reflect executives' stated values, especially when they seem not to.

R. J. Dourney, president of Hearthstone Associates, recommends maintaining your "stable point" in a turnaround situation by systematically building on changes and sustaining each, even after you have shifted focus to the next issue:

> I've done [turnarounds] in our acquisitions. The first thing that we're going to talk about is getting our arms around our people and taking care of our folks and making sure that they're happy. Do they have health benefits? Does the dishwasher have a 401(k)? I'll be candid with you. In six months I'm not going to be talking about that as much as I am going to be talking about wowing our guests and the quality of service that we give, but we're still going to talk about the 401(k). You have to have a building block approach, but you can't shift complete focus. You can't abandon whatever it was that you said you were going to do on Monday.

Think about change as a process of building, and communicate about it in this way. When employees lose the sense that the company's learning is a cumulative process, they tend to get a sense that the change—which is uncomfortable—lacks meaning—which is intolerable. Acknowledge continuity, and also acknowledge change as growth—and communicate a lot about both. By giving employees a meaningful story, you can help keep flavor-of-the-month cynicism at bay.

COMMIT: MEAN IT, AND KEEP IT UP

A pitfall flagged by several executives is insufficient executive commitment to change efforts. Most serious efforts call for substantial follow-up in coaching, performance appraisal, hiring, and perhaps even terminations. And changes typically require time—sometimes years—in order to bear fruit. Failing to allocate enough time and attention is another route to the flavor-of-the-month club. You roll out a change with great fanfare. After a few months, it fizzles. For whatever reason, nobody makes the effort to overcome the obstacles and sustain the program. The management team tries something else, which is again rolled out to the blare of trumpets, and the cycle repeats. All the while employee cynicism steadily mounts.

Commit. Mean it, stick to it, and make it work. Decide with 100 percent certainty that your actions are going to continue to line up with the promises made in the rollout—or you risk your credibility. If you are not willing to make that decision, rethink your rollout. Bob Fox, vice president of human resources for Carlson Hotels Worldwide, draws an analogy to trendy diets:

> It seems to me that with any of these diets and exercise videos, the issue is not whether they're good or bad, because they're almost all good and will give you the desired results—if you stick to them. But folks get caught up with something and don't stay the course—particularly around these weekend seminars and things like that.

If you call for change without allowing for the time and effort, you get the hassle of change without its benefit.

Darryl Stickel, founder of Trust Unlimited, a consulting firm, highlights the importance of evaluation:

> One of the main complaints I get from clients is: "Yes, we do training. People will come back from a workshop, and we will ask, 'What did you learn?' They'll say, 'San Diego is really cool.' Or 'The person who stood up was really funny.' But nothing else. Nothing seems to stick." So there's frustration around that you're getting these training sessions or this flavor-of-the-month stuff, and nothing seems to be permanent. There seem to be no evaluation criteria; there seems to be no follow-through on this new approach. So, my company pushes to evaluate, pre- and post-.

Companies and executives promote flavor-of-the-month cynicism when they pull support for programs before they have been given enough time to work. Sometimes effective change means continuing the effort for two or three years before you see returns. It is hard to maintain that kind of time horizon in the face of more immediate performance pressures. I never said leadership was easy. A second way to preserve word-action consistency through the change is to build in follow-up and accountability all around when planning the effort. Without follow-up, the program risks falling back into the dustbin with previous fads. If you intend the change to stick, you need to remind people about it and openly assess their efforts to implement the change on an ongoing basis. If you do not do that, employees will question whether you ever intended to make a lasting difference or were merely dabbling.

Discuss the Temporary and Tentative

Not every new policy, strategy, or approach merits deep commitment of time, effort, and follow-up. It might be untested, or it might be a response to a short-term need. You can still use a tentative or temporary approach if you let employees know how tentative or temporary it is. The risk, of course, is that the sunset of the policy comes as a surprise, or, more likely, the policy suffers the slow death of obscurity.

When you describe a tentative direction as permanent, then future changes in direction undermine your credibility. When you share the tentative nature of the direction, you can explore and experiment without risking the power of your word. Bob Fox captures this difference:

> [Suppose] I say to a group, "This is our new direction, and we are committed to this direction. I look forward over the next two years to us really energizing this and picking up momentum." If then I change in three months, it's an integrity issue. On the other hand, [suppose] I say to the group, "We are in trouble. We've got to find a new direction. I have some ideas, and I'd like you all to put your noses to the grindstone and try this. In three months we're going to come back and check in and see how we're doing, and if this is working, we'll stay the course. If it's not working, I'm looking for your input in what different strategies we might want to use." That's a different message.

Phil Kiester openly discusses with his team the false starts involved with experimenting:

> In order to get the benefits of trying new things, we need to acknowledge in advance that things may not work out the way we want them to. That doesn't mean we shouldn't have tried. It's not an indictment of the effort or the process when things don't go exactly as we'd hoped.

By being frank about a tentative plan up and down the organization, Phil preserves a culture of exploration and learning while minimizing the disappointment and surprise that so often lead to cynicism.

A good approach to experimentation is setting up small trial programs with explicit sunsets. Judith Kalfon, general manager at the Radisson Plaza Hotel in Minneapolis, described trying out many new programs in her first months at another hotel:

> I'm trying to be clever about implementing new programs, basically experimenting without undermining credibility. All the incentives that I've done here are very short term. "Come to work for the next busy weekend, and you get a chance to win a fifty-dollar Wal-Mart certificate. Everybody who comes Friday, Saturday, and Sunday gets one entry." If that doesn't work, I've got a three-day kind of program. I'm trying to build in the sunset, because I don't know what will work. This approach has let us try some fun short-term incentives to see what our associates react to and enjoy.

The experiments are low risk and do not pretend to be permanent changes, though Judith is open to the possibility of making successful programs permanent. To be sure, some extra communication might well become necessary to avoid employees' taking experimental programs for granted. The second time the Wal-Mart certificate is offered, people may well come to expect it and to see any eventual change in the incentive as yet another shift in policy. So experimentation of this sort probably needs to be followed up with a public announcement of "This worked, and we will keep doing it," or "This did not work, so we . . ."

Several executives I spoke with recommended talking openly about the tentative nature of experimental programs. This approach makes it less likely that the enthusiasm and high hopes of new converts to a new management approach will lead to cynicism if the program changes. Based on their initial enthusiasm, those converts make and imply many promises to others and are then forced to break them when the program is discarded. The second or third set of dashed promises can reduce managers' credibility to a shambles. In being openly tentative, the executive makes fewer promises and cautions the middle manager against overextending in promises made.

ALLOW HUMOR

Some executives go further than acknowledging the tentativeness of an experiment: they openly acknowledge the silliness of frequent change even while supporting such change. By allowing management to be in on the joke, these executives affirm a shared humanity and a shared fate with workers. They say, in essence, that we are all in this together. They also invite employee reactions to change—good, bad or indifferent—into the conversation, which allows them to be addressed. Alison Smith pokes fun at the glut of jargon that has accompanied Carlson's change efforts:

> We're open to new ideas, right? So if there isn't an acronym for something, we *will* create it! And in fact one of the new ideas for our next strategy symposium, which will be hilarious—we're going to do some *acronym bingo*. We're not doing brain surgery here. We are providing hospitality, and our mission is great hospitality built on great relationships. First and foremost, we are relational. So it doesn't matter how perfect or wonderful or elegant or simple an idea is, you know—if it's going to get in the way of a relationship, it's not going to fit in much around here. And it has to help us to produce awesome hospitality.

By officially running a game of Acronym Bingo, where employees listen for buzzwords and mark them on a playing card, Carlson's executives poke fun at their own change efforts. The joke, however, does not undermine the message of the change effort itself or the fundamental Carlson value of relationships. To the contrary, it reinforces them, just as a good speaker's touch of self-deprecating humor acknowledges a shared humanity and draws an audience in.

John Hillins, in his role as a senior human resource executive with Honeywell, similarly found that humor served to reduce cynicism:

> We came up with a way to address [flavor-of-the-month cynicism]. I'd go into these divisions with something that was the flavor-of-the-month club, and I'd say, "I'm here from corporate, and I'm here to help you." They'd crack up. Just crack up!

By joking with employees about frequent change efforts, these executives create a sense of continuity amid change. They build relationships and reduce barriers. By acknowledging and joking about flavor-of-the-month, they foster humor rather than cynicism.

SUMMARY

The flavor-of-the-month club is a real danger to leadership credibility and to behavioral integrity. Where change efforts pile up on one another, where previously novel approaches are neglected in favor of the latest and greatest, and where jargon and acronyms proliferate into a meaningless jumble, cynicism breeds. Employees learn to second-guess their leaders' talk of new direction and to sit out shifts they find personally uncomfortable.

Yet there remains a real need for leaders to continue to learn and experiment—to stay engaged, respond to new circumstances and challenges, and adopt the occasional mousetrap that really is better.

Into Practice

Consider

- What changes has your company undertaken in recent years?
- Have the change efforts been sustained?
- How have the cumulative change efforts been understood? What is the story told about them?
- What effect have these changes had on leaders' credibility?
- Have experimental changes been communicated as such?
- How might humor cut through any resulting cynicism?

Act

- First and foremost, slow down in considering new approaches. Take the time to carefully consider payoffs and challenges to implementation. Use dry runs or discussions to gauge employee reactions and the reactions of your team without putting your credibility on the line.
- Choose and implement only the changes that make sense to multiple constituencies and draw on themes and techniques that seem to have endured the test of time. Be selective.
- Appreciate and discuss elements of continuity, not just change. These elements give employees and other stakeholders something they can hold on to. They form your company's identity.
- Help employees to make sense of changes in the light of enduring values. Creating continuity and making it vivid are critical aspects of managing the change without generating cynicism.
- When you take on a change, commit to it. Give it enough time and resources to work. And show you mean it. If you are not ready to do that, do not roll out the program.
- Acknowledge the tentative and the temporary. Tell employees what the program or policy success criteria are. Keep them in the loop. Any time they are surprised by your change in policy, you risk alienating them and generating accusations of the flavor of the month. So reduce the surprises.
- Let management be in on the joke, and openly laugh at the silly aspects of the change process. When you openly acknowledge the humor in the exploration process, you defuse the frustration and cynicism that so often accompany the perceived flavor-of-the-month pattern. You also highlight personal relationships, which can form the continuity that is so vital to effective change management.

PART FOUR

BROADER APPLICATIONS AND SUMMARY

CHAPTER TEN

THE INTEGRITY DIVIDEND AND OUTSIDE STAKEHOLDERS

The previous parts of this book have focused on behavioral integrity as a touchstone of leadership, and so they look mostly inside the company. Trust, though, is of huge value in almost all business relationships, and so, as previewed in Chapter Two, there are aspects of the integrity dividend to be reaped outside the boundary of the company as well. Relationships with customers, suppliers, unions, regulators, board members, and many others will be colored deeply by the extent those parties see they can count on your word. When they know they can count on you, they usually become more loyal and more helpful. Those qualities tend to make your business dealings more efficient, which yields the dividend.

Managing behavioral integrity outside the boundaries of the company can be harder than managing it inside the company. Outsiders usually form their opinions based on fewer interactions, which leaves a smaller margin for error in any given interaction. They often interact with several different representatives of the company, but they may form a single assessment of behavioral integrity and trustworthiness of the company as a whole or of the relevant senior executive. That means that integrity outside the company depends in part on the morale, reliability, and integration of your employees and systems. Still, the principles developed through this book apply. This chapter highlights a few key challenges in managing the power of your word with customers, suppliers, and unions.

CUSTOMERS AND THE BRAND PROMISE: ALIGNMENT AND RECOVERY

If a company keeps the promise it makes to its customers, the company builds its brand. Duane Knapp, president of BrandStrategy, calls it a brand promise and has titled his latest book exactly that: *The BrandPromise: The Essence of Success.*[1] This promise forms the core identity of a company for its customers, and it should form the organizing principle of the company's operations. Building and preserving behavioral integrity with customers is about making sure the customer experience lives up to the brand promise. A tremendous amount can be learned and said about this goal. This section discusses two challenges: aligning the different people and systems in your company to support that promise and recovering when you foul it up.

L.L. Bean provided high-quality mail-order sporting goods long before the Internet and overnight delivery made it fashionable to shop that way. Consumers were understandably skeptical about purchasing items without trying them on, and L. L. Bean addressed that skepticism head-on with an unconditional money-back guarantee. How conspicuously does the company live up to that promise?

A few years ago, a neighbor of mine ordered a dress from L.L. Bean, and it arrived while she was out of town. To avoid an extra run to her house, the UPS driver delivered the padded envelope to my house instead. Nobody was home at the time, except my white sled dog, Abbie, an otherwise sweet creature, who was tied up outside with access to the porch and her water dish. Abbie took an immediate and inexplicable dislike to the package or perhaps its unfortunate carrier. When I came home, I found a padded envelope that had been enthusiastically chewed. I sheepishly put the package, along with a note, in my neighbor's mailbox. The next day, a landscaper was driving a truck to another neighbor's house. A bee flew into the cab, which caused him to panic and smash his truck into the first neighbor's mailbox—the one containing the already tattered package. The mailbox was destroyed. When the neighbors returned, they opened the now badly mangled package, and the enclosed T-shirt dress was found to have suffered a pinhole from all this abuse. Here comes the amazing part: L. L. Bean replaced the dress because of its unconditional money-back guarantee. The operator laughed on hearing the story, but there was never any question about honoring the guarantee. The company kept their promise under extraordinary circumstances. I will never again doubt them.

Contrast this story with what happened at Hampton Inns in the early years of its 100 percent satisfaction guarantee. The policy said that the room was free if anything was not as the guest wanted: a blown bulb, a bad air conditioner or TV, noise at night—anything. The idea was to make a marketing statement— a brand promise—and at the same time drive quality improvement. Operations people were pretty nervous about the policy because they knew how often small things go wrong. Skip Sack, former executive vice president of Applebee's International, tells the story of Chris Hart, a consultant charged with implementing the program:

> At Hampton Inns, when they first started the program, Joe, the regional manager, would call up the individual hotels and say, "How many rooms did you comp last night?" And Jim, the manager of the Hampton Inn in Ithaca, New York, would say, "I comped eleven rooms." And Joe would say, "What are you, crazy, Jim, are you out of your mind, eleven rooms? What the hell kind of an operation are you running there?" By the next time Joe called, Jim had purposely violated the principles of the program: he hadn't comped rooms he should have comped because he didn't want to incur Joe's wrath. Jim had comped maybe two rooms instead of the ten rooms that he should've comped. And Joe calls and says, "Two? Okay, that's good, Jim, that's great."

Chris called the regional managers together and told them that their approach would likely doom the program and undermine the brand. He encouraged them to focus on the reasons that rooms were getting comped and to channel resources into fixing the underlying quality problems. In essence, he instructed the regional managers to support their hotel general managers in operating successfully within the word and the spirit of their brand promise. Absent that intervention, the incentive system, which emphasized profitability, would have gutted the guarantee and rendered it a corporate hypocrisy.

A brand promise need not take the form of a guarantee. Motel 6 makes and systematically keeps a promise of low prices. According to Georges LeMener, former president and COO of Accor North America,

> We have based the success of Motel 6 on the fact that we are the lowest priced of any national chain. And over the years, our customers have trusted us. Most of them don't even check. They go to a Motel 6 directly because they know; they don't need to check. We are going to be the lowest priced of any national chain in the area.

Customers don't even need to check. Why not? Because Motel 6 does it for them:

> For example, every month we call every competitor in the area to make sure that we are really the lowest priced. For me, vis-à-vis the customer, it's critical to be clear about what you are as a brand, what you deliver, and not play games.

Behind Georges's approach is a genuine accountability at the top to ensure that the promise is being kept throughout the enormous Motel 6 chain.

CUSTOMERS AND SALES

In most industries, sales are extremely competitive, and most salespeople feel constantly pressured to promise more. The easiest way to sell (if you are not too worried about the long run) is to promise that your product or company will deliver whatever the customer wants most. Many sales representatives are incented not to concern themselves about the long-term consequences of the promises they make. For ease of tracking, most incentive systems focus on the initial sale or contract. Sales representatives are often uninvolved with actual service delivery or long-term follow-up.

Rich Panico, president and CEO of Integrated Project Management Company, highlighted the consequence of even small misrepresentations in the sales process:

> If we misrepresent ourselves to a client and don't have the subject matter expertise required to address their issues, we are going to lose any trust and future business. I would expect the client to question everything from that point forward. Even if we continued to work together, the obstacles and distractions would consume time and energy.

Salespeople are tempted to exaggerate and reassure clients that they and the company can address their needs. However, where the reassurances are inaccurate, they undermine customer faith in the integrity of the company and in its brand.

Steve Wells is the president and co-owner of American Food and Vending, a corporate dining and catering service with clients in fifteen states. As his company grew, it was strategically critical to preserve credibility by making sure clients already on contract were satisfied with their service. They aligned their sales representatives' pay system to reflect this brand promise:

> In our industry, most salespeople are compensated by incentives. Ours make a straight salary, and the salespeople are also responsible for ongoing service. If they sell something that operations can't live up to, they are responsible for dealing with that client. Our philosophy is that we can't lose any business. If we get a call from a client who's not happy about something that was said by the salesperson, that salesperson is right back in there. Forever. They can't walk away from business that they've sold. They have to be accountable.

Make a mess? Clean it up. Or, as Steve says, bring in "business that will fit for the long term." The approach has worked admirably for American Food and Vending: as it has grown over the past seventeen years, it has never lost a client. Their very first clients are still with them.

Service Recovery

Kelly Services, the global staffing agency, faces special challenges in its contracting. Its contracts often cover five- or ten-year periods across dispersed geographical locations and, despite Kelly's extraordinary size, fewer than one hundred client companies make up most of its business. Over the course of a multiyear contract, the original people involved often turn over—on both sides. Local and global economies can change dramatically, such that a profitable staffing contract one year might easily become a money loser the next. Carl Camden, the president and CEO of Kelly Services, preserves the excellent reputation of his company through a fierce emphasis on good contracting and making good his company's promises:

> It comes down to making a promise consistent with our corporate values, with our belief system, so that regardless of the actors, regardless of the culture, regardless of the passage of time, there should be a consistency to our fulfillment of the promises. The promise has to be consistent with all those core values, with all of our core practices, so that we know that over the course of time the promise is going to endure even if the people don't.

The way to write contracts that survive the passage of time and turnover and geographical dispersion is to make sure that the contract resonates with the core identity of your company. In this case, the promise draws strength from Kelly Services' culture, which tells new employees how to keep the promise. Carl's insistence that contractual promises align with the company's core identity parallels, in larger scale, the idea of internal alignment discussed in Chapter Six: integrity as a personal discipline. When you make promises without ambivalence, you keep them.

But even a great contract has limits. When circumstances change around a multiyear contract—anything from a glutted local employment market to drastic technological change—once-profitable contracts can cease to be profitable. When that happens, local managers tend to want to exercise the exit clause that is in every Kelly Services contract. Sometimes the exit is gradual, as they try to operate profitably by performing services at less than the agreed-on level. Customers understandably get unhappy about subpar performance. In these cases, Carl has instituted a strong policy: he insists that his people perform to the level specified in the contract before they exit. This approach is designed to protect the brand, and it pays off:

> We are not going to exit the contract until we're in a position of being judged by the customer as having met all its terms. In other words, we will fulfill the written promise, even if it is not congruent with some of the intent, because when I exit an account, I want to exit with the customer not being able to say, "Kelly didn't do what they said they would do."

Carl's goal is to exit exclusively from a position of strength and compliance with the contract—and with integrity. "And at that point," he adds, "we're often successful in renegotiating the contract" rather than actually exiting. When integrity has been restored by compliance with the contract, most customers are willing to sign a new, and profitable, contract with Kelly, a company that honors its word.

Carl tells the story of the meeting that led to this policy early in his tenure at Kelly. He was a newly appointed director of sales, and he walked into a meeting with a long-time client. He had been told by his office that the clients were satisfied and wanted to meet him:

> I walked in. They had about ten people there, which I thought was unusual. They had PowerPoint presentations, and they didn't seem to be particularly happy. I sit down, and they detailed for an hour all of the promises made by the previous head of sales that weren't being fulfilled by Kelly. They really beat me up. We were just doing a bad job all across the board.
>
> So we spent six months and returned all of the metrics to the point where they should have been. Now we were fulfilling the intent of the contract as well as the metrics on the contract. Then I went back in. They said they were happy. I documented for them how much money we were losing by fulfilling this contract. And I said, "My predecessor never met a promise he wasn't willing to make. He just didn't believe in keeping them." I said, "You're going to find me making very few promises, but we will keep 100 percent of what we make. So now I'm telling you: we have fulfilled the promises here that we made, even though they were stupid promises. We're not going to do it any longer. We're going to resign the account." That customer is still a very good account today, and very much respected the honoring of the promise.

Carl was faced with the results of a broken promise, cleaned the mess up effectively with a service recovery, and charted Kelly's commitment to integrity.

This story applies many of the principles of managing behavioral integrity to customer relationships. It is a service recovery, which is a form of apology for a promise unfulfilled. The apology is offered cleanly as an acceptance of responsibility and ownership of the problem, without extensive explanation, and service is restored. The promise is ultimately kept. Then Carl describes his intention to make fewer promises but to hold to them. He says, "I'm always telling salespeople that we have no credibility with the customer until we tell them 'no.' And I believe that the earlier you can tell them 'no' in a relationship, the better the credibility you're establishing." Apparently his customers approve of integrity in long-term relationships.

SUPPLIERS: MANAGING OPPORTUNISM

In most industries, supply chain relationships that have mutual trust provide a tangible payoff in service. To build those trusting relationships, you must show genuine concern for the welfare of the other party; it cannot be faked. A key challenge to behavioral integrity in these relationships is avoiding the opportunism that presents itself as chances to squeeze just a little more out of the deal. That pull appears as chances to rig or tweak a bidding system, as short-term discounts proposed by rivals and as the chance to legally delay payment. The problem is that displays of those forms of opportunism make any avowal of relationship building sound like hypocritical efforts to extract better prices.

BUILDING STRONG RELATIONSHIPS

Strong relationships with suppliers pay off in extra service and flexibility when the unexpected happens. But how do you create those relationships? Jay Witzel is the president and CEO of Carlson Hotels Worldwide, one of the world's largest hotel companies. His perspective is that

> the best way to have a great relationship with suppliers is to sit down and talk to them. And tell them where they stand in your

value chain. Make sure they understand that you understand *their* cost structures. We try to have an open conversation about what prices we like to pay, at what cost they can produce, and whether there is any way that we can work together to either take out costs or improve the quality—one of the two.

Jay steers clear of bidding as the central point of the conversation and strictly avoids threats that suggest Carlson would "switch you out tomorrow for a nickel." He wants a long-term relationship, and he wants the supplier to know that. Jay views relationships that focus only on price as "parasitic":

> One party will live, and one party will die. We want vendors who are healthy. We want that health for *their* longevity because we don't have to change vendors, and we want that health for *our* longevity because we believe a healthy organization can probably find ways to increase its efficiency and still make the margins it needs. [We seek] a relationship based on the knowledge of each other's business. And to the extent that we're good at that, we've had the same vendors for a very long period of time. Our pricing is rational, and we think it provides good value to the overall enterprise. We hope it does.

By building a relationship based on mutual understanding and respect, Carlson enjoys long-term supply relationships with companies that genuinely consider themselves as partners in the Carlson Hotels enterprise.

Ted Ratcliff is a senior vice president for Hilton Doubletree Operations East. He shares the concept of partnering with suppliers and the sense that you cannot abandon a supplier because someone else offers a good deal in the short run:

> We operate on a cost-plus contract—we want your costs, and this is the markup. [But] it's easy to go outside that and say, "I'm going to buy the canned tomatoes from somebody else because they're five dollars cheaper a case this week." You certainly can find that. The supplier's competition is more than happy to lose money in the beginning or to throw things out there that could be attractive.

> But that's not what it's about. It's about the whole market basket of goods that you've contracted for, and you need to live up to that. Otherwise, you get a pretty sour reputation. You need loyal suppliers. When you really need a supplier to assist you because you have

made an error on ordering or whatever, or you need somebody to run something out on the weekend, they'll bend over backward for you if you deal with them straight-up.

One of the pitfalls to managing supplier relationships with integrity is the temptation to switch, or to dabble, in response to an appealing offer. If your stated intention is to build a relationship with them, you need to act like it. That means talking to them, learning about and supporting them in managing a successful business, and keeping the big picture of their performance in mind. If you genuinely operate as though the relationship were worth something, they will tend to reciprocate when you most need them.

"YES, BUT WHERE'S THE CHECK?"

The single greatest tension between suppliers and their corporate clients—and the greatest temptation for opportunism—arises out of one simple question: "Where is the check?" We heard from Pete Kline, a partner with Seneca Advisors consulting firm and the former CEO of Bristol Hotels and Resorts, on that subject in Chapter Two. Is the invoice paid promptly, or is it "aged"? Different departments within your organization may prefer to answer differently because they maximize different kinds of performance. There is a financial benefit to aging those invoices just a few more weeks— but there is a hidden cost as well.

The timing of payments is especially critical for small companies that have to manage their cash flow closely. Pete recalled being on the receiving end of slow payments in the early days of his hotel company:

> I can remember us as a small struggling hotel company dealing with some of the major corporations in Dallas. These were *huge* companies, and they would just routinely take sixty to ninety days to pay us. To us, it was a critical problem. To them, it was not a big deal. That was just the way they handled their payables and their cash flow.

Suppliers in general greatly prefer to be paid promptly, and that goes double for smaller companies. Pete's recollection of this pattern is just one of several I have encountered. When I asked about maintaining trust with suppliers, many executives replied simply, "Pay on time."

I am not saying that slow payment is necessarily calculated; sometimes it emerges from bureaucratic complications like needing multiple sign-offs, and sometimes the checks are being cut by a central office that tends to the largest accounts first or has other priorities. But these circumstances make little difference to the small business owner who has to scrape by because your company takes too much time to pay. In the interest of improving the relationships, and what you can get from these relationships, it might make sense to streamline the payment process to support your company's behavioral integrity.

Pete submits that early payment can be a positive (and profitable) strategy, at least in an industry where payments are widely delayed by the larger players.

ORGANIZED LABOR: GETTING PAST THE ADVERSARIAL STANCE

Unions and management often have a long history of doing battle and of thinking of the other side as an adversary. Of course, every new contract is promoted as ushering in "a new era of partnership," and therein lies the integrity pitfall. The new era is typically as short-lived as a honeymoon, and business as usual involves a game of "gotcha" that does not resemble partnership.

In Chapter Two I described "Nancy Kimber's" experience of a labor strike in a major city and the local union's lack of trust in the hotel chain's local management. The lack of trust was natural because the local manager had made it obvious he hated unions. Nancy described solving the problem by replacing the manager with someone who was willing and able to deal with the union sincerely, in alignment with Nancy's own precept. The change made a huge difference in how union employees regarded their work. Speaking to Nancy about what they liked about the new manager, they said, "She talks to us. She listens to us. And she doesn't give us everything we want, but she tells us why she can't do something if she can't do it. She answers us. We're getting the truth."

Nancy's story makes a major point about relations between companies and unions. Noncommunication is a poor option. Where organizations deal with unions, it pays to keep communications open and active, not only at negotiation time but between contracts as well. Honest conversation is how you create and maintain partnership. It is necessary if you are to enact your promise to behave as a partner.

The more basic challenge of practicing behavioral integrity in relation to unions is that company managers are often extremely ambivalent about what kind of relationship they want to have with organized labor—if any at all. Few companies welcome unions. Many management teams dislike unions but work with them as a practical matter. Feelings range from hate to respect. An organization can take either a partnering or an adversarial stance and still align its words and action. But an organization's managers cannot take both and still capture the integrity dividend.

THE BOEING 2000 STRIKE AT PUGET SOUND: "WE LOVE OUR WORKERS BUT HATE THEIR UNION"

In the Puget Sound area, two-thirds of Boeing's workforce was in one or the other of two unions. Boeing's well-educated, highly qualified engineers were represented by the Society of Professional Engineering Employees in Aerospace (SPEEA). In spring 2000, Boeing experienced its first (and thus far only) engineers' strike. It was one of the largest white-collar union strikes in U.S. labor history.

Managers at Boeing describe SPEEA before the strike: "For many years it was more of a society than a union. Some people called it a discount buying club. The company bargained with SPEEA in good faith, and by and large things had always come out okay in the end." Charles Bofferding, former executive director of SPEEA, agrees and comments that the union dealt in good faith as well. It is, after all, a union of engineers—professionals proud of their problem-solving skills.

In the late 1990s, a merger with McDonnell Douglas had brought Boeing under the control of new top leadership that secretly decided to attack the unions and try to drive them out.

One part of its basic strategy became to offer less to union members than it offered to its nonunion engineers. This strategy ended a long-standing policy by which Boeing offered pay and benefits to nonunion workers basically equal to those it negotiated with the union.

As negotiations began in 1999, the change in corporate strategy was obvious to everyone. The company negotiation team was given its assignment but was asked to maintain the illusion of honest bargaining:

> The PR campaign started from corporate about how ugly and stupid people were to be in a union in the first place. The negotiation was going to demonstrate that people in the union were not going to get what people outside the union had already—there were to be reductions in medical benefits and pay and all kinds of what unions call "takeaways." It was absolutely a direct challenge to the union. In charge of the labor relations since the merger was a guy with a railroad background. He hated unions, and he had strong support from the board and other people.

> When the contract went up for a vote, out of one side of his mouth, here's our corporate leader talking about how "people are our greatest asset, we're all one team, and we all share in the risks and rewards of our company." But at the same time, he is beating the crap out of a very important part of our population in Puget Sound.

Only a few managers and executives were directly involved in the negotiations, and those on the outside were appalled at what they saw happening. They tried "to convince our corporate leaders that this approach would be devastating." The response, according to those involved, was,

> "You don't know what you're talking about. We trust these people. They won't really walk out. They're professionals." It was such an interesting thing. On the one hand, they'd say, "They're like animals because they're in a union." On the other hand, "They're professionals and they won't strike."

> Well, they were and they are professionals. They've all gone to college. They've got degrees. They've worked to build a career. Even the name of their union says "professional." But at this point they had been attacked so much—they were backed into a corner.

In response to widespread and accurate perception that Boeing executives were bargaining in bad faith, SPEEA voted to strike, and production soon stopped. After forty days, the strike ended with "a complete collapse at the corporate level." The union got everything it wanted and even things it didn't really expect or ask for, including a closed shop.

Despite total victory at the bargaining table, union members' trust in management was destroyed. Workers became hypervigilant about perceived slights and often resorted to work-to-rule slowdowns. Any management initiatives aimed at increasing productivity were seen as precursors to layoffs and thus to be resisted. The events surrounding the strike had turned the SPEEA into

> a very aggressive union, and one that now felt really good about what they had just done. They went out as partners in arms. They won this war. They got what they wanted. And they showed those SOBs that they were important after all.

The timing of this shift could not have been much worse, as Boeing faced new competition in the form of state-subsidized Airbus and grappled with consistently declining market share. Caught between competitive pressures and internal inefficiencies, the company's survival was in jeopardy. It would have been a good time to have an energized, engaged workforce to help create a turnaround. That was not the workforce that management's inconsistency and belligerence had inspired.

The story has a fairly happy ending, though. Over the next three years, starting at the local level, the leaders at Boeing Commercial carefully orchestrated collaboration and incented managers for morale improvement. Eventually they were able to turn around the morale crisis and improve productivity by 60 percent from its low point. But the company should not have reached that low point in the first place.

TELEMAR PHONES IN BRAZIL: FORGETTING TO CARE

The adversarial stance in labor relations is not limited to management. When a sense of perennial struggle envelops the relationship between labor and management, it is easy for everyone to forget that their mission is to work together toward a common goal. Given that the official rhetoric on both sides invariably reflects this ideal, it quickly becomes an integrity issue.

Steve Zaffron is the CEO of Vanto Group (formerly Landmark Education Business Development). His team worked with a group of Brazilian telecommunications companies a year after the Brazilian government had privatized the industry. Telemar, which served Rio de Janeiro, was made up of sixteen companies that had all been part of the government a few months earlier. They were going through tremendous upheaval, and they had to improve performance in order to qualify for expansion into lucrative wireless communication. The previous employee climate was more oriented toward logging hours than toward performance, and Steve's team was tasked with creating a shift.

They conducted workshops for over a thousand people over the course of six months. They had participants introduce themselves at these workshops, and one guy raised his hand:

> His introduction, was, "Long live the union." A bunch of union people cheered. He was a pretty nondescript small guy, but very tough and old-school union. One of the representatives of the union was also in the program. So when he said, "Long live the union," he looked at the union representative, and they both kind of winked and said, "Yeah," and that's how they began the program.

The guy did not say much through the course of the program, but he seemed to be paying attention. At one point, the workshop leaders asked people to write letters during a break. The letters weren't meant to be sent; they were a way to practice addressing difficult issues with people without blaming them:

> So on the last day of the course, we say, "Who has a letter?" And this guy is waving his arm wildly, and it's like, "Oh my god, what is he going to say now?" And he got up, and his letter was addressed to the vice president who was the head of this division—and to the union representatives. He said that for fifteen years he's been working in this company, and he never saw this company as really important. He saw his job as important, and keeping his job as important, but he really didn't have much concern for the quality of his work.

And, he said, as he's going through this program, he started to see that he wanted to have pride in his work. And he also acknowledged that he saw that the success of the company was critical—not merely for him to keep his job, but for all of the people he liked in the company—for them to keep their jobs.

At the end of the letter, after acknowledging what he now saw was really important, he said, "I have a few requests. My first request is I want my toolbox to be complete. I'm missing a number of tools in my toolbox—specialized screwdrivers and circuit testers and so on—but I haven't really cared about it because I didn't really care what I did much. If I didn't have a tool, it was fine with me, I just didn't do that job." Then he said, "I really need a new truck. My truck is always breaking down, but my team and I never cared because, in fact, when it broke down, then we didn't have to go and work. We'd just wait until it got fixed. But now I want to work. So I want a new truck." That's how he ended his letter.

Very quickly he got a new truck and a new set of tools, let me tell you! He became one of the strongest advocates for the work we were doing with people. He would come by the course—we would do it almost every week—and he would tell people, "Look, sit through this. It won't make sense in the beginning, but it really works—it's been great."

To me this story says something about integrity. In labor relations, it is easy on both sides to forget the fundamental basis of your employment agreement: that workers and managers are to work together to get the job done. When people lose sight of this fact, they sometimes work without integrity. That lack drives performance down. It also exacts a human toll, along with its toll on integrity dividends.

SUMMARY

The principles of integrity as developed in this book apply powerfully to aspects of business that deal with stakeholders outside the company, be they customers, suppliers, or union representatives—or, for that matter, board members, regulators, or even friends, lovers, or family. People are people, and relationships are relationships, and the value of your word is something that, properly safeguarded, yields a powerful dividend. People really do notice, and trust pays off.

The challenges to integrity in these different settings differ a little, and there is a tremendous amount more to know about each of them. Each is worth its own book. In this chapter I've mentioned that when you are dealing with customers, your greatest integrity challenges are likely to involve the question of selling without overpromising, aligning internal incentives to deliver on your brand promise, and cleaning up the mess when you fail. With suppliers, it is avoiding the temptation to exploit as you try to build relationships. With unions, it is remembering that ultimately you have to function as a team to get work done.

Perhaps your greatest integrity dividend will come from doing as much as you can to think of and deal with outside parties as though they were not "outsiders" at all. The more you can both promise and act on the idea that you look out for their interests as well, the more you will build and maintain the trusting, collaborative dealings that sustain excellent performance. Greg Oxton is the executive director of the Consortium for Service Innovation. He says:

> The distinction between customers, partners, and employees is often not helpful. You should think of people as people first, and think of them as human beings, not as resources, with emotions and a multitude of competencies and abilities to contribute. That awareness is totally counter to the silos-compartmentalization view of people, and the fact that we have really strong barriers between our employees and our customers. When you operate that way, you unleash a level of capacity and capability that we've never really been able to capitalize on before, which more than offsets the cost. It drives the level of loyalty and connection with the company, for both employees and customers.

Ted Teng, former president and COO of Wyndham Worldwide Corporation, offered that the best way to maintain integrity is to "love your stakeholders." That way, you do not have to hide your agenda.

Into Practice

Consider—and Act

These questions on dealing with customers, suppliers, and unions may also be relevant to dealings with other outside parties.

- Integrity with customers
  - Define the promise on which your brand identity rests. This is an important decision; if you have not already done so, draw on the expertise around you to develop a meaningful brand promise.
  - Are sales incentives aligned with delivering on that promise?
  - Are incentives elsewhere in the company aligned with delivering on the promise? Are there any other structures that get in the way?
  - Do the executives at the top have a reliable way to know how well the promise is being fulfilled? The credibility of the whole company depends on it.
  - What routines are in place for service recovery when your company fails to keep its promises? Do you apologize, take ownership, and correct the problem?

- Integrity with suppliers
  - Notice how often you depend on unusual service from suppliers.
  - Are your supplier decisions based on long-term profitability or short-term pricing? Have you struck the correct balance between competitive bidding and relationship building? Is your bidding process transparent?
  - How promptly do you pay your suppliers?
  - Do your suppliers know your business model? Do you know theirs?
  - What can you do to make those relationships more trusting and more profitable?
  - Where might your suppliers see your word as broken? Consider asking them. Address the problems that come to the light.

- Integrity with organized labor
  - To what extent does your company's management and labor work together to solve problems in a way that is effective and mutually respectful?
  - Is there a shared awareness of interdependence?
  - What can you do to make those relationships more trusting and more profitable?
  - Where might your union representatives see your word as broken? Consider asking them. Address the problems that come to the light.
  - Consider establishing as a ground rule for negotiations a 100 percent commitment to honoring any resulting agreement and to getting others to do so.

Chapter Eleven

Capturing the Integrity Dividend

The point of this book is simple: any leader's word is his or her most potent tool, and an effective leader devotes much attention to developing and preserving the power of that word. It is not about being nice. It is not about being ethical. It is about being more effective by developing and preserving your credibility. Most managers undermine their own credibility in big and small ways. They make their word less effective as a tool for persuasion and for creating change.

Taking charge of making our word impeccable is a daunting challenge. I cannot honestly report that I have mastered it. But the work I have done convinces me that there is vast power in it. If your word is law, at least with regard to your own conduct, people listen more closely. And you yourself are more closely shaped by what you say: you gain more self-control and in ways that you did not previously consider as self-control. It affects how you manage your time and what commitments you make. But it also affects how others react to you.

Behavioral integrity is not everything it takes to lead, but it is a necessary ingredient of huge consequence and huge challenge. Many others have recognized it as part of a larger picture of effective leadership. But it deserves focused and sustained attention because nothing else works without it and because it is really challenging in this complicated world. Look around you: people of impeccable word are rare. Companies and teams that foster an impeccable word are rarer still. Become one of those people, and create one of those companies or teams, and watch success follow.

I began by reporting a hotel study in which employees' sense that their managers lived by their word was shown to drive hotel profitability, accounting for over 10 percent of the differences between high- and low-profitability hotels. From there I set out to explore how behavioral integrity—perceived alignment of one's word and action—generates this integrity dividend and how that integrity can be achieved at individual and company levels. There are many challenges to credibility at each level, and many forms of the dividend too.[1] The integrity dividend can be seen in hard financial payoffs, but also appears as more loyal and cooperative relationships, a more engaged and directed workforce, and better change implementation.

BEHAVIORAL INTEGRITY AT THE PERSONAL LEVEL

You need people's trust if you want to lead them or do efficient business with them. If they are to trust you, they need to see your word as good. A reputation for living by your word pays off but is hard to build and maintain. To see why this is so, I presented a model of the factors that contribute to or detract from your impeccable word, and others' perception of it.

One challenge is the inevitable unpredictability of the business environment. Another may be problematic aspects of your company's culture or structure, such as misaligned incentives or patterns of poor communication. A third general area of challenge lies within you: a relative lack of awareness about inconsistencies in your own motivations and actions or a lack of practices to keep your words and deeds aligned. A fourth challenge is the subjective nature of the integrity assessment, as observers respond to misunderstandings by reducing trust. The challenges are multiplied by a natural human tendency to desensitize oneself to one's own inconsistencies in order to preserve a positive self-image, which means that inconsistencies breed further inconsistencies. The challenges are multiplied again by the fact that those observing your behaviors are often primed to cast them in a certain light, according to their own historical baggage and their previous experiences of you.

One way to increase behavioral integrity is to promise less but do it more often. By selecting and focusing on just a few values, you can send a consistent message to different employee groups and put programs and practices in place that affirm those values and hold people accountable to them. A list of ten or more values is way too long; it only fosters cynicism. Choose three or four key values, and use them as a touchstone for everything you say or do. This level of focus allows the values to live vividly in employees' hearts and minds and allows you and your company to live by your word.

If you communicate well and completely, you can more easily live by your word and avoid perceptions of broken promises that erode your credibility. We often unintentionally say things that others hear as commitments. We do this sometimes out of politeness or because we would rather not acknowledge uncertainty or personal limitations. We too often express our judgments as facts and our hopes as commitments. Fairly or not, misunderstandings undermine our credibility. It is our charge to manage them and eliminate them if we can.

Integrity potholes come up when we make mistakes or are asked to evaluate the performance of others. It can be difficult to own up to our failings, limitations, or simple broken promises, and efforts to save face for ourselves or others can undermine integrity perceptions. It is, by definition, hard to discuss awkward truths, and often we would rather not openly express our negative judgments for fear of emotional fallout. These patterns also lead others to perceive us as inconsistent between word and deed. The course of greater integrity is to be more transparent about our thoughts and values and to encourage constructive debate.

Behavioral integrity thrives on systematic attention to the process of asking for and getting commitments, because mutually understood promises are far more likely to be kept. Follow these three steps every time you commit or contract:

1. Ask for a commitment, specifying the conditions of fulfillment and the due date.
2. Wait for a response. Allow for a "yes" or a "no" answer. Negotiate if necessary.

3. Follow up after the fact to remind both parties of the commitment, whether or not it was fulfilled.

Behavioral integrity calls for personal discipline—and may even be the same thing as it. We can work to strengthen the needed muscles. Most of us need to overcome deeply patterned, sometimes automatic habits of small social deceit and replace them with greater honesty. Most of us are not good at delaying gratification and choosing longer-term benefits over short-term gains. We need to handle fear more effectively and become more aware of our feelings in general and how they drive our speech and action. If we focus on making commitments very deliberately, hold ourselves to a standard of 100 percent delivery, and keep at it, the muscles will grow and the barriers will fall away.

If you take on the challenge of building your integrity muscles, find a good coach, mentor, close friend, or circle of supportive peers to discuss it with regularly. Their job is to keep you from turning back at the moments when you stand to learn the most. Such people must be capable of brutal honesty and committed to delivering it when necessary.

Here are other practices and exercises for self-development:

- Develop a phrase that reminds you of your larger mission, purpose, and values. Reflect on that phrase to align with it before engaging in leadership activities.
- Combine all your commitments and obligations in a single list, and then work systematically to fulfill or renegotiate each and every promise.
- As you make any new promise, first reflect sufficiently to be certain that you completely want to make and fulfill it. Consciously take the task's challenges and your competing priorities into account before you commit.
- Practice recording *every* commitment you make. Follow up on each one about whether or not you kept the promise.
- Deal with breakdowns with a simple, sincere apology (explanations may be largely irrelevant) and a renewed commitment. Follow up with a promise kept.

Along with such practices, a deep conviction that your word is your bond can and will profoundly enhance how you see and conduct your everyday life. Build that conviction by making and keeping promises to yourself. Start with your personal daily to-do list.

Managing Integrity in an Organization

Middle managers face a serious behavioral integrity challenge simply because of their position in the middle of an organization. Typically their superiors are much less aware of their problem than are the middle managers themselves.

The middle managers' dilemma is how to respond to mandates with which they disagree. Most consider (and senior managers agree) that one major requirement of their job is to champion all initiatives from above. Good middle managers grapple with the question of how to do so without violating their own consistency, as apparent inconsistency would undermine their subordinates' trust in them. The problem needs to be addressed by middle managers themselves, and also by those above them.

If you are a middle manager, you need to express your considerations about a given policy to senior management. Senior management can then allay the expressed concerns and so persuade you, or be persuaded by you, or at least equip you with justifications you can share. Failing that, it comes down to your trusting in senior managers' judgment and the possibility that they have information that is not available to you.

Find honest ways to promote policies about which you have reservations. If you see an upside, share that; if you trust in top managers, share that; if you see a challenge to be overcome, share that. Subordinates are likely to notice dishonest endorsements on your part, and those endorsements cost you credibility. As a middle manager, also develop a clear sense of what ethical lines you are unwilling to cross and what price you are willing to pay for those values.

As a senior manager, you can minimize middle managers' dilemmas through participative management. Discuss with middle managers the importance of buy-in, share your decision justifications, and seriously consider their input. You can retain final decision-making authority, but tell people when you do that so they do not feel your invitation to participate was a ruse. Welcome the expression and constructive resolution of dissent. Consider inviting anonymous expressions of concern, such as the sticky note exercise described in Chapter Seven. When these steps aren't enough, fall back on your bank account of trust. Most important overall, though, is to simply be aware of middle managers' dilemmas, and support their efforts to minimize the toll on their credibility and their subordinates.

When integrated with coaching, modeling, and other good practices, performance appraisals are probably the most potent tool for creating a corporate culture of accountability and integrity. Many managers avoid the performance appraisal process because it can require hard conversations with marginal performers. Other managers undercut the effectiveness of appraisal in efforts to preserve smoothness and morale. Watch out for your own inconsistent messages or opaque, apparently capricious judgments. Support effective appraisals with clear communication, transparent measurement and reliable consequences, and ongoing feedback and skill development. These steps demonstrate consistency and promote alignment, and so build trust. A company's senior executives need to personally demonstrate the conduct they espouse for others.

Organizational change of any sort is a challenge to behavioral integrity, as new and old values and policies may seem to clash and so provide evidence of management hypocrisy. Managers' ambivalences and confusion can give rise to real and perceived behavioral inconsistency. To maximize behavioral integrity through organizational change, pay attention to clear communication and impeccable alignment of performance management practices. Such attention is also a good idea in relatively stable times.

Address the realities and perceptions that your organization may have joined the flavor-of-the-month club. This common executive obsession with novelty in management ideas gives rise to inconsistent practices and jargon, poor follow-through, and ultimately a coldly cynical and unresponsive workforce.

The primary tool for managing the flavor-of-the-month-club is to slow down in choosing and implementing new approaches. Choose carefully, solicit input before committing, and then commit to sustaining the effort. Support employee perceptions of consistency and continuity by discussing the mix and the interconnection of old and new ideas, and show how elements of the old carry into the new.

Experiment and try out new ideas in trial programs. Acknowledge openly where they are temporary and tentative. Laughing at the process of organizational change and the inevitable jargon also seems to help dissipate cynicism from those below.

OUTSIDE THE COMPANY

Consider the impact of behavioral integrity in relationships outside the walls of your company. There are integrity challenges in those other relationships as well, and an integrity dividend to be reaped from successfully addressing those challenges. This book discusses relationships with customers, suppliers, and unions, but behavioral integrity also plays a critical role with regulators, owners, executive boards, and other stakeholders. Consider the impact of behavioral integrity on your personal relationships as well.

When you deal with customers, the integrity dividend is brand identity. How well your company keeps its brand promise defines the marketing durability of that promise.

Watch out for overpromising during the sales process. Attend to how sales representatives are incented and how they are held accountable. Also make concerted efforts to recover when services or products do not perform as promised. A good recovery clarifies the identity of the company and the level of service for which it stands. A part of recovery is a sound apology process, like the one described in Chapter Six.

Supplier relationships can be troubled by excessive opportunism and by legally permissible late payment. Paying bills promptly, especially to smaller accounts, can elicit surprising favor. A supplier relationship can be improved in part simply by assigning, communicating, and demonstrating whatever value you place on it. Whether you consider the relationship to be special or not, transparency supports integrity.

Union relationships are often plagued by histories that perpetuate uncooperative and hostile behaviors despite collegial words on the surface. Those covert drivers can be toxic. They need to be surfaced and at least held in abeyance in order to build any sort of trust-based relationship. A simple insistence that any agreement requires full commitment to its successful implementation can shift the dynamic profoundly.

TOWARD THE FUTURE

The principle that leaders should nurture the power of their word is hardly new, but it has only begun to be the focus of systematic research. There is much, much more to learn. For example, how do assessments and consequences of word-action alignment differ across national cultures? Communication in some parts of the world relies much more heavily on contextual cues than it does in the United States, and integrity judgments are probably affected by such differences. Is the emphasis on keeping one's word particular to the United States? Certainly attitudes toward written contracts appear to differ in different parts of the world: U.S. businesspeople often see a contract as a formal definition of a whole relationship. A typical Chinese businessman, in contrast, is likely to understand the contract as a symbol of a much more complex implicit agreement. Where communication is expected to be inferred more than spoken, alignment between word and action may take on a very different meaning.

There are other aspects of word-action alignment to explore as well. Not surprisingly, scholars have already found that behavioral integrity makes a big difference in the effectiveness of coaching. But different employee groups seem to be differentially affected by word-action alignment, some noticing it more acutely than others. Some values will be more important to employees, and alignment on those particular values is critical for employee trust. It is possible that we assign people multiple levels of integrity depending on the topic, as, for example, a friend who might be perpetually late but is deeply caring about you as a person, or a boss who is sincere when he talks about customer service but not when he talks about participative management. How do we reconcile a person's different levels of consistency? How important is behavioral integrity relative to other drivers of trust, and how does this relative importance change in different situations? How does managers' behavioral integrity affect subordinates' stress levels? What strategies most effectively recover from failure? A growing group of management scholars has embraced this framework as a new way to consider and explore questions about relationships, leadership effectiveness, and ethics. We are still learning about how behavioral integrity affects performance and how leaders can most effectively manage it.

The idea of word-action alignment is profoundly simple, but the impediments to it are not. There is much more to be learned as managers consciously struggle to live by their word and to be seen as doing so. Managers contribute to our growing understanding of it by reflection and informal conversation and scholars by scientific exploration. Both should continue this journey of mutual learning. I see good evidence that sustained and focused attention to the management of our own word will make us all more effective, both individually and in groups and companies.

Some say talk is cheap. And it is, in the sense that it is easy to say stuff, whether or not you really mean it. But in terms of consequences, talk is not cheap; it is expensive. When a leader says something and fails to visibly follow up with action, it costs that person credibility. The credibility of leaders makes or breaks companies. Credibility with managers and workers. Credibility with customers and suppliers. Talk is not cheap. It is the most valuable thing a leader does. Make it more so.

NOTES

Chapter One

1. For a full theoretical treatment and concept definition, see Simons, T. "Behavioral Integrity: The Perceived Alignment Between Managers' Words and Deeds as a Research Focus." *Organization Science,* 2002, *13*(1), 18–35.
2. Dirks, K. T. "Trust in Leadership and Team Performance: Evidence from NCAA Basketball." *Journal of Applied Psychology,* 2000, *85*(6), 1004–1012.
3. Dirks, K. T., and Ferrin, D. L. "Trust in Leadership: Meta-Analytic Findings and Implications for Research and Practice." *Journal of Applied Psychology,* 2002, *87*(4), 611–628.
4. Cohen-Charash, Y., and Spector, P. E. "The Role of Justice in Organizations: A Meta-Analysis." *Organizational Behavior and Human Decision Processes,* 2001, *86*(2), 278–321.
5. Zhao, H., Wayne, S. J., Glibkowski, B. C., and Bravo, J. "The Impact of Psychological Contract Breach on Work-Related Outcomes: A Meta-Analysis." *Personnel Psychology,* 2007, *60*(3), 647–680.
6. If I were to run the survey again, I would probably engage illiterate employees through use of voice-recognition telephone technology, which has advanced considerably in recent years. The read-aloud tables too often created a social atmosphere and wasted time.
7. Colquitt, J. A., Scott, B. A., and LePine, J. A. "Trust, Trustworthiness, and Trust Propensity: A Meta-Analytic Test of Their Unique Relationships with Risk Taking and Job Performance." *Journal of Applied Psychology,* 2007, *92*(4), 909–927. Harrison, D. A., Newman, D. A., and Roth, P. L. "How Important Are Job Attitudes? Meta-Analytic Comparisons of Integrative Behavioral Outcomes and Time Sequences." *Academy of Management Journal,* 2006, *49*(2), 305–325. Jaramillo, F., Mulki, J. P., and Marshall, G. W. "A Meta-Analysis of the Relationship Between Organizational Commitment and Salesperson Job Performance: Twenty-Five Years of Research." *Journal of Business Research,* 2005, *58*(6), 705–714. Riketta, M.

"Attitudinal Organizational Commitment and Job Performance: A Meta-Analysis." *Journal of Organizational Behavior,* 2002, *23*(3), 257–266. Cohen-Charash, Y., and Spector, P. E. "The Role of Justice in Organizations: A Meta-Analysis." *Organizational Behavior and Human Decision Processes,* 2001, *86*(2), 278–321. Cohen, A. "Organizational Commitment and Turnover: A Meta-Analysis." *Academy of Management Journal,* 1993, *36*(5), 1140–1157. Tett, R. P., and Meyer, J. P. "Job Satisfaction, Organizational Commitment, Turnover Intention, and Turnover: Path Analyses Based on Meta-Analytical Findings." *Personnel Psychology,* 1993, *46*(2), 259–295. Cohen, A., and Huducek, N. "Organizational Commitment-Turnover Relationship Across Occupational Groups: A Meta-Analysis." *Group and Organization Studies,* 1993, *18*(2), 188–209. Beadles, N. A., Lowery, C. M., Petty, M. M., and Ezell, H. "An Examination of the Relationships Between Turnover Functionality, Turnover Frequency, and Organizational Performance." *Journal of Business and Psychology,* 2000, *15*(2), 331–337. Dalal, R. "A Meta-Analysis of the Relationship Between Organizational Citizenship Behavior and Counterproductive Work Behavior." *Journal of Applied Psychology,* 2005, *90*(6), 1241–1255.

Chapter Two

1. Knapp, D. *The BrandMindset.* New York: McGraw-Hill, 2000. Knapp, D. *The Brand Promise.* New York: McGraw-Hill, 2008.

Chapter Three

1. Richard D'Aveni aptly calls this state of affairs "hypercompetition" in his book by that name: D'Aveni, R. A., with Gunther, R. *Hypercompetition: Managing the Dynamics of Strategic Maneuvering.* New York: Free Press, 1994.
2. Shapiro, E. *Fad Surfing in the Boardroom.* Reading, Mass.: Perseus Publishing, 1996.
3. Kramer, R. "Divergent Realities and Convergent Disappointments in the Hierarchic Relation: Trust and the Intuitive Auditor at Work." In R. M. Kramer and T. R. Tyler (eds.), *Trust in Organizations: Frontiers of Theory and Research.* Thousand Oaks, Calif.: Sage, 1996.
4. Lewicki, R. J., and Bunker, B. B. "Developing and Maintaining Trust in Work Relationships." In R. M. Kramer and T. R. Tyler (eds.), *Trust in Organizations: Frontiers of Theory and Research.* Thousand Oaks, Calif.: Sage, 1996.

Chapter Four

1.   Kay, M. Z. "Memo to a Turnaround Boss." In G. W. Dauphinais and C. Price (eds.), *Straight from the CEO: The World's Top Leaders Reveal Ideas That Every Manager Can Use*. New York: Simon & Schuster, 1998.

Chapter Five

1.   Solomon, R., and Flores, F. *Building Trust in Business, Politics, Relationships, and Life*. New York: Oxford University Press, 2001.

Chapter Six

1.   DePaulo, B. M., and Kashy, D. A. "Everyday Lies in Close and Casual Relationships." *Journal of Personality and Social Psychology*, 1998, *74*, 63–79. DePaulo, B. M., and others. "Lying in Everyday Life." *Journal of Personality and Social Psychology*, 1996, *70*, 979–995.
2.   Slim, W. (1957) *Courage and Other Broadcasts*. London: Cassell, 1957.
3.   Goffee, R., and Jones, G. *Why Should Anyone Be Led by You?* Boston: Harvard Business School Press, 2006.
4.   Mintzberg, H. "Strategy-Making in Three Modes." *California Management Review*, 1973, *16*(2), 44–53. Mintzberg, H. "The Manager's Job: Folklore and Fact." *Harvard Business Review*, 1975, *53*(4), 49–61. Kurke, L. B., and Aldrich, H. E. "Mintzberg Was Right! A Replication and Extension of the Nature of Managerial Work." *Management Science*, 1983, *29*(8), 975–985.

Chapter Seven

1.   Axelrod, R. H. *Terms of Engagement: Changing the Way We Change Organizations*. San Francisco: Berrett-Koehler, 2002. Axelrod, R. H., Axelrod, E. M., Beedon, J., and Jacobs, R. *You Don't Have to Do It Alone: How to Involve Others to Get Things Done*. San Francisco: Berrett-Koehler, 2004.

Chapter Eight

1.   Hemdi, M. A., and Nasurdin, A. M. "Predicting Turnover Intentions of Hotel Employees: The Influence of Employee Development Human Resource Management Practices and Trust in Organization." *Gadjah Mada International Journal of Business*, 2006, *8*(1), 21–42. Mani, B. G. "Performance Appraisal Systems,

Productivity, and Motivation: A Case Study."*Public Personnel Management*, 2002, *31*(2), 141–160. Mayer, R. C., and Davis, J. H. "The Effect of the Performance Appraisal System on Trust for Management: A Field Quasi-Experiment."*Journal of Applied Psychology*, 1999, *84*(1), 123–136.

2.   Welch, J., and Welch, S. *Winning*. New York: HarperCollins, 2005.

Chapter Ten

1.   Knapp, D. *The BrandPromise: The Essence of Success*. New York: McGraw-Hill, 2008.

Chapter Eleven

1.   Another good source on this topic is Kouzes, J., and B. Posner, B. *Credibility*. (Rev. ed.) San Francisco: Jossey-Bass, 2003.

Acknowledgments and Dedication

I wish to acknowledge and dedicate this book to several people who helped make it a reality by believing in me and my work.

My wife, Kathie Hodge, and my son, Cole, tolerated my obsession and even kicked in a few pearls of insight.

Darrell Cheung and Heather Allen volunteered as research assistants and insisted that they got value simply by participating in the project. They were joined briefly by Jacqueline Bolda and David Boisvert. This team provided both critical practical assistance and moral support.

Bob Wright, Jim Kouzes, and Dick Axelrod are my advisory board. Each of them has expressed belief in me at some critical juncture, and their wisdom has been invaluable.

All of the people I interviewed—those I quote in this book and those I do not—moved my thinking on integrity forward and deserve full credit. And three of them—Robert Gass, Michael Kay, and Charles Feltman—each contributed insights that essentially shaped a chapter.

I dedicate this book to these wise souls, in gratitude.

ABOUT THE AUTHOR

Tony Simons is an associate professor of management and organizational behavior at Cornell University's School of Hotel Administration. He holds a Ph.D. from the Kellogg School of Management at Northwestern University.

His research examines the causes and consequences of trust in leadership, team decisions, negotiations, and supply chains. He speaks, trains, and consults for organizations in a variety of industries.

Simons has published over twenty-eight articles in academic journals such as *Journal of Applied Psychology, Academy of Management Journal,* and *Organization Science* and also in practice journals such as *Cornell Hospitality Quarterly* and *Harvard Business Review.*

INDEX